The education of Gypsy and Traveller children

Action-research and co-ordination

The Proceedings of a Conference organised by the
Centre for Gypsy Research
Université René Descartes, Paris

with the assistance of the
French Ministry for Education and the
Commission of the European Communities

UMETLD

and held at the
Ecole Normale de l'Aude in Carcassonne, France
5–12 July 1989

This edition has been translated from the original French
and edited by the
Advisory Council for the Education of Romany and other Travellers

with financial assistance from the
Commission of the European Communities

This translation was first published
1993 in Great Britain by
University of Hertfordshire Press
Library and Media Services Department
University of Hertfordshire
College Lane
Hatfield
Hertfordshire AL10 9AD

British Library Cataloguing in Publication Data

Education of Gypsy and Traveller Children:
Action-research and Co-ordination –
The Proceedings of a Conference Organised by the
Centre for Gypsy Research, Université René Descartes, Paris
I. Advisory Council for the Education of
Romany and Other Travellers

ISBN 0-900458-50-X ✓

Designed by Beverley Stirling

Cover design by Ecole normale de l'Aude
and the Centre for Gypsy Research

Diagrams by Colin Boyter

Page layout by Robert Smyth

Typeset at University of London Computer Centre

Printed by Antony Rowe Ltd

Contents

Editors' Note
Sally Naylor, Mary Waterson, Mary Whiffin

Foreword
Raymond Courrière

Preface to the English Edition
John Evans

Preface to the French Edition
Jean-Noël Loubès

Part 1 Setting the Scene

Part 2 Action-research and Co-ordination:
the Situation in Different States

Editors' Note

The English edition of *The Education of Gypsy and Traveller Children: Action-Research and Co-ordination* has only been possible through the generous help of our co-translators, some of whom have dealt with more than just one chapter. We are deeply indebted to:

Mike Baldwin
Alan Bream
Liz Kwast
Jenny Lindop
David Middleton
Lady Plowden
Helen Powell
Sinead ni Shuinear
Margaret Wood

We would also like to thank Bridget Auger and Janet Whiffin who managed to decipher the editors' hieroglyphics and put the text on disc; John Evans – who chaired the Traveller Education Sub-committee of the Swann Committee – for making time to read the text and write a preface for the English edition; Jean-Pierre Liégeois for his support and advice and Bill Forster who, on behalf of the University of Hertfordshire, took on the publishing and whose guidance has been invaluable.

Sally Naylor, Mary Waterson and Mary Whiffin
Advisory Council for the Education of Romany and other Travellers

December 1992

Foreword

Liberty, equality, fraternity are values of the highest importance for this College of the French Republic – the Department of Aude College of Education – host to the University Summer School.

The steps which contribute to educational success must be the constant focus of our attention. The fact that half of those who are members of the Gypsy communities are under sixteen makes the question of education even more important for those communities. Schooling is a fundamental right. The demand for schooling exists. Schools must respond to that demand in a welcoming and flexible manner.

Relevant in-service training of teachers plays an essential role in improving the quality of teaching.

The Department of Aude is honoured to welcome the University Summer School. It is happy to assist in the dissemination throughout Europe of the ideas and propositions emerging from this Summer School.

Raymond Courrière
Chairman of the Aude County Council

Preface to the English Edition

I am very pleased to have the opportunity of commending the English version of the Carcassonne Seminar Report to those who have an interest in and concern for the entitlement to education of Gypsy and Traveller children. The papers evidence a discipline and rigour in their analysis that represent a major step forward.

The Seminar enjoyed the impetus of meeting within weeks of the 22 May 1989 Resolution of the EC Council and Ministers of Education about measures "to overcome the major obstacles to the access of Gypsy and Traveller children to schooling". The inaugural keynote speech set the context of the debate by throwing down the challenge of devising a programme of action-research, with a collaborative European-wide basis, to overcome the stark reality in which only one-third of these children on average attend school with any sort of regularity, that fall-off in attendance is marked and progressive as children become young people and that underachievement is endemic.

The contributions of the working groups in particular are commendable in facing up to the challenge of producing a structured work programme with defined priorities that are capable of being translated into a coherent action plan. Not surprisingly the groups struggled with varying degrees of success to define a programme that offers complete sense and avoids the repetition of the short-term, piecemeal approaches that we know so well.

Various points emerge from the national contributions. Sites remain a critical consideration. Where they are not available, educational provision is built on sand. Where they are available, attendance rates can rocket to 90 per cent. The experience of the Netherlands, where sites are found in relation to practically every town and village, should be heeded. Secondly, it is common European experience that teaching and learning approaches and materials have to be sensitive to the children's experience and values. The successs of the curriculum has to be seen in terms of the experience that each child takes away from school. Teachers need training programmes to help them provide the 'differentiation' that is now a standard expectation in relation to the National Curriculum. The successful outcomes of teachers and Gypsy parents working together, as experienced in Andalucia, will offer encouragement to those who accept the shared nature of educational enterprise.

The evidence from the Gypsies and Travellers themselves underlines their frustration tinged with anger, as their reasonable requirements and expectations continue to be neglected. The contribution from Santino Spinelli touches every sensitive nerve and supports the suggestion that we must learn from the Gypsies and that they should be used to inform public opinion. Other priorities identified are the need for exchange of information, the establishment of a repertoire of good practice and the need for committed Europeans to work together. Jean-Pierre Liégeois' concluding chapter on action-research is a 'tour de force' expounding a rationale for an action-based participative research programme rooted in the realities of working experience.

All in all, these papers are a good read and show how concerns have matured from national meetings of the like-minded to an international determination to seek out sound and well-considered action plans that may be presented to those who need to be reminded constantly of their responsibilities to all within democratic societies.

John Evans
Executive Director of Education and Leisure Services, Kirklees Metropolitan Council

September 1991

Preface to the French Edition

I have had the honour, for the second year running, to assist Professor Jean-Pierre Liégeois in organising the University Summer School devoted to the schooling of Gypsy and Traveller children.

This enormous and complex problem has been addressed in an exemplary manner by sixty-five specialists representing ten countries of our European community.

The Carcassonne meeting is taking place at a time of intense educational debate while the 'loi d'orientation sur l'education' is being prepared in Paris. The schooling of Gypsy children directly questions our institutions. It has been necessary to speak of failure and exclusion and it has been stated again that democratisation within education is not about assimilation but about the acceptance of the need for more differentiated strategies.

The participants remember well the intensity of the debates. Exchanges and proposals have been exceptionally rich as this report bears witness.

It is necessary to guard the memory of the work that has been achieved by the teachers and the parents of pupils who have participated in these days at the École Normale in Carcassonne and by all those who have not been able to attend. Many of them provide training for men and women who will be capable of adaption, creativity and solidarity and of taking full responsibility for their personal, civic and professional lives.

I must express my grateful thanks to the Council of the Department of Aude, the Ecole Normale and the Centre for Pedagogic Documentation of the Department of Aude who have made this French edition possible. Thanks to them this synthesis of the work of the University Summer School of 1989 will reach all parts of Europe. I must also thank all those who contributed to the quality and the success of the seminar: the town of Carcassonne, the Paul Sabatier School, the teachers and others who gave their time and effort to ensure that our European friends were welcomed according to the best traditions of the Department of Aude.

It certainly is no simple matter, in the context of a world undergoing radical changes, to lay the foundations for a European education for the children of Gypsies and Travellers. We must pay tribute to the participants from all over France, from Belgium, Spain, Greece, Ireland, Italy, The Netherlands, Portugal, Germany and the United Kingdom because it is their work and their devotion to equality of opportunity and to a particular view of schooling which has produced such a solid body of work.

Finally, thanks are due to Professor Jean-Pierre Liégeois and his team: Maria Alcaloïde, Benoît Gramond and Arlette Laurent-Fahier. Their great skill and personal commitment have succeeded in creating a dynamic force capable of advancing at a European level the idea of schooling open both to the world and to families and capable of facing up to the differing cultural characteristics of young people. This is in accordance with the great principles which we have been commemorating in this bicentenary year of the French Revolution, the right to knowledge for all and a spirit of tolerance and solidarity.

Jean-Noël Loubès
Inspecteur d'Académie du Département de l'Aude

Introduction

Jean-Pierre Liégeois, Director of the Centre for Gypsy Research, University René Descartes, and Consultant to the Commission of the European Communities

A European conference was held at the Ecole Normale in Carcassonne (department of Aude) from 5-12 July 1989 which dealt with the schooling of Gypsy and Traveller children. About sixty-five delegates from ten member states of the European Community attended the conference entitled *The Schooling of Gypsy and Traveller Children: Action-Research and Co-ordination.* This was the result of the unification of two projects proposed by the Centre for Gypsy Research of the René Descartes University (Paris), and two separate institutions, the French Ministry of Education, Youth and Sport and the Council of the European Community.

The French project took the form of a 'Summer University', the term used for a vacation course for teachers and other educationists. The Ministry puts the proposed course out to tender to all interested institutions of higher education. If the idea is adopted, candidates can apply to join the course and the organisers select participants from these applicants. The process involves two separate voluntary groups – academics willing to establish the appropriate course and candidates agreeing to participate during vacation time. Only highly motivated people apply which explains the strength of feeling and involvement of these courses, especially the one described here.

The participants, who came from all parts of France, teachers, education-ists and inspectors, were selected for their experience and competence within the framework of this Summer University. Highly qualified candidates from all three categories had to be turned down; this suggests that there is a real need for training and information in this field which existing in-service courses do not cover.

The preparation and setting up of this Summer University under the direct auspices of the Centre for Gypsy Research was undertaken by Jean-Pierre Liégeois in collaboration with Maria Alcaloïde and Benoît Gramond (both teachers of Gypsy and Traveller children and members of the Conseil d'Administration du Centre de Liaison et d'Information Voyage-Ecole – CLIVE) and Arlette Laurent-Fahier (Centre d'Information pour la Scolarisation des Enfants de Migrants de Paris – CEFISEM). Locally the collaboration of Monsieur Jean-Noël Loubès (Academy Inspector), Madame Marie-Claire Biau (bursar), Monsieur Michel Milian (course tutor) and Mademoiselle Marie-Jo Hirigoyen (PhD student) ensured very favourable conditions for the working party at the Ecole Normale.

The project submitted to the Council of the European Community concerns the education of Gypsy and Traveller children within the local authority framework. The fact that on 22 May 1989, several weeks before the conference, the Council and Education Ministers of the twelve member states of the European Community had adopted a resolution concerning the education of Gypsy and Traveller children (cf Appendix 2), emphasizes the importance of this conference. There were representatives from Belgium, Spain, Greece, Ireland, Italy, the Netherlands, Portugal, the Federal German Republic and the United Kingdom. In cases where there already exist national or regional associations of teachers and others working in the field of Gypsy and Traveller education, the delegates represented these associations. Where such associations do not exist they were, as far as possible, representing groups of teachers and other interested parties.

Including France there were representatives of ten countries from the European Community. There was no-one from Luxembourg since at the moment there are no teachers specifically concerned with this subject, nor from Denmark where, although there are people working in this field, there is a language problem. One of the criteria for participation in this conference was a good knowledge of French, the language of the host country, since for practical and financial reasons it was impossible to organise the provision of interpreters. Nor was it possible to invite representatives from each region of the different member countries, e.g. the different autonomous regions of Spain, Scotland or Ulster, although each area presents particular problems. Moreover, unexpected last minute developments – always a problem when planning so far ahead – meant that certain countries were poorly represented. There was only one delegate from Greece, one from the Federal German Republic and there was no-one from Walloon. Some people were there in a private capacity; Gypsies and Travellers could not be official delegates as they were not members of the teaching profession. It is intended that future working parties and committees will be set up where they will be able to analyse the situation and express their own opinions and priorities.

It was necessary to plan the week-long conference with great care, thereby enabling the participants to pool their ideas in planning for the future. The programme for the conference, key documents and questionnaires were distributed in advance and, in certain cases, preliminary meetings provided material for discussion groups. During the conference, a number of methods of working were adopted. A presentation of the seminar and of the context of the work, followed by a brief presentation of their concept of action-research by representatives of the different countries, was made to the whole group. Also in plenary session, a series of ten lectures was given on the situation in the ten countries represented, as well as a statement by those Gypsies and Travellers present. Delegates also worked in groups: this took up an important part of the time; over a period of four days the delegates had to present an analysis, come to a conclusion and consider future developments of a variety of suggested topics; thematic groups then considered each of the themes previously established and reported briefly on their conclusions. Two meetings were held to enable delegates to give their opinions and propose a plan of action for co-ordination of the work to be carried out on both French and European levels. Most evenings there was an organised activity: documentary videos from France, Italy, Portugal, UK; a film; a musical entertainment provided by Santino Spinelli (one of the Gypsy delegates, a professional musician and director of the music school of Lanciano, Italy); a visit to the city of Carcassonne; sampling of regional specialities. Educational material from different countries was displayed in several parts of the Ecole Normale. Finally, numerous documents, sent by the Council of Europe, were distributed to the delegates.

It is obvious that a report cannot give an entire record of the work completed during a meeting of this kind, especially with regard to its intensity during a week behind closed doors, and the inevitable conflict between participants, representatives of different states, Gypsies and non-Gypsies, the essential being the education derived from it and more important, concern for a constructive plan for the future. This type of conference provides a unique and necessary meeting place for the growth of new individual and collective attitudes arising from a critical evaluation which leads to new ideas which other lengthy and costly means have failed to produce. At the final meetings in the groups discussing co-ordination, there were many who felt determined, once they returned home, to develop in their colleagues the efforts necessary to realise this essential co-ordination. Apart from the institutional effects of this meeting, it is certain that the participants came away enriched by this intensive collaboration which went far beyond a simple exchange of ideas. In most cases the spin-off within the framework of personal and professional practice, particularly from the educational viewpoint is important – in fact, essential.

Keynote Speech

Jean-Pierre Liégeois, Director of the Centre for Gypsy Research, University René Descartes, and Consultant to the Commission of the European Communities

I intend to be as brief and as clear as possible here, my purpose being to place this meeting, its bases and objectives firmly within the context of school provision for Gypsy and Traveller children as it stands today. Looking at these aspects will shed light on the conditions under which we will be working and the shape which that work will take.

Background to the Meeting

I shall not repeat here the analyses, guidelines and recommendations which are to be found in the various documents emerging from projects carried out under the auspices of the European Community and the Council of Europe. You have already read these reports as a pre-condition for participating in this seminar (see Appendix 1). You are thus familiar with the various projects undertaken by these European organisations, the different stages covered over the last few years and the conclusions and guidelines arrived at through study and consultation.

The study launched in 1984 by the European Community raised expectations on all sides for parents, associations, teachers, administrators and others involved in work of this kind. Generally speaking, attention has been focused on what is being done and what it will be possible to do. Some may feel that progress is slow, yet if we were to describe in detail what has actually been accomplished over the past five years, there is no doubt that movement has, in fact, been rapid. Throughout this period there has been a major event of some kind at European level at least once every six months. A range of Community institutions has been involved in meetings and examination of and follow-up of information dossiers.

This movement has, through its various publications and the projects it has initiated, slowly established points from which to operate. It has recently gained a solid base with the adoption, on 22 May 1989, by the European Council and the Ministers of Education meeting within the Council, of a Resolution on school provision for Gypsy and Traveller children (Appendix 2). This Resolution provides a framework for action, enabling us to go beyond the preparatory stages in which we have been involved up to now. It is a document of enormous value both historically and symbolically, recognising the existence of Gypsy and Traveller culture and the necessity for respecting it. It lays out guidelines in the field of education for Member States and for the Community as a whole. The next stage must be to develop a working programme that is to establish priorities since some needs are more urgent than others and since, for reasons both financial and organisational, everything cannot be done at once. Having outlined priorities we shall be proposing plans for action.

This meeting, mere weeks after the adoption of the Resolution, takes on particular significance. These priorities and action plans will be formulated here. A few days ago, at the opening of a Spanish seminar which I had organised at the request of the Spanish authorities and the Council of Europe, I emphasised the importance of meeting to discuss a concrete theme: teacher training. We are gathered here today to discuss much broader issues – action-research and co-ordination – and I want to emphasise the same point once again. I would also like to remind each of those participating here today of the responsibility we bear. Over the next few days, we have an important contribution to make to the body of information which brings us together here.

My final point, in recalling the bases of our work, is to remind you of the most basic point of all, as outlined in the documents already mentioned, namely, that the situation of Gypsy and Traveller communities is, as a result of their difficult history, very grave, particularly with regard to school provision. In the Member States of the European community only 30-40% of Gypsy and Traveller children attend school with any regularity. A very low percentage get as far as secondary level and results, particularly with regard to reading and writing, are not in keeping with the amount of time spent in school. Such are the effects of the existing situation, the causes of which are analysed in detail in the documents already mentioned, for some 600,000 children in the twelve Member States of the Community.

It is thus vital, urgent, and just, that the various partners concerned should address themselves to improving this situation. Schooling has become a fundamental factor in the cultural, social and economic future of Gypsy and Traveller communities, notably through the tools which it can provide to facilitate adaptation to a changing cultural environment. Gypsy and Traveller parents themselves are increasingly aware of this and the demand for schooling is rising accordingly.

Objectives and Content
This seminar has several interrelated and complementary objectives. As in any Summer University or other meeting of this type, there is an éducative function for those participating in it. At both national (French) and European levels, it aims to facilitate dialogue and exchange between those directly involved in a professional capacity in school provision for Gypsy and Traveller children. The information we gather here, and the guidelines we evolve, will serve as a basis for planning action at both individual State and at Community level. Our two themes are action-research and co-ordination. I shall carefully avoid defining these terms here at the introductory stage, because it is we who

must, through a dynamic process of dialogue, arrive at an operational definition and evolve proposals for their implementation. I shall limit my comments
to reminding you that the Commission of the European Communities'
Orientation Document for Reflection and for Action, simply written and widely
distributed (see Appendix 1), places very clear emphasis on the necessity for
creating favourable conditions for 'co-ordination' at both national and Community levels, particularly between teachers and other personnel, and to set up or
step up 'action-research'. Both themes are particularly vital in the context of
school provision for Gypsy and Traveller children. (The document introduces
these topics under the headings "Action-research" and "Consultation and Co-
ordination", and puts forward a synthesis and consensus of views expressed in
many studies and at many meetings by the various bodies concerned).

In July 1988 the Centre de Recherches Tsiganes organised the
Montauban Summer University, a project supported and funded by the French
National Ministry of Education. The theme was "Gypsy Children in School:
The Training of Teachers and Other Personnel". Approximately sixty participants from all over France – teachers, inspectors, teacher trainers – selected
for their expertise in this field were thus able to spend a full week exchanging
ideas. There were also three guest participants – one each from the Netherlands, Spain and the United Kingdom – whose presence was deemed essential,
so much so that they stayed for the whole week. Participants were unanimous
in their demand that similar opportunities for exchange be initiated at inter-
State level. There was a convergence of conclusions too: a demand for national
and European co-ordination, and for a stepping up of action-research within a
coherent network, echoing the conclusions of the 1983 and 1987 international
seminars organised by the Council of Europe. (Details of the documents
outlining the conclusions of all three meetings are given in Appendix 1).

This demand for contact, co-ordination and communication in a spirit of
enquiry and with a willingness to evaluate, is widely shared by and is an
expressed priority for teachers and other personnel from Community Member
States. It tallies with the expressed goal of the Commission and of other
Community institutions as well as of national authorities, to encourage
dialogue and exchange between colleagues from different States.

Which is how we come to be gathered here today, focusing on themes
proposed by the Commission of the European Communities as well as the
French Ministry, with a view to initiating action by those involved. This
meeting will enable the Commission, various Community institutions and the
relevant Ministries to pool the analysis, advice, aspirations, recommendations
and proposals of those working in the field. All this information is essential in
preparing for action.

Our work here is also connected with action undertaken within the
Council of Europe, notably in the Council for Cultural Co-operation.

The task facing us here today is vital and concrete: to take stock of what has
been, and is being, done, to analyse these approaches and to expand upon them.

We must also formulate precise proposals for various institutions both
national and international.

A well-thought out, structured work programme is needed both in action-
research (suggestions for implementation at national and European levels) and
for co-ordination (exchange programmes and platforms where representatives
of various organisations and associations can discuss their work with colleagues and other partners, within each State and between States). The aim of

all this is to develop the exchange of ideas, teaching materials and experiences and to establish the principle of active, sustained collaboration. In effect, our task (and here I refer again to the published reports listed in Appendix 1) is to put an end to the isolation of those working in this field and to avoid the fruitless repetition of short-term piecemeal approaches often doomed from the start by their unsuitability to the task in hand and indeed by their very isolation. The result is a waste of time, money, energy and human resources.

The documents mentioned amply demonstrate the necessity both for co-ordinated in-depth thinking, such as will be made possible by the structured approach of action-research, and for liaison between those involved, at all levels. The present seminar, an opportunity for reflection, analysis, and formulation of proposals, aims to establish the bases for this co-operation which is indispensable and universally reecognised as such. The importance of this co-operation is emphasised in the Resolution of 22 May. It is thus clear that our role here is an essential one and of crucial importance.

Outline for the Meeting

All of us come to this meeting forearmed with both practical experience and familiarity with the preparation documents; we thus have a basic minimum of shared knowledge. Insight into our dual theme has been greatly sharpened by a series of documents emerging over the past few years. We are not here to go over the same ground but to use these observations as our starting point. That is why it is so vital that, as I have insisted, participants be thoroughly familiar with the documents listed in Appendix 1.

Practical experience and theoretical preparation imply that participants will already have devoted some thought to the themes which bring us together. Some headings have been suggested to help group various topics. These headings are simultaneously thematic axes for reflection on action-research and axes for work to be undertaken after the meeting in order to implement the action-research and co-ordination proposals evolved here.

In other words, each axis pertains to stages before, during and after this meeting. Before the meeting there has been stocktaking, evaluation and analysis. During the meeting there will be presentations of analyses, groupwork and the formulation of work programmes. After the meeting there will be co-ordinated implementation of work programmes.

We will work together, in 'plenary sessions', as well as splitting up into 'workshops'. Each of these smaller groups, comprising representatives of different roles (inspector, teacher, teacher trainer, etc.) and different geographical areas, will have four days to devote to a study of all the themes of our seminar. Participants have prepared by reading and studying various documents; now they will pool their analyses and reflections with the aim of compiling a brief report stating their collective conclusions and proposing priorities and methods for tackling them. This report will be completed and submitted by the end of the fourth day and distributed among all the participants.

The original workshops will then re-form into new groups each of which will spend the next two days concentrating on a single theme, developing the proposals put forward by the original workshops and suggesting ways in which they can be implemented. Our final day will be devoted to reporting and subsequently discussing the findings of the thematic workshops.

As you can see, the framework in which we shall be working is well defined, by the context in which we find ourselves, by the fact that we meet in the wake of the passing of the Resolution, and, most concrete of all, by our timetable. These will be demanding days, filled with intense work but the burden will be eased by your conscientious preparation. There will also be 'planned' days run to a strict schedule. It is always difficult at meetings of this sort to strike a balance between spontaneity and efficiency and between freedom and direction. Given the circumstances and our responsibilities, the objectives of this meeting and their implications, we, the organisers, have opted to fit these seven working days into a clear framework in the hope that this will maximise our chances of success. At the same time, you will note that neither in the preparatory documents nor in these introductory lines has content been anticipated. What to cover and how to cover it, is entirely up to you. For similar reasons, each workshop will appoint a co-ordinator to ensure that our objectives are covered in the allotted time, yet each will develop its own dynamics and working pattern and will evolve its own programme and priorities. If I stress that the written reports arising from these workshops must be of limited length, I do so because they must be read by all participants as immediate working documents before we go on to the second, thematic stage, and also so that they can afterwards be published 'in toto' (without the arbitrary editing to which over-long documents are fated) and, last but not least, so that they will actually be read.

I am counting on you to make optimum use of the coming days, and am confident that, thanks to your skill, your experience and your hard work, we shall reach our objectives. The fact that your recommendations will be widely implemented may weigh heavily but it should also encourage you; rarely can one be certain that one's voice will indeed be heard and heeded. I myself will be applying your conclusions in a range of contexts and I can assure you that the Commission of the European Communities will be listening very attentively to what emerges from your work here.

Action-research, Myth or Reality

Claude Clanet, Director of the Centre for Research & Study into Inter-cultural Matters, Lecturer at the University of Toulouse

It is difficult to use simple and clear language when talking about action research because this term covers a variety of realities. We will try to pull together some common characteristics. Without doubt the lack of clarity about the term forms part of its attraction as everyone will find something to serve his/her needs in the action-research myth. Drawing together the words 'research' and 'action' can actually suggest that the difference in views of the scientific and the practical camps is decreasing and that the gap between those two disciplines is lessening.

For the moment, we will leave those two views behind us and concentrate on our understanding of action-research. Firstly, we will look at it from a historical point of view and contrast this method with more classical methods and afterwards, we will try to establish some characteristics which seem to identify this type of work. Finally, we would like to raise some of the problems and difficulties posed by action-research.

Kurt Lewin and 'Action-research' (1)

The invention of the term action-research has been attributed to Kurt Lewin who used it at the end of the 1930s to define a particular type of research. Lewin is a psychologist. He began working in Germany, specialising in in experiential and Gestalt psychology. In 1933 he was forced to emigrate to the United States and there is no doubt that this forced break in his career led him to develop his interest in new phenomena: those that underlined the psychological and social changes in real life. Thus he became involved in action – political, economic, militant – by his attempts to introduce research into action-processes and by his desire to make a 'practical science' accessible to the man of action which would enable that man to evaluate the relations between his efforts and the results. Lewin knew the methodological difficulties of such an approach. In spite of this, he and his co-workers chose to leave the comfort and security of a university behind to do research on the ground, in workshops and offices. This is how 'action-research' was born.

Everyone in the education sector knows the experiment on 'authority environments', conducted with Lippitt and White, in which Lewin sets up a rigorous experimental procedure to ensure that the relational environment in each of the three groups could differ artificially only where the researchers wished it to do so.

I would also like to recall a well-known piece of action-research on the changing of eating habits. The starting point for this research was the conclusion that shortages of certain foods would occur in wartime, the best pieces of meat being kept for the army, and that it would be necessary to introduce into the diets of the American population meat of lower quality such as heart, tripe and kidneys, then widely rejected as unfit for human consumption. Lewin set about researching into the modification of eating habits by studying two series of problems: those underlying the distribution of meat (Who supplies the shops? What is the reasoning adopted for supply and what criteria are used?) and those underlying the food shopping pattern of American people (attraction of the food, preferences and dislikes of members of the family, necessary preparation time). These problems create tensions and conflicts which translate into the shopping pattern, for example, a certain frequency of buying a particular item.

The research took the form of concrete action simultaneously with distribution channels and with the public. Lewin compared the reciprocal effects of different forms of intervention under identical circumstances. He observed seminars with specialists and also group discussions between housewives and dieticians. In this way, Lewin discovered that the differences between the two methods of action in effecting changes of habit could be ranked from 1 to 10.

Lewinian action-research demands various attitudes and activities on the part of the researcher:
■ sometimes s/he will evaluate the situation and is led to formulate a diagnosis
■ sometimes s/he constructs an experimental environment of conditions which allows validation or invalidation of certain suppositions used as a base for the diagnosis. This work is followed by a theoretical interpretation which tries to explain the relevant processes
■ sometimes the researcher plays the role of instigator or agent of change, intervening directly in the lives of the people subjected to changes.

In this way, one can define several characteristics of action-research as Lewin used it. Firstly, the researcher is at the centre of action-research: s/he is the one to elaborate hypotheses, put the different sequences of research into action and become the agent of change. All decisions, interventions and interpretations are made by the researcher.

Secondly, the action-research develops in a simple institutional context. This explains the omnipotence of the researcher in action-research. The action-researcher works along the lines of a commander: s/he is servicing the initiators and the people responsible for the project and shares entirely in their objectives. There has been criticism of this integration of Lewin's and one important difference between that and current action-research is apparent. This context has, however, the merit of a certain institutional transparency and has also enabled results to be obtained, both at a theoretical and practical level which is more difficult in a complex institutional context, be it through conflict or merely through ambiguity.

Thirdly, the researcher is permanently in the field. To obtain results it is necessary for there to be voluntary participation and effective co-operation and liaison, both with social participants and with systems because the research develops in real environments. Therefore, the researchers also need to research their own attitudes and their own involvement.

From a global point of view, Lewinian action-research can be seen as the most efficient type of research to introduce socially desirable changes. Its procedures can provide inspiration for changes in education.

Finally, from an epistemological point of view let us emphasise Lewin's pre-occupation with advancing simultaneously on the fronts of experience, action and research. For Lewin the object of research can only be studied in the light of its relations with other objects in its environment: Lewin introduces the notion of a 'research field' which constitutes one of his important contributions to the development of psychological science.

Strangely enough, and in spite of the interest in action-research along the lines of Lewin and his collaborators, rapid dissemination of action-research outside the United States did not take place. Without doubt, pedagogical experiments in France during the 1960s, both institutional and otherwise, can be linked to concrete experience in action-research but without a mention of the term and without effecting any move towards Lewin's action-research. Here the starting point was different and the institution was at the centre of the research.

The term action-research was used and developed in West Germany between 1968 and 1975. In the French language the term action-research was not used until early 1977 except within certain associations. However, confusion about the concept has set in since this period: diverse activities are regrouped under the term 'action-research' which do not really have common characteristics. It can also be said that there are various strands of action-research.

The reference to Lewin gives us a starting point and allows us to give relatively defined and solid antecedents to the term. Now we can try to contrast action-research with other forms of research by indicating what is not action-research. Then we will indicate what action-research is, or what it seems to be, in the context of our research.

What Action-research Is Not
We can differentiate between action-research and the traditional, or classical, empirical research. We would also have to distinguish it from most forms of applied research and from most problems of or analyses of concrete social practices.

Action-research Is Not Classical Empirical Research.
In classical research, the term research is more or less synonymous with verification: the researcher knows from his initial hypotheses what it is he wishes to find out and consequently constructs an empirical path to verify, or disprove, these hypotheses. In other words, it is not the real events which are most significant but the choice of those elements of the reality destined to conform to the coherence introduced by the researcher. This process conforms to a certain number of norms and expectations linked to a certain scientific

concept in a humanities context:

- research of causality: the relationship of cause and effect between two sets of facts. Because these facts are isolated in a more or less arbitrary way, one commonly establishes simple causalities, sometimes linear and always partial
- the assumption of separability and of analytic priority: all reality can be separated into simpler 'elements'; therefore, it is from the start a limited reality on which the researcher constructs his/her proofs
- the non-involvement of the researcher: the object is thought to exist independent of the researcher and the logical, psychological and institutional structures to which it refers
- the public character of knowledge: once identified, the knowledge can be communicated and will remain valid as long as others do not refute it
- the possibility of generalisation due to the universal character and the timeless nature of 'laws'.

It is only to fuel the debate that we list, albeit somewhat arbitrarily, some of the norms of traditional research. Those listed seem to indicate, above all, a means of ordering, a research of coherence. Now, the stronger the coherence, the more one sees the lack of significance, the loss of real meaning. Lewinian action-research as we have seen in our examples takes as its starting point a practical problem which makes sense in a real context. It seems, therefore, that meaning is put unambiguously ahead of coherence. This leads action-research to reject the norms of empirical research as the absolute basis of knowledge and only to accept them as relative and temporary elements, subordinate to the search for meaning.

Action-research endeavours to establish new relationships between meaning and coherence by giving priority to meaning but bearing in mind that developing meaning as sole norm and control (the rejection of any coherence) will lead to abandoning the very idea of research.

Action-research Is Not Applied Research

Applied research is concerned with the application in practice of the conclusions of empirical research. The two should not be confused. However, some stages in research or sectors of research have all the characteristics of applied research. For example, parents and teachers may respond to a questionnaire on educational attitudes and behaviour, then participate in information and training sessions, then again respond to a new questionnaire with the assumption that there will be a modification of educational behaviour and attitudes. In contrast to applied empirical research, action-research will integrate those questionnaires and sessions in a much more deliberate and complex whole and, above all, the techniques could be more refined, analysed and modified with the participation of the interested parties. There is modification of the boundaries between the subject and the object of the research or rather, mutual knowledge, instead of merely the exterior knowledge and assumptions of a single researcher.

Action-research is not an investigation of concrete social practice carried out by the practitioner after the event

This type of investigation and analysis can be absorbed into an evaluation, a training aim or personal research. One cannot deny the involvement of the practitioner in such an analysis nor the modification of practice which may result. Such an investigation can form part of action-research, for example, research groups can be established to analyse teacher, parent or researcher practice. But such groupwork differs from carrying out an isolated investigation as in applied research. These groups are only sub-groups of a larger whole. Above all, reciprocal control needs to be maintained through video recording and control after the investigation through written records. Thus a variety of methods and perspectives is needed to place the investigation in both the theory and the practice of action-research.

Action-research: What Is It?

The action-researches in which we have participated have certain similarities with Lewin's models. On the other hand, they differ in other dimensions, in particular, in the complexity of the institutional context, in the status and function of the researcher. It is, therefore, difficult to define action-research in terms of functions, objectives or specific characteristics. In general terms and without losing sight of the relative nature of our point of view, we can try to define action-research.

Research can be undertaken on concrete, social practice, i.e. existing independently from the research institute and, therefore, not created by the researcher to verify hypotheses or theories. Ginestous' action-research focused on education for Traveller children in the light of relations between different agencies (school, research team, organisations, Traveller community) and protagonists of those different agencies.

Research can focus on a problem to be resolved through the medium of a project. The aim is not solely the gathering of knowledge but also to induce a transformation in the human group affected by the problem. The problem to resolve here is the lack of adaptation by Traveller children to school and also the lack of adaptation of schools to Traveller children. The project consists of changing relationships between agencies (school, agencies, research team, Traveller community) and also between the various participants (teachers, social workers, researchers, Traveller children). One of the objectives is also to encourage Traveller parents to participate in the project which they have not been able to join directly.

The changes to be introduced affect the various social actors (teachers, researchers, social workers) not to deny their specific work but, on the contrary, to gather knowledge about it and to locate it in the overall dynamic context of the education of Traveller children. This involves looking at interaction between participants at different levels: personal, relational, organisational, institutional, in the systems concerned. In more general terms it is evident that the project can be described as one of socio-cultural change whilst promoting a model of inter-cultural society in which cultural minorities are not only recognised but are allowed to develop and exchange as equal partners with other cultural communities in the national life. Therefore, the project is referred to explicitly as a project of socio-cultural change with all the ambiguities and uncertainties which such a reference implies.

There can also be research in which the researchers and the different actors are all involved. Every researcher, in one way or another, is involved in his/her research. In action-research, the involvement of the researcher and the various protagonists is in itself the focus of study. It would, in effect, seem impossible to develop a situation in concrete and complex research in which the various actors could be excluded. The analysis must be carried out at different levels. On the psychological level the motives of each of the participants in the research are examined and each personal problem is related to the general problem of the research. On the relational level the tensions and interaction between different groups and, in particular, between different cultures are analysed. On the institutional level the place and status of everyone involved in the situation (the researcher, the teacher, the social worker) and the resulting power dynamic is included in the analysis.

This analysis of involvement is not done to regularise the situation (the resolving of tensions which will inevitably interfere) but forms one of the objects of the research. Therefore, these changes in attitudes and relationships need to be included. In one way or another, we must make them apparent and include them in the general problem of research into socio-cultural change.

We can be faced with an extremely complex situation where the very nature of the subject to be studied changes. Action-research uses numerous theoretical and methodological procedures. We have already indicated that action-research intends to produce and study socio-cultural changes at different levels: personal (references to the social psychology of relationships and groups), organisational (references to the analysis of organisations), institutional (references to institutional analysis) and so on. References to sociology, economics, history, if not appearing directly at any operational level, guide and influence action-research at other levels: the level of the global project and the presentation which can be given at any moment during the research and the action.

The approach to this complex reality of socio-cultural changes must, therefore, incorporate a variety of disciplines, or better, the use of a multi-disciplinary team with the attendant difficulty of co-ordinating the different points of view and ensuring that all participants take cognisance one of the other.

Action-research might appear to be, by definition, contradictory in the pursuit of its double objective. First, is the production of knowledge of a certain scientific character which has to coincide with established norms of knowledge. Second, are socio-cultural changes and transformations at a level of concrete social practice. These form one part of a 'political' project and, therefore, are located in value systems of a given social structure.

In Ginestous' action-research the placing of researchers in a research centre, the preoccupation with analysis and 'objective' controls and the theoretical justification of events (often after the event and in an interpretative way) focus on the first objective. The continuous adjustment of intervention in relation to the developing situation and the various protagonists on the one hand and, on the other hand, general adaptation of the whole project focus on the second objective.

The praxis of action-research exists without doubt in this project which, if not entirely reconciling contradictory objectives, at least aims to take them into account.

Problems and Difficulties of Action-research
One of the main difficulties of action-research which we have experienced is the ambitious nature of the projects which it tries to tackle. We aim to introduce socio-cultural changes at different levels and we aim to understand and explain those changes. Of course, it is much more a question of an intention or an objective to be studied rather than an accomplished reality, albeit in a fragmented manner. One of the problems is to circumvent and

control this characteristic incomplete quality of action-research by checking against the objectives.

Lewin and his collaborators had many problems with controlling the abundance of variables of their action-research whose objectives seemed less ambitious than those of current action-research projects. It was necessary for Lewin to change variable components such as aggression or the consumption of food in a precise institutional setting in which the researcher conducted the entire operation. In action-research concerned with education and socio-cultural change, the problem appears to be more complex: the changes to be introduced are much less pragmatic, hazier and more difficult to alter in relation to values or in relation to a more or less Utopian project in society. We are talking here of changes of 'mentality' or changes of relationships.

Action-research broadens out in the direction of institutional structures which it now takes into account. Power is no longer possessed by the single researcher with a mandate from a single financial backer. Several institutions, e.g. research, schools, associations, each possess part of the power and part of the project. Action-research, therefore, cannot economise on negotiations at the institutional level or on institutional analysis.

In addition, action-research broadens out in the direction of psychological structures and processes where it envisages more fundamental changes and which it tries to study by analysis of the involvement of all the participants. This aspect used to be experienced only in action-research but nowadays it has become an object of study in itself.

Action-research tends to involve the different participants more and more in the actual setting up of a piece of action-research and in the decision-making process. Therefore, one could say that action-research participates more and more in the socio-drama through the relationships between the action (practitioners) and the research (researchers) and also in certain multi-disciplinary approaches through the relationships between researchers from different disciplines.

These collected difficulties should induce in us a certain prudence which could be translated into certain methodological or technical precautions in the setting up of an action-research project. We will now present some of these procedures as elements for reflection.

The Control of Complexity and of Systematic Analysis

The setting up of an action-research project must be accompanied by a systematic analysis covering the areas of action and investigation. Certainly, several 'systems' are likely to be productive in the socio-cultural area: institutional and organisational systems, power systems and even systems of beliefs and opinions. It is necessary to analyse those systems most relevant to the objectives assigned to the action-research. The elaboration of these systems, the acknowledgment of gaps between the various points of view of the participants and the 'negotiation' around those gaps already introduce us to the field of action-research.

As an example we intend to present a systematic global approach to the socio-cultural field. This general scheme of analysis, attributed to Roland Colin (2), divides the socio-cultural field into different productive segments with the total socio-cultural area as a reference. This area is then divided into six secondary segments, six layers which are grouped into three groups of two segments with particular affinities. A disciplinary approach can be globally attached to each of these subgroups which allows us to avoid reductionism and synchronism and also allows us to establish an interdisciplinary articulation.

This division of the socio-cultural area takes us from the level nearest to nature, the field of primitive ecology, through progressively more complex levels.

1st level: Technology and Techniques
These are the work procedures which transform 'nature's gifts' so that they may fulfil human needs or objectives, e.g. agriculture, the environment or clothes.

2nd level: The Economy
The products are classed by the social group as goods or services and organised by the group according to their objectives of production, redistribution and consumption. These two levels, technological and economic, are closely linked and are considered as the foundation or infrastructure on which the social construct is based.

3rd level: The Political
There is always a power system which establishes a social order and defines the interaction between the various members of the group. The power system is concerned with problems in the infrastructure and also with forces at other levels.

4th level: The Socio-Familial System
This is the structure of the family, the basic unit of society. This level is very close to the political level and often interacts with it in societies 'without a State' or where the chief of the clan also has the political power. The 3rd and 4th levels are 'environmental structures', the mesostructures, which simultaneously touch both the infrastructure and the superstructure, playing a role more or less linked to one or the other, depending on the type of society.

5th level: Psychological Organisation
The basic social units are composed of persons, that is, human beings with their own psychological structures (cognitive, emotional and relational) produced or reproduced by an educational system and, therefore, manifesting different characteristics from one culture system to another.

6th level: Ideologies and Values
This is the level of 'representations of the world' which take an ideological, philosophical or religious form. It is the level of the values which makes sense of the world according to the perceptions held by the social group. The 5th and 6th levels are often called 'superstructures' because they are the 'highest' structures of the socio-cultural model.

All these levels or processes which are the result of a developing analysis are in constant interaction with each other. When something changes at one level, the total structure is involved: either because the other levels change to retain consistency or because they block or reduce the initial change. One can establish that there are fifteen sets of interaction to be considered between those six levels.

The purpose of a systematic analysis, other than to introduce dynamics by the exchanges and interactions which it provokes, is to allow us to position the various areas in which action-research is carried out with the minimum of ambiguity. Thus, the areas of intervention and investigation can be defined with the utmost clarity.

The Control of Involvement and Clinical Analysis
As we indicated before, it has been possible for the past ten years to identify a number of levels of involvement.

Structural-Professional Involvement
This takes place at the structural-professional level of research and analysis into the social practice of various participants in elements which are relevant to the socio-economic structures of present-day society. If one initiates action-research in education one runs the risk of "studying one's own role and function as researcher and specialist in the society, that is to say, of accepting an enquiry into one's own values and attitudes on which the equilibrium of one's personality depends. This will always provide a contradiction with the historical and existential project and also with the structural reality of the professional action with its constraints and economic, political and scientific limitations".(4) The personal project, taken over and absorbed by social institutions, is at risk of going in a contradictory direction to the objectives which were initially envisaged. What, for instance, is the sense of integrating Gypsy/Traveller children at school when they are certainly going to be excluded from society when they reach adolescence? It seems that the only freedom in action-research is based in contradiction rather than in compromises. As Daniel Hameline said, "The agent of change is a double agent, always busy serving two sides."

Historical-Existential Involvement
The researcher and the educational practitioner are part of an intellectual environment, generating habits, perceptions and thoughts and developing a system in which their practices can be encompassed. On the other hand, everyone is a product of a social class of origin in which one has been socialised as a child. At the level of historical-existential involvement, it is, therefore, necessary to take into account the original social class of each of the participants in the research. If a social participant originates from the working class s/he is unable to approach cultural practices in the same manner as someone from the 'upper classes'. "The rift with the original environment, the loss of roots, degrading by contrast with the elevation of another, are too common not to interfere in research in an educational area. It is towards those tensions and conflicts that the researcher uses his/her intuitions and hypotheses and becomes acquainted with the dilemma of a socially undefined position between 'them' and 'us' as is often said in working class circles." (6)

However, the historical-existential involvement of the researcher is not entirely dependent on his/her past. The personality, which can be partly attributed to previous influences, holds a dialogue with actual social practice through an individual and collective project. The praxis of the project is not solely determined by the past: it also shapes the project. "Everything changes if one considers that society presents a future prospect to everyone and that this perspective goes to everyone's heart providing the real motivation for their future conduct."(6)

Examining the historical-existential involvement of the social participants involves them in situating their praxis in their own personal history and relating that to their sector of the project and to the action-research project as a whole.

Psycho-Affective Involvement
Without doubt, this is the involvement that immediately springs to mind. The object of investigation always involves personality structures. Certain wishes of the researchers having their origins in infant experience are realised in response to questions posed by the research. For example, one of the problems with which a researcher in education is confronted is that of his/her authority: how can involvement be legitimate, what right does s/he have to work in this way rather than in another way? This authority model is, according to Gérard Mandel, nothing but the emphasising, exploitation, the reworking of a primitive guilt, a result of the aggression felt by the child towards the adult and its consequence: the fear of being abandoned, which "induces the child and later the adult, in a quasi-automatic conditioned reflex, to submit to a 'grown up'." (7) Other attitudes and tendencies, such as the 'wish to know', ingrained in a research activity, the 'parenthood wish', giving birth to a group, creating and disseminating ideas, have psycho-affective implications which need, without doubt, to be controlled, clarified and then used as a source of personal strength and increased awareness.

It is certainly difficult to differentiate between these various levels of involvement or, indeed, to prove their existence. In our view, this can be achieved only by a clinical analysis of the motives of the various participants. The analysis can, for example, make use of a control group and certainly an external facilitator for the research. This clinical analysis of involvement provides a privileged means of gaining knowledge about the processes of personal change during the action-research as well as ways of articulating the psychological and socio-cultural structure.

The Relationship Between Research and Action

One more difficulty, and certainly not one of the least, is the problem of the relationship between research and action or between theory and practice. This relationship depends on our ways of viewing complex and concrete realities and systems that constitute educational situations. We have plotted three paths of gaining knowledge about the reality which corresponds with three types of interaction between theory and practice. (8)

The Phenomenological-Subjective Path
This consists of a direct approach to the phenomena as they occur, as 'natural' and 'self-generated'. In this approach to reality theoretical knowledge and concrete action are almost inseparable. This type of approach certainly does not miss its objective, the educational situation, but a methodological incapacity of distancing itself, of researching the demarcations in an objective fashion, often make the determination of a theory implicit and always personal. In this approach theory can appear as a 'sub-product' of practice, destined to be justified after the fact, sometimes by orientation in directions based on the desires of only one individual or on the values of one institution.

The Scientific-Objective Path

This is the traditional research which we referred to before in which the rigorous methodology makes it possible to put objectives at a distance and to gain access to the proposed theory. The object of the study is never educational practice but always its components, abstract and timeless. Everything happens as if there were a prior scientific truth in relation to research activities: there will be some principles or phenomena which can be revealed or discovered which, once revealed in their essence, will be subjected to practice. Why, in this method, does not the practitioner wait for the researcher's 'revelation' to put those discovered 'truths' into practice? Unfortunately, these 'truths' only exist by the grace of the methods and technologies of the researchers who have defined them. Hence the difficulty and, realising the 'truths', the near-impossibility of research in the field of educational practice.

The Knowledge-Through-Praxis Path

This "not only has the system of objective relations, as used in the objective research method, as an objective but includes the responding relations between those objective structures and the structured situations in which they exist, that is, the twofold process of interiorisation of the exterior and exteriorisation of the interior" (9). It is not only necessary to study an objective but also the structure in which the objective was determined as well as the researcher him/herself and all the facts which, in one way or another, reproduce or create the objective of the research. This method could very well be that of action-research.

Nevertheless, as Edgar Morin (10) has said, in order to take a phenomenon into account it is not enough simply to associate contradictory notions in a compare-and-contrast manner and to affirm in the abstract that a dialectical relationship exists between, for example, theory and practice, thought and action, subject and object of research. The character of this relationship needs to be considered. It is not only a comparison of terms but of "their integration at the heart of a meta-system which transforms each of the terms in the process of a retro-active and recurring cycle." Each notion or action only makes sense in and by means of the cycle or rather in a system of cycles which interact and whose interactions need to be studied. Therefore, no theory can exist independently of any practice which in itself only makes sense through its interaction with the theory. The same goes for action and thought, subject and object.

It is worth dwelling on Morin's proposition that "...the idea of a cycle embodies a principle of knowledge which is neither atomistic nor holistic. It means that one can think only through cognitive praxis (active cycle) which interacts with sterile thoughts when they are disjointed or contradictory. It means that all explanation, rather than being reductionist or simplifying, must pass through a retro-active and recurring cycle which becomes a generator of knowledge. It is a necessary mediation, an invitation to productive thought."

Thus the cycle generates itself at the same time as it generates finding its sustenance in the observation of phenomena and animated by the cognitive activity of the thinking subject. Therefore, the cycle has no essence, no substance, not even reality without the interaction between the subject and the object. There is thus no system as a starting point for knowledge, real, material or objective, but a circular play which generates systems which appear as moments of production. Thus, the inexorable oppositions between systems such as Spiritual/Material, Freewill/Determinism, etc. disappear... the exclusion of the observer-subject in the deterministic or materialistic explanations places them in the same metaphysical sphere as the spiritual and idealistic explanations.

According to Morin "the real debate and the real alternative are embedded between complexity and simplification". Such simplification puts knowledge at the disjunction of concepts (subject/object, order/disorder) and complexity which associates primary concepts with a cycle, or rather with a system of cycles. Complexity or simplification is, therefore, not only situated at the level of observation of phenomena and of elaboration of theories but also on the level of the very principles of elaboration of thinking and knowledge. "It is the level of patterns that change the vision of reality, the reality of vision, the face of action that changes the reality."

Finally, I would like to remark that if the pattern of complexity opposes the absolute pattern of simplification/ disjunction, it integrates the simplification/disjunction so that it becomes the relative principle. "The pattern of complexity is not anti-analytical, is not anti-disjunctional: the analysis is a moment that recurs again and again, that is to say, it is not submerged in the totality synthesis itself but neither does it determine the analysis and that goes on to infinity in a process of producing knowledge."

The central idea of Morin's discourse is that the constitution of a new area of knowledge cannot intervene in opening the frontiers but can act on what generates the frontiers, i.e. the very principles of the organisation of knowledge. It is at this very transformation of frontiers between theoretical knowledge and practice that action-research can make a significant contribution through its systematic analysis, by taking into account involvement as an object of study. We should always recognise – and deplore – the fact that the pattern of complexity, having been recognised for more than twelve years now, has not been overtaken by the systematic elaboration of a methodology of complexity.

Current action-research workers can contribute to the elaboration of a methodology of complexity: their aptitude in this sector of knowledge can be an irreplaceable contribution.

References

1   HESS, Rémy. Histoire et typologie de la recherche-action. *Pour* 90 (June-July), 1983, 9-16. Toulouse: Privat,1983.

2   COLIN, Roland. La situation interculturelle, analyse et interpretation. *Les Amis de Sèvres* 4, 1982.

3   CLANET, Claude and BATAILLE, Michel. Une recherche-action sur la co-action éducative. *Psychologie et Education* 3 (2), June 1979, 109-140.

4   BARBIER, René. *La Recherche-Action dans l'institution éducative.* Paris: Gauthier-Villars, 1977, p73-74.

5   BARBIER. Op. cit., p70.

6   SARTRE, Jean-Paul. *Critique de la raison dialectique.* Paris: Gallimard, 1960, p125

7   MENDEL, Gérard. *Pour décoloniser l'enfant.* Paris: Payot, 1971, 245.

8   CLANET, Claude and BATAILLE, Michel. Op. cit., 120 et sequ.

9   BOURDIEU, Pierre. *Esquisse d'une théorie de la pratique.* Genève-Paris: Droz, p163.

10   MORIN, Edgar. *La méthode, la nature de la nature.* Paris: Le Seuil, 1977, p380.

Part 2 Action-research and Co-ordination: The Situation in Different States

Paper 1   Belgium
*Koen Van Ryckeghem, Vlams Overleg Woonwagenwerk (VOW)
and Alain Reyniers, Coprodev*

General Data

Numbers
■ Flanders and Brussels: 800 families in trailers (census carried out by VOW in May 1989) and an unknown number living in houses. This is the total number of Travellers, Rom and Manouche Gypsies.
■ Walloon: an estimated 7,000-8,000 people of whom 2,000-3,000 live in trailers.

Groups
■ Travellers: defined as itinerants or trailer inhabitants of Belgian origin. The majority of Belgium's Traveller population.
■ Manouche Gypsies: estimated Belgian population 1,500, mixed (by familial and economic links) with the Traveller population.
■ Rom Gypsies: 400 persons.

Geographical Distribution
■ Flanders: 30% of Flemish communes have trailer dwellers on their territory (this includes showmen). Forty communes (12%) have more than five families within their boundaries. The average is 3.5 families per locality.
■ Walloon: no accurate figures.
■ Rom Gypsies: concentrated in the large urban areas (Antwerp, Brussels, Charleroi).

Languages
■ Travellers: Dutch or French but spoken with a strong local dialect, interspersed with slang.
■ Manouche Gypsies: generally speak Manouche interspersed with many

words borrowed from French or Dutch spoken in a Manouche style. Second language: Dutch or French but of a very limited vocabulary.
■ Rom Gypsies: generally speak Romanes. Second language: limited French.

Educational Organisation
Under Belgian education policy there is no specific or separate provision. In general there is no policy for Travellers. All the projects and provisions taken are the result of initiatives emanating from organisations for Travellers.

Degree of Schooling
It is estimated that 60-80% of parents are illiterate or functionally so. Schooling for the children is becoming the norm: at least 80% of primary aged children (six to twelve years) regularly attend school. After the age of twelve (secondary level) the level of attendance diminishes. Between fourteen and sixteen this diminution is considerable. However, in a generation the maximum percentage has risen from 20% to 80%. The exception to this rule are the Rom who, apart from those living in Brussels, do not go to school. Those without formal education are principally the children of families who still lead an itinerant life.
■ Walloon: one can see a relationship between schooling and the fairly high level of housed families. Housed Travellers are most often salaried and to become thus they require a minimal level of education.
■ Flanders: there is great dispersion of the children into the schools close to the sites rather than a massive concentration in certain schools.

Major Problems
Generally the children's attainment levels range from poor to average. The transition to secondary level is problematic. The school leaving age has been raised to eighteen (with the possibility of part-time attendance between sixteen and eighteen). The Travellers stay on because they have to rather than out of a choice for professional training. Almost without exception they choose a practical course rather than an academic one. There is no known example of a Gypsy in Belgium entering higher education.

Action-research
Action-research is about theoretical reflection and research (study) of practical experience with a view to an eventual modification of this practice. There is no systematic action-research on the education of Gypsy and Traveller children in Belgium. Work on travelling people in general and the study of their educational situation in particular is principally left to initiatives by private organisations. The public authorities invest very little to support these initiatives and conversely the results obtained by these private initiatives do not change general policy. The development of sites remains the priority question.

Organisations for Travellers in Belgium
■ Flanders and Brussels: Vlaams Overleg Woonwagenwerk Asbl is a grouping of eight Flemish organisations which have co-ordinated their activities since 1977. Size: three staff on an unlimited contract and two employed on a contract known as 'troisième circuit de travail' (third work system) who deal with a whole range of problems: site development, social and administrative problems,

community work, basic literacy, getting children into school etc.
■ Walloon and Brussels: Coprodev (Committee for the Advancement and Defence of Travellers Asbl) was created in 1987. Size: one co-ordinator.

The two organisations are recognised as valuable intermediaries by the authorities of the two linguistic communities. They are seen as competent and representative to deal with problems facing Travellers. Nevertheless, grants are not much increased: in 1989 one person and a half were subsidised (one co-ordinator for Flanders and a half-time co-ordinator for Wallonie).

The VOW and Coprodev maintain regular contact and collaborate in their approaches to the authorities. They share the same hopes and priorities. Co-ordination between the two organisations is similarly essential because the movement of the travelling population goes beyond the boundaries of the Belgian communities. Since 1988 the VOW has had a specific department dealing with education which could take on the responsibility for action-research. At present in Belgium there is no organisation involved in this field, not even at a local level.

Recognition of the Importance of Action-research
The two organisations recognise the importance of action-research. However, in practice, it has only taken place in the Flemish Community in view of the lack of staff and resources in the south of Belgium. It can not be over empha-sised that the public authorities are only beginnings to take an interest in the education of travelling children. One cannot expect any initiatives in the area of action-research to come from this quarter. Action-research must then be made at the same time as a study of much wider problems.

Priorities for a Comprehensive Study
Apart from the research report, *The Education of Gypsies and Travellers in Belgium*, there is no scientific publication about the education of Travellers. This absence of basic analysis necessitates, in the first stage, a survey of all aspects of education:
■ a survey of the parents' level of education
■ the parents' expectations of education, training in general and/or professional training
■ the children's and adolescents' expectations of education, training in general and/or professional training
■ the influence of circumstances and economic activities on motivation in respect of schooling, training in general and/or professional training
■ the relationship between 'nomadism' and schooling and between 'settling' and schooling.

Priorities for Action-research
■ relationship between site provision, the establishment of relationships with the local community and the level of school attendance
■ study of the needs/expectations of parents, children and adolescents
■ study of the education authorities from specific local situations
■ transfer to secondary level: Travellers' expectations of training in general and professional training
■ qualitative improvements to the education received: reasons for failure in relation to motivation.

Co-ordination

The organisations for Travellers, VOW and Coprodev, work within the same terms of reference, methods and priorities. Given the limited means at their disposal they focus mainly on raising the awareness of authorities at local, community and national level and provoking action. Given the monopoly of the two organisations in this area, they fulfil, de facto, a co-ordinating role.

Independent Education: since 1988 Catholic education has concerned itself with the problem of Traveller education. (This is the greatest teaching resource in Belgium covering about 70% of the country's schools.) 1988-1989: mainly an introduction to the problem and raising of awareness. Planning 1989-1990: study and first project about the results and retraining of teachers who work with Traveller children. Instrument of co-ordination: "Overleggroep Nationaal Sekretariaat van het Katholiek Onderwijs – Vlaams Overleg Woonwagenwerk".

National and community authorities: nascent interest in the problem created by pressure from the independent sector.

Co-ordination Initiatives and Priorities
There is a need to develop an instrument of co-ordination to take over the different networks within the local teaching ministeries. This body should have the following structure:
- competent cabinet member
- competent government officials
- representatives of the different networks
- Traveller organisations.

Its aim would be to determine a policy on the schooling and the professional training professional of Travellers and to furnish the means to realise this policy.

Its tasks would be to:
- study the attendance of children in school, learning circumstances, academic results, the teachers (educational and instructional problems)
- organisation the training and re-training of teachers
- skills participation in the body representing the different networks.

This is already operational for the Catholic network.

Reference

1   REYNIERS, Alain. Centre de Recherches Tsiganes. *La scolarisation des Tsiganes et Voyageurs en Belgique et au Grand-Duché de Luxembourg* (The Education of Gypsies and Travellers in Belgium and the Grand Duchy of Luxembourg: a research report presented to the General Department of Employment, Social Affairs and Education). Commission of the European Communities, 1985.

Paper 2   France: The General Situation

Maria Alcaloïde and Benoît Gramond, Teachers of Gypsy and
Traveller children, Members of the Administrative Council of
the Centre for Liaison and Information, Travel-School (CLIVE).

Facts given in the three French presentations which follow were drawn from
the sources given in the bibliography at the end of the final paper (Paper 4)
and specific references in the text of each paper are to the list of references at
the end of Paper 4.

The Gypsy Communities

It must be remembered that the generic term 'Gypsy' (Tsigane) is not used by
the communities themselves. On French soil there are communities of
Manouche or Sinti, Gitane or Kale, Rom and Yenish. Within these groups there
are sub-groups:

■ Manouche
German Manouche or Gadzkene
Piedmontese Sinti
Spanish Manouche
Alsatian Manouche
■ Rom
Kalderash Rom
Lovara Rom
Curara Rom
Yugoslavian Rom
■ Gitane
Catalonian Gitane
Andalusian Gitane
Portuguese Gitane

    The geographical labelling was probably correct at some point in history
and to a certain extent still is today. To these Gypsy communities may be
added the Yenish, Travellers of European origin. The term Traveller is common

to all these communities and as such takes on an identifying role: "To say that you are a Traveller is first of all to say, and maybe that is all it says, that you are not a Gauje." (1)

Numerical Importance
In France it is estimated that the various communities number between a minimum of 220,000 and a maximum of 320,000 (1). Therefore, France is in second place in the EEC after Spain. This estimate draws attention to the fact that 50 per cent of this population is under the age of sixteen. These figures must be re-estimated on a regular basis because of the implications of a large increase in a section of the population.

Geographical Migration
In the absence of any national survey it is difficult to be precise about the geographical migration of the different communities. The organisation CLIVE (Centre de Liaison et d'Information Voyage Ecole: Centre for Liaison and Information, Travel-School), founded in 1901 and, since 1985, bringing together members of the National Education Board, commissioned a survey (3) which gives us some idea, albeit a partial one, about children receiving school provision. It would appear that the Rom, Manouche and Yenish groups are spread throughout France whilst the Gitane groups remain strongly concentrated in the south-west and south-east of France (Bordeaux, Toulouse, Perpignan, Marseille). It is difficult to pinpoint the exact movements of the Yugoslavian Rom communities.

Languages
Romanes, the Gypsy language, has become diversified with the passage of time and through migration. An important number of dialects has emerged from this diversification. In France the following dialects can be found (4):
■ Sinto dialects: these comprise several dialects influenced by the German language which have spread throughout Italy and Germany. Alsatian, Manouche and Piedmontese Sinto are much in evidence.
■ Kale dialects: this group of dialects, reduced to a state of 'slang', is in use in France, the Iberian peninsula and in North Africa.
■ Vlax dialects: heavily influenced by the Romanian language, whether in Walasia, Moldavia or Transylvania, these dialects can be found in almost all parts of the world. In France the Kalderash, Curari and Lovari dialects are spoken.

Finally, not all Gypsies in France speak these dialects; the other languages in use are French, 'Traveller slang' (the language spoken by Gypsies of Sinto-Manouche origin who have forgotten their own language or who have intermingled with non-Gypsy nomads, fairground people or others), as well as Spanish (Castilian, Andalusian) and Catalan more or less padded out with Kale, Romanian, Serbo-Croat and Turkish. The question of bilingualism applies particularly to the Gitane Kale groups (Marseille, Perpignan, Bordeaux).

School Provision for Gypsy/Traveller Children
In the interests of clarity, we have again used the information from the European synthesis report (2) together with the results of the CLIVE survey (the results can be found in (3)). Seven class models, either defined by individual schools or by the State programme, are on offer to Gypsy/Traveller

children on school entry. In the studies made from the information collected from the different States – and in the CLIVE survey on the different locations used for school provision – there is almost always a dichotomy between 'special classes' and 'ordinary classes'. However, different interpretations are possible here; the term 'special class' must be used with caution because there are classes everywhere which are 'special' by virtue of the children in them or by status, and there are classes which are 'special' by law, that is, having such status accorded to them by the authorities and correspondingly by the 'specialist' status of the teachers who work in them.

Classes denoted 'special' by law often come under the aegis of the AIS (Adaptation et Integration Scolaire), the State Education Department responsible for the education of children with a 'handicap', whether physical, mental, social or other. These classes remain affiliated to the main Department of Education, with a specialist inspector offering his support for the everyday functioning of these classes. These classes are called "Perfection Classes" (in England: Special Needs Classes), and take in children with learning difficulties often associated with behavioural difficulties. There is a special qualification for teachers in the form of a diploma, the Certificat d'Aptitude Pédagogique Spécialisée Adaptation et Integration Scolaires (Certificate in the Teaching of Special Needs Education). This entitles the holder of the certificate to priority of appointment to a special post over teachers without this qualification. Side by side with the "Perfection Classes" run "Adaptation Classes" which offer pupils a special programme facilitating their return to the mainstream curriculum after a short period of time.

Special Classes for Traveller Children
Classes adapted for the reception and teaching of Traveller children while maintaining relations with mainstream classes within the school (Lézignan, Nantes, Valence, Romainville, Trappes primaire, Herblay Jean Jaurès).

Mainstream Classes in a Mainstream School
These classes take in all new children who are then divided according to age and the academic level they have reached. In practice children are placed in a class with others differing in age by not more than one or two years (Montauban Verlhaguet, Toulouse, Eragny, Herblay Jean Jaurès, Jean Moulin, les Chênes).

Classes Decreed Special by the Authority
The CLIVE survey uncovered a significant number of special classes. Of 168 classes in twenty-three schools, twenty-four were officially Special Needs.

Bordeaux	3	Orléans	3
Villeurbanne	1	Lézignan	5
Valence	1	Romainville	1
Clermont-Ferrand	3	Trappes	1
Montauban	2	Herblay	2
Narbonne	2		

Special Classes for Traveller Children Without Access to Mainstream Classes
These classes are not integrated with the rest of the school (Bordeaux, Lézignan, Villeurbanne, Argenteuil).

Classes Permanently Situated on an Official Site
These classes are 'special' by law or by nature and open only to Gypsy/Traveller children.
■ Aurillac: one nursery class, special by nature
■ Dijon: one class on site, special by nature
■ Montauban: known as 'the wood pigeon', special by AIS law
■ Orléans: two special classes by AIS law
■ Trappes: one nursery class, special by nature
■ Nantes: three classes on 'ground set aside for the purpose'/site schools

Mobile Provision on Unofficial Sites
Generally private, affiliated to state education and comprising preschool education and acclimatisation to school provision; ASET (Association pour la Scolarisation des Enfants Tsiganes/Association for the Education of Traveller Children) in the Paris region (Val d'Oise); four mobile classrooms with three and a half ASET teachers and a half-time State teacher. It is also sometimes possible to maintain school provision for a family group wishing to ensure continuity while the group is travelling: Clermont-Ferrand (the travelling school of Auvergne).

Mobile Provision on an Official Site
This arrangement is similar to the pattern of domiciliary tuition (the travelling school of Auvergne).

The Boarding School Model
This is not common and is mainly rejected by families. For example, the State School for the children of bargees at Conflans Ste Honorine is reminiscent of the children's homes in Belgium.

Summary of the Results of the CLIVE Survey.
Of the twenty-three schools involved or having to face up to the issue of school provision for Gypsy/Traveller children, there is provision at nursery level in sixteen and at elementary level in twenty. Out of a total of 168 classes, twenty-four are specialist by law.
It should be noted that in a single school several systems can be in operation. In one school there could be X classes of which N are specialist, closed, open, and/or mobile. Nor does this 'rigid' structure reflect the choices made in practice by the different schools in the management of the posts to which they are committed.

Examples of Flexible Management
Some examples of the staffing arrangements in specific schools and the manner in which the teaching teams operate:
■ Herblay Jean Jaurès: six ordinary posts, two specialist posts and one support post specifically for the teaching of Gypsy/Traveller children. Flexibility in the use of the two specialist posts allows eight ordinary classes; one post can be kept free for computer and library work; the 'Gypsy-Traveller' teacher is kept

available for specific support. Eventual integration into the mainstream is the norm.

■ Lézignan: fourteen posts including specialist posts. There is a flexible structure for the specialist posts, with the aim of swift integration into the mainstream but with support provided as necessary at transfer from primary education and even beyond.

■ Nantes: six posts including one with responsibility for non-readers. This particular post of special responsibility offers little flexibility within the basic curriculum. During the afternoon when less structured activities take place, specific support can be offered to children newly integrated into the mainstream.

In the Val d'Oise, an administrative innovation has been the creation of support posts to the schools and no longer to the children when they have a large number of Traveller children.

The appointment and management of these 'Traveller' posts have two main objectives: to avoid the specialisation and personalisation of a post closed to mainstream classes by the allocation of a half-time post to a school; it is used for Gypsy children (either by regrouping children or by team teaching with the class teacher). The rest of the time it is envisaged that without extra support for this school, the responsibility falls to the whole of the teaching team to welcome the children and provide education at all levels.

The Education Process

The following figures should be treated with caution. In the absence of any official government information, they are based on the 1979 estimates in the *Ecole Libératrice* (a Union newspaper) which suggest that 65 per cent of Traveller children are not attending school together with the figures given in the synthesis report (2) which estimates that there are 120,000-150,000 Gypsy/Traveller children in France.

population under 16	120,000	150,000
attending school	42,000 (35%)	52,500 (35%)
not attending school	78,000 (65%)	97,000 (65%)

If all these children were receiving education up to the age of sixteen they would represent (on a base of 150,000 Gypsy children) 1.5 per cent of the ten million children in school in France at this level. It must be remembered that a very large proportion of these 35 per cent of children in education leave school between the ages of twelve and fourteen.

In conclusion, we can say that a great variety of situations exist with a corresponding variety of evaluations ranging from the very optimistic to the very pessimistic. Our survey so far has found evidence that:

■ there are Gypsy children attending school and transferring to secondary level without problems

■ the vast majority of questionnaire replies show a level of education corresponding to that of the end of the second year primary at the point of leaving the primary sector

■ that experience of nursery education from a very early age is a good basis for success in reception classes and that the child's reception and the taking into account of the Gypsy child's life experience ease his socialisation in the first instance and then enable his future education to proceed.

Other voices have, however, made themselves heard:
- there still remains a very strong resistance on the part of the communities to school methods and customs for those who have attended school
- after the elementary level education for the majority is not continued
- a lack of innovation in the way they are received persists
- there is a lack of official recognition of the importance of working conditions (smaller classes, special funding, stability and continuity of teams)
- there is continued widespread refusal by teachers to accept these communities because of general lack of information and training (initial and in-service)
- there is relatively little opening-up of school provision apart from the special classes accorded recognition by law for children suffering social, intellectual or physical handicap – despite a tendency which would invalidate the figures given by *l'Ecole Libératrice* in 1979, showing at that date 80 per cent of Gypsy children being educated in special classes.

The CLIVE survey confirms a tentative opening of mainstream or special classes (support, adaptation, Gypsy/Traveller-orientated etc.) specialist by nature but created and intended for these populations in the framework of respect for cultural minorities. The sole objective in the long run would be to phase out special provision after the transformation of a too rigid educational system which was conceived without reference to the educational needs of the Traveller communities.

Paper 3   France: Some Thoughts on Action-research

Arlette Laurent-Fahier, Centre for Gypsy Research and CEFISEM

"In most human beings the aptitude for research is either asleep, somnolent or awakened. Just as one can improve oneself by education in the same way, through research, one can and should deepen one's understanding". (5)

The Necessity for Action-research by the Practitioners Themselves
In a changing society where most values are being questioned, the process of education can no longer rest on an immutable ethic of training for tomorrow's world. Pedagogical research (research into teaching and learning) enables the school to evolve. But what research and what new training does this imply for practitioners?

Research in Education
"Pedagogical research, applied or pure, is divorced from the activity of the educational system" (Schwartz Report). There is a crisis in education; it hides its failures and it no longer addresses the expectations of the young. According to Louis Legrand (6) "research into teaching methods can fulfil several functions in the evolution of the educational system:
■ to increase knowledge of the act of learning and the conditions which can lead to improvements in learning. That is its best known function. Dissemination of research findings to the teaching force and to those in training would be necessary to augment knowledge and improve good practice
■ to initiate experimental projects based on proven research, with all the necessary precautions, and possibly with the assistance of consultants and research workers
■ to promote knowledge of scientific developments throughout the world of education. This could reinforce teaching strategies underpinned by a pedagogical rationale."

Pedagogical research is thus linked to practice in the classroom and to its difficulties and problems. It must not be merely a statement of what exists but must be dynamic and participate fully in the process of change.

In addition, teacher training should include research, the relationship between theory and practice and the construction of theory based on practice, carried out by the teachers themselves. Educational research is not new in France and so we may question why it plays such a small part in the transformation of educational practices:

■ the conservatism of teachers, their lack of interest in research work and their fear of their methods being questioned are often put forward as arguments to explain the uneven progress associated with initiatives for reform in schools
■ in addition practitioners do not hesitate to point out how far removed research projects are from their own daily experiences; it is taken out of their control.

It would seem that common ground could be found if experiments for proposed innovations were carried out in the field, in conditions as close to reality as possible. If the observations are to be meaningful, it is essential that teachers and researchers work in close collaboration throughout the action-research process programme:

■ choice of the problems to be studied
■ elaboration of the hypotheses
■ methodology of data-collection
■ data analysis
■ pedagogical conclusions.

Nevertheless, in order to achieve this, teachers must be 'actively initiated into research' as emphasised by G. de Landsheere in his work, targeted specifically at educationists (7). In fact, action-research by the practitioner him/herself in his/her own class, poses a large number of considerations which s/he will have to record and then analyse:

■ methodological problems; how to reconcile action strategies with research strategies? How to be objective about everyday activities? How to participate and to observe?
■ problems concerning professional duties; is the practitioner able to concentrate his/her efforts, in other words his/her time, on a single aspect of his/her work? Can s/he conduct a piece of research concerning the children without the children themselves being involved in its planning, the control of data-collection, the analysis and the putting into practice of the results (Children's Rights)?
■ considerations of value; what kind of knowledge can be built up by this type of research?
■ considerations of status; what will be the status of the teacher-researcher (salary, time)? What will be his role in the school? There are many other considerations.

The Nature and Future of Research in Education

There will be no transformation of the educational system without making a real attempt to innovate by giving power to the practitioners: the innovatory process must be liberated. If research, associated with innovation, has a fundamental role to play in this, it must also be liberated and we are forced to the conclusion that action-research by the practitioner him/herself, on his/her own territory, is without doubt, a vital necessity.

The practitioner is the only one who knows and is able to keep account of the specific parameters of the teaching/learning situation for which s/he is responsible. Why should research by the practitioner be impossible? There are still researchers who make this claim but such research already exists and can actively include all those concerned, in this case Gypsies and Travellers. This is a question of rights and dignity.

Research is a common good of which there can be no monopoly. Nobody can delegate responsibility for research to others when it concern one's own social and professional life. Consequently, the social actors must become acknowledged as competent and responsible practitioners, innovators or researchers, and be given the means to become so. Thus arises the inevitable old question: can the positions of the scientific researcher and the subject to be researched be reconciled?

A certain number of practitioners, confronted with difficulties or goaded into action by researchers' ideas or by political or social ideas, have changed or are about to change their methods of working and are committing themselves to a new approach. Very quickly, they are obliged to step back, make a space, observe and analyse – in short to enter into a research process to evaluate the effects of their experimentation.

One can be a practitioner engaged in research without becoming a researcher of one's practice, i.e. a practitioner-researcher whose status must be examined closely so that the appropriate training and resources can be placed at his/her disposal. In particular, s/he must be afforded the opportunity to collaborate with others through networks where practitioner-researchers, researchers, trainer-researchers, specialists in various disciplines and all the social actors are working together. Obviously one cannot be a researcher in and of one's own practice without establishing relations with one's peers and with the research, whether it be directly within the networks between practitioners and researchers or indirectly through familiarity with the results of research. Thus the practitioner-researcher has an original and vital role to play in linking practice with research and the social demands with practice.

In addition, any educational initiative brings with it a particular vision of society and reflects its values. Is it possible to think of a research project with the aim of transforming the educational system? Whatever it is, an ambitious policy owes it to itself to muster all the forces of research. Even diverse, many-faceted, productive research by the practitioner, based on the practical experience culled from the field, and using the available tools of the trade (methods, resources, institutions, structures etc.) sometimes still meets the scepticism of certain university researchers because this research would be seen as empirical, tainted with subjectivity, would not present the required scientific features and would not meet the necessary scientific criteria.

In order to improve university researchers should educate practitioners in scientific rigour, in the epistemological status of research in education and help to create the appropriate tools for action-research by the practitioner him/herself in his/her own field.

What is a Practitioner?
Innovation, to initiate, to research, to act, to discover that little extra something which will allow progress... hope for more efficiency... There is an inevitable element in all the pedagogical situations in which the teacher finds him/herself: dissatisfaction. Therefore, the teacher seeks in his/her work, in a

practical sense, solutions which will afford him/her satisfaction. S/he re-searches, innovates, renews, does not know. However, what s/he does know is that s/he is making progress. S/he researches into his/her own practice because if this is a need, a compulsion, it is also to find a 'better way of doing things'. The teacher sets out on the route towards active change to understand his/her own daily practice, to deepen his/her own research, to form his/her theories while developing himself/herself (self-training). It is by embarking on an analysis to understand his/her practice that s/he re-emerges by conducting a synthesis towards this development, this theory which will free the practitioner from being once again a stranger to his/her research and to research in general.

From the starting point of his/her own life, personality and experiences, the teacher goes through four stages. First of all, dissatisfaction. There is a period of reflection: the teacher observes his/her surroundings and observes himself/herself in his/her own practice. S/he tries to understand for himself/herself the phenomena which are unfolding. Then follows a period of consideration. S/he looks for solutions for and in himself/herself in relation to aims and objectives which are his/hers. During a period of foundering s/he often loses direction, then looks for new pedagogical strategies both within and outside of himself/herself.

The time for evaluation arrives... that is when the teacher must theorise to ensure the maximum possible coherence in the triangle of aims, objectives and practices. Through a methodology, at least partially coherent, the teacher very often passes through the arena of innovation which is personal and peculiar to him/her. This also calls upon the imaginary... imagination, creation, creative power, do-it-yourself... for is not the fantasy of every teacher 'the Pygmalion effect', the creative anticipation...?

From Innovation to Research

Innovation is a novelty which appears as a break in the continuity; it engenders restructurings which answer to the needs and/or the wish of the innovator. It exists in reaction to an earlier, inadequate situation. The need to innovate corresponds to the necessity to adapt oneself to an environment. Faced with an urgent situation, it is necessary to find the means to correct it in practice and improve effectiveness. One cannot exclude the part played by the will of the innovator; in fact, an innovation can correspond to an ideological concept. The word contains a positive connotation. It is a relative value – is innovation for one innovation for others? What is positive for one may be negative for others. For the innovator this could be an ideal. It is a process which has a limited duration in space and time. Innovation is a perpetual readjustment.

Schema of Innovation

Environment	Means	Concept
Needs	Innovation	
Wishes		

In response to the environment, either through need or wish, people provide themselves with the means for innovation. For the innovator, innovation can be an ideal. The innovator innovates in order to adapt to the problems raised (creative adaptation... strategy and the dynamic of change): the principle of necessity. Will this person continue to change for the pleasure of it and not through necessity (the principle of pleasure) or will s/he analyse, deepen and theorise?

To innovate is to act in a different way, to upset the status quo: "Non, les braves gens n'aiment pas que l'on prenne une autre route qu'eux." (No, good people don't like you taking a different path from theirs. Georges Brassens).

Action Survey of Ongoing Research

As preparation for the Summer University a questionnaire was put to some teachers and teams of teachers asking the following questions:

1. Do you consider your actions and experiences could be incorporated into a network of action-research?
2. Are these actions the product of individual or group work and, in the latter case, who are the other people concerned?
3. What would you expect to gain from belonging to a network?
4. What resources might be at your disposal?

The responses to the first question can be categorised by type of research (number of responses):

■ research into learning (11)
■ training of and dissemination of information to teachers (13)
■ the impact of a project and its diversity for the school, the children and the parents (4)
■ school follow-up, continuity/breaks in continuity (5)
■ school structures, types of support, their adaptability, flexibility and n readiness to embark upon initiative (10)
■ curriculum content (3)
■ university studies, action-research (6)

Paper 4 France: Co-ordination

Jean-Pierre Liégeois, Director of the Centre for Gypsy Research,
University René Descartes, and Consultant to the Commission
of the European Communities

The Present Situation

The balance sheet regarding co-ordination in France tips towards the negative
side. Without oversimplifying it can be said that people are all working in their
own little corner, unaware of what is going on elsewhere, however near or far
that may be. This accounts for the sense of isolation, or even total abandon-
ment, which is the fate of most of the teachers involved. They are excluded
from all opportunity to collaborate with colleagues and are deprived of the
benefits of organised information and liaison.

This springs from the fact that in France, as in most neighbouring
countries, for reasons explained in the various reference documents for this
conference, no overall structural policy has been adopted regarding the
education of Gypsy and Traveller children. Conscientious work was, and still
is, going on according to chance or the necessity of the moment, and is
dependent upon the determination or goodwill of individuals. If news of
projects emerges beyond the classroom walls, more often than not it goes no
further than that particular team of teachers, if indeed there is one. We are
thus wasting time, energy and money. Having teachers, advisers and local
inspectors working in isolation does not lead to innovation, if indeed there is
any, nor does it favour the necessary flexibility and encourage the school to
adapt to the child. In France, at national, regional and academic levels, there is
no structure and no individual responsible for co-ordinating, passing on
information and organising co-operation in the field of Traveller education. It is
a completely unworkable situation and one which astonishes our neighbours,
particularly in a country where there has been a long tradition of centralisa-
tion. The situation has arisen, mainly as a consequence of policies of
assimilation.

This compartmentalised way of working is widespread, even where co-ordination, meetings, collaboration and the dissemination of good practice could be extremely easy. Just to give one example, this is exactly what happens in teacher training, particularly in-service training, which is, as various seminars have stressed, of special importance in our field. In France, the structures do exist; there is the relatively well-resourced and flexible network of Training and Information Centres for the Education of the Children of Migrants (CEFISEM). Since 1979-80 the Ministry has also made them responsible for training in the teaching of Gypsy children. In fact, 'Gypsy' education courses are not only extremely rare (the effect being that hardly any teachers of Travellers have attended a course at these Training Centres) but additionally, to pursue the theme of co-ordination, they have given an impression of being very disorganised. Poor co-ordination of activities and publicity means that so far, in most cases when a CEFISEM has planned a course, recruitment of participants has been random, information has not been circulated effectively, people involved have been identified haphazardly, there has usually been no guarantee that they will be allowed to attend and the selection criteria have not been apparent. This all means that on the same course there would be beginners and highly experienced people, newcomers and veterans. The participants have enjoyed the meetings, in spite of the problems, simply because of their infrequency and everyone's sense of isolation. It is always good to meet and to share problems and complaints, particularly if you do not have the chance to improve the position directly. In other respects, the lack of co-ordination has so far prevented the proposal of more advanced training modules, a step by step progression through courses which would bring together teachers from a wider geographical area. This teacher training example demonstrates the possible drawbacks of not having someone to co-ordinate people and activities: not only do we fail to make progress in our thought and actions but we are also being counterproductive in the sense that participants are dissatisfied and become disillusioned or tired, not to mention the fact that the 'training' aspect of most of these courses is questionable.

The report of the French University Summer School at Montauban in 1988, where it refers to co-ordination, is clear both in its analysis of deficiencies (particularly those highlighted in the summaries of the working groups' discussions) and in its proposals for remedying the situation. Here, we see clearly the need for a structured and, therefore, co-ordinated, approach. Odd efforts remain localised and there emerges an impression of immobilisation due to institutional inertia and to a lack of global planning. The most pressing demand is for collaboration, co-ordination and organised information. This French conference concluded that teachers have "the legitimate feeling that there is no way for them to put forward and develop new ideas; this is because there is no framework for them to fit into, nothing to support and maintain them, no structure for cross-fertilisation to allow discussion and validation of new ideas".

It is only very timidly that here and there the situation is changing such as at very local or local authority level where co-ordination is developing for a combination of reasons which we do not have time to analyse here. The changes are linked to the pressure of circumstances, the determination of one or two people, the appearance of an inter-cultural movement and the need to accommodate Gypsy and Traveller children highlighted by the European institutions using the means they have at their disposal: information, seminars, studies, publications. For the same reasons, the whole attitude is starting to change within most central institutions. This development, if it continues still further, will probably enable the necessary action for co-ordination to be intensified.

Liaison Between Teachers and Others

Opportunities for liaison are an important means of help for teachers. They allow comparison of ideas and practice, provide support and advice and give teachers the feeling that they belong to a supportive network and are not working in isolation and fumbling individually in the dark. Liaison may be possible by various complementary means: for example, a teacher, an adviser or an inspector could be appointed across several districts or a whole local authority. However, in France this is only part of the timid innovations already mentioned; the role of those concerned is not always very explicit and their availability for the task may not be sufficient. That is why, in this context, the setting up in France of an association for people employed in Gypsy and Traveller education takes on a special dimension.

The idea – or one should say the need – for a national association had emerged during the first national meeting for teachers organised in 1980 in Dijon by the Centre for Gypsy Studies in conjunction with the local teachers' team. It was not until 1985, however, that the CLIVE (the Centre for Liaison and Information Travel/School) was set up. The aim of the association is "to encourage a better match between the home culture of the Gypsies and the demands of the education system". This is why it proposes to distribute information about educational issues relating to Gypsy/Traveller children and to act as a discussion and resource centre in close contact with the staff who are directly involved. It appeared crucial to put an end to their isolation, to offer support which would enable them to reflect on the issues and to keep sight of the educational situation. A consensus seemed to emerge on a number of points, namely:

■ an acknowledgement that there was no coherent policy regarding the education of Gypsy children. There had been odd attempts and even political initiatives but these had never been transformed into reality

■ there is no one answer to the questions asked about the education of Gypsy children. It should be possible, in particular through the specialist frameworks, to develop a network which would look into means of making provision for children

■ it is vital that there should be liaison between all those involved so that experiences can be described and the results evaluated, circulated and understood

■ it is urgent and necessary to establish a coherent policy which should be developed under four headings: awareness raising, information, training, research

■ in the area of training, one proposal of the CLIVE is that teachers working with Gypsy/Traveller children should be recognised as having a role to play in the training of colleagues and that they themselves have a priority need for training on in-service courses.

The CLIVE is pursuing its collaboration with the Centre for Gypsy Studies at the René Descartes University so that all initiatives likely to improve the education of Gypsy children may be developed.

In 1989 the CLIVE had just redefined its working methods. At the last Annual General Meeting it was noted that after several years of existence the executive can no longer represent all the members (now fifty-seven); its present over-centralised set-up no longer allows for effective decision-making and any over-rigidity in this area leads to inefficiency and sometimes discourages colleagues. The 1988 University Summer School at Montauban led to the setting up of branches in different regions of France. Discussions revealed the diversity of problems from the viewpoint of Gypsy cultures and of the school structure. The idea of a regional CLIVE network was proposed by the Marseilles members. Maintaining collaboration with the Centre for Gypsy Studies and the support of the CEFISEM will broaden the association's scope for thought and action. The different regions, which were defined according to the distribution of members, are: Centre-Rhône-Alps, South West, South East, Paris Area, Loire Valley, West, East.

The following new approaches have been adopted. We take more account of regional interests when considering problems and their solutions. The new executive committee will include representatives of all the regional CLIVE branches. The main subjects for consideration will be the adaptation of the Gypsies to the constraints of urban living and long-standing settlements in a region, educational implications, respect for cultural identity and the setting up of educational initiatives; the exchange of diverse educational experiences linked to the local context and the publication of these experiences.

We should also remind you of the existence in France of the Centre for Gypsy Studies which has been recognised for several years at French and European levels for its work and, notably, its co-ordinating role with and for the European Community and the Council of Europe. A state-owned University body set up in 1979, it is part of the Social Science Training and Research Unit of the René Descartes University. Its activities in research, training, information, advice and co-ordination are essential in the field of Gypsy and Traveller education.

Evaluation

Any evaluation one can make is brief and contained already in the preceding remarks. Until now the education authorities in France have had no policy of co-ordination in the field of Gypsy and Traveller education. Furthermore, if one lists the achievements in this area one will notice, on the one hand, that most of the initiatives (teachers' meetings, seminars, studies, publications and University Summer Schools) have not been set up by the French education authorities and, on the other hand, that the authorities played no role in facilitating any of the projects. Compared with certain neighbouring countries the contrast is striking and all the more so, I stress, since France has a totally centralised education policy. It is certainly desirable, and even essential, that the authorities should not monopolise initiatives or the actual carrying out of projects but the advantage of a centralised system is that it can allow for and support, for example, pilot schemes in different places. The outcome, the good and the bad points and suggestions for setting up similar schemes can then be made public. This is one advantage that a decentralised system, where any activity is scattered and isolated, does not have. A centralised system is logically ideal for developing co-ordinated action. If it does not do this the participants experience the negative aspects of the system without enjoying the benefits.

Evaluation of the few efforts at co-ordination with which we are familiar at the local level in France is positive. When a teacher, a trainer, an adviser or an area inspector has managed to develop co-ordinated action the benefits to the teachers, their pupils, the administration and numerous other partners have been rapidly felt: better adapted activities, personal enthusiasm benefiting from the support of a team, an evaluation of projects, making the best use of everyone's knowledge, exchanging ideas. Moreover, it is easy to demonstrate that there is a saving in time, energy and money, issues on which all educational administrators are sensitive.

What conclusions can we draw from this? It was, in fact, only ideas and ideologies deriving from policies of assimilation that previously prevented us from providing ourselves with the means to argue and work for a cultural minority on the way to extinction. This hindered the co-ordination of projects to which one did not wish to draw particular attention. Times have changed and now nothing, apart from a lack of determination, stands in the way of developing structured and co-ordinated projects. We are working on this and are hopeful of moving things forward.

Hopes and Plans
The hopes and plans emerge from a summing up of the situation. The answers to the survey we sent out at the beginning of the year are clear on this subject. The questionnaire, linked to our preparations for this conference, was devoted to action-research, a description of on-going projects as well as hopes and plans for the future. To the question 'What do you hope to gain from belonging to a network?' the answers are significantly grouped around the following ideas: contacts, meetings, liaison, the struggle against isolation, mutual exchanges, critical reflection, support for discussion of ideas, sharing information, creating a resources centre. We see that, in response to an open question about the advantages of action-research, we come back to matters which have been considered for years (for example, refer to the Dijon conference in 1980 (9)) as basic necessities: such as co-ordination through liaison or a resources centre. Equally significant is the fact that very few of those who answered expect financial support from an action-research network. This does not mean that no money is needed but that it is not a priority and that any investment in co-ordination is soon recouped through the benefits it brings.

People's hopes and plans were clearly expressed at the 1988 University Summer School at Montauban and we agree whole-heartedly with the needs identified when the European Community's study was issued (2 and 11). I shall quote a number of extracts but the documents do need to be re-read in full:

"Fragmented action is, more often than not, doomed to failure; a global and comparative approach is thus necessary and this implies meetings and co-ordination between the various partners, particularly the Gypsy parents and organisations both locally and nationally. Co-ordination would allow ideas, projects and funds to be cohesive and complementary according to defined objectives. It would avoid repeatedly working through trial and error, endless fresh starts and the accompanying disillusionment." (See Summary and Recommendations in Report 2, point 43.)

"In the field of education, co-ordination implies working in a wide educational team including teachers as well as advisers, inspectors and, maybe, other partners. This lends itself to a sharing out of tasks and mutual support, it prevents the rapid isolation of those who specialise, saves them and their pupils from the ghetto-effect and avoids isolated pockets of activity. If several partners are grouped and co-ordinated around a common task this enables them to avoid administrative and ideological hurdles more easily." (Summary and Recommendations in Report 2, point 43.)

"The teachers would like to see links and exchanges set up with other colleagues at a national and European level. They underline the need to set up contact networks and study-visits for those working in education. To this end we propose:
■ at the national level the setting up of a body that would bring together professionals from the Education Service, a national association for specialists (CLIVE), a structure at the University level to vouch for the quality of information and research (CRT: the Centre for Gypsy Studies at the René Descartes University) and an official organisation to take responsibility for the practical aspects of disseminating information, mainly by publishing a liaison report. (CNDP: the National Centre for Educational Information.)
■ at the local authority and regional level the setting up of a regional network to circulate information with representatives such as the School Resources Centres in each area which could be called upon in case of difficulty. The national body should produce a list of the people responsible for resources based upon the information that has been collected; the local and regional networks should facilitate meetings and opportunities to exchange experiences at ground level." (From Working Group Summary, University Summer School at Montauban, Report 8).

This summary is representative of the hopes expressed in the other Working Groups. For example, "We propose the setting up of a Resources Centre with a hierarchical network (i.e. a national centre with regional branches) but where information can readily be passed upwards or downwards. This Centre would generate a resources bank responsible for collecting and sending out information and details of research, publishing scientific and literary works concerning Gypsies and Travellers, and various teaching materials (audio-visual, computer software and teaching packs etc.). It would provide information and training by running courses in the School Resource Centres and would include teachers who have acquired skills through on-the-ground experience, researchers, advisory teachers and Gypsy and Traveller organisations." (idem). Yet another group said: "It is absolutely essential to establish a national resources centre in order to co-ordinate ideas, research and training in collaboration with the various partners involved."

Establishing Priorities
The priorities are clearly defined, the consensus is so strong. They are repeated over and over again at local and national meetings and they link up with the European priorities: we must develop methods of co-ordination, particularly by setting up a National Centre linked to local branches. Another priority, contained in the first, is the publication by this Centre of a liaison report in conjunction with a European publication having the same purpose of liaison and information. Details of setting up a framework for co-ordination are contained in the various publications quoted both at the French and at the European level where co-ordination of initiatives is just as essential. I do not wish to repeat the reports quoted in the reference list but I do recommend

referring to them as a source of inspiration for various initiatives in the area of co-ordination and an analysis of projects already underway.

We will conclude by quoting again one of the recommendations of the European report (number 2, point 65) which certainly applies in France: "When the different partners wish to get away from specialist structures which may lead to segregation in a variety of areas and especially schooling, competent people who have been specially trained and selected must have the opportunity to provide support, information and co-ordination. The authorities (local, regional and national) must all play their part in collaboration and co-ordination as previously described and offer mediation, consultation, technical assistance, information, encouragement and help with decision-making. It is not about creating structures which will soon be ossified and ossifying but about providing the opportunity for people to get together within a flexible system which ensures the participation of all partners, co-ordinated action and continuity. It is about making sure that the Gypsies are not 'left out'. In the past their voices have not been heard in the political game and, if we are not careful, once again they will be dealt with in the framework of authorities and institutions which do not concern them and were set up without them and with others in mind such as groups considered globally poor, maladjusted, second-class, delinquent."

After this rapid outline of the general situation in France and some thoughts on action-research and co-ordination we are optimistic about the outcome of this meeting and the efforts of each and every one to make a fresh step forward by developing initiatives, by reflecting upon what we are doing, by carrying out action-research in various places and by keeping in touch and co-ordinating within a flexible and solid framework.

Bibliography

LIEGEOIS, J-P. *La scolarisation des enfants tsiganes et voyageurs (School provision for Gypsy/Traveller Children) Rapport de synthèse (Synthesis Report)*. Commission for European Communities, 1986

CENTRE DE RECHERCHES TSIGANES. *Les populations tsiganes en France (The Gypsy Peoples of France)*. Centre de Recherches Tsiganes et Direction des Ecoles du Ministère de l'Education nationale, under the direction of J-P Liégeois, 1981.

CLIVE. *Situation 1 - 1989*. Centre de Liaison et d'Informations Voyage-Ecole (CLIVE), 1989.

References

1   WILLIAMS, Patrick. La société. *Les populations tsiganes en France.* Ministère de l'Education nationale, Direction des Ecoles/Université de Paris V, Centre de Recherches Tsiganes, 1981.

2   LIEGEOIS, Jean-Pierre. *La scolarisation des enfants tsiganes et voyageurs: rapport de synthèse.* Commission des Communautés européennes, 1986.

3   CLIVE. *Situation 1 - 1989.* Centre de Liaison et d'Informations Voyage-Ecole (CLIVE), 1989.

4   CALVET, Georges. La langue. In: *Les populations tsiganes en France.* Ministère de l'Education nationale, Direction des Ecoles/Université de Paris V, Centre de Recherches Tsiganes, 1981.

5   LABORIT, Henri. *Apprentissages en Sciences sociales et Education permanente.* Paris: Editions Ouvrières, 1971.

6   LEGRAND, Louis. *Pour une politique démocratique de l'Education.* Paris: Presses Universitaires de la France (PUF), 1977.

7   DE LANDSHEERE, G. *Introduction à la recherche en Education.* Paris: Colin-Bourrelier, 1975.

8   CENTRE DE RECHERCHES TSIGANES. *Les enfants tsiganes à l'école: la formation des enseignants et autres personnels.* Report from the Summer School organised by the Centre for Gypsy Studies at Montauban, France from 4-8 July, 1988. Conseil de la Co-opération culturelle, Conseil de l'Europe, DECS/EGT (88) 42. Council of Europe, 1988.

9   LIEGEOIS, Jean-Pierre. *La scolarisation des enfants tsiganes et nomades, rapport des Journées de Dijon.* Ministère de l'Education nationale, Direction des Ecoles/Université de Paris V, Centre de Recherches Tsiganes, 1980.

10 CENTRE DE RECHERCHES TSIGANES. *Les enfants tsiganes à l'école: la formation des personnels de l'Education nationale.* Report from the Summer School organised by the Centre for Gypsy Studies at Montauban, France from 4-8 July, 1988. Montauban: Centre départementale de Documentation Pédagogique, 1988.

11 COMMISSION FOR THE EUROPEAN COMMUNITIES. *La scolarisation des enfants tsiganes et voyageurs. Document d'orientation pour la réflexion et pour l'action.* Produced by the Commission for the European Communities, document V/500/88.

Federal Republic of Germany
Katharina Lenner, Adult Literacy Teacher

I am happy to take part in this conference although I am not an expert in the education of Sinti and Rom children nor am I in any way responsible for this education. Neither am I an official.

My participation is due to the fact that since 1980 I have been responsible for the basic education of Sinti and Rom adults in Munich. In this way I am personally concerned with the problem of the basic education of the children.

In the course of my preparation for this seminar I tried to find out whether there were in Munich, or in West Germany generally, any officials or teachers involved with the education of Gypsy children at a national level but I found no-one.

The Gypsies themselves, that is to say the 'Zentralrat Deutscher Sinti und Rom', did not answer my questions and suggestions and made it known that they "could not see any possibility of taking any action". This is bad news. It is an indication of the problems faced by this minority when structures are based on the needs of the majority and vice versa.

I am, therefore, not here in any way as an expert but to learn. I hope very much to learn what is happening and what is proposed in other European countries. I hope I shall be able to take away from here some ideas and some suggestions which it would be possible to put into effect in the Federal German Republic.

In Germany the position is as follows. According to the information given by *Der Spiegel* , issue 23, 1989, there are 30,000 Sinti and Rom in the Federal German Republic. The majority of the Sinti have lived in Germany for generations – they are Germans and have German passports. Those who survived the concentration camps and the war now live on the outskirts of towns on special sites or more and more in council housing. Traditional work opportunities and travelling are becoming more and more difficult.

Assimilation or integration into the way of life of the majority of the population happens to some extent but this also poses great problems.

On the other hand there are Rom who, especially over the last few years, have been arriving in Germany from Yugoslavia. Their situation is even worse. There are only a few towns which are prepared to receive them, to give them sanctuary and to make life easier for them – these towns are Cologne, Bremen and Hamburg. In 1986/87 there were several hundred Rom in Munich for several months but they disappeared as fast and as spontaneously as they had arrived. They lived in appalling conditions in tents on a municipal site. There was no question of any education for them because of the shortness of their stay and their complete lack of any knowledge of the German language. We had considered a course of German and of basic literacy for the adult women but the week before the course was due to start all the Rom had gone...

The School Situation

There are several cities in the Federal Republic of Germany (e.g. Munich, Karlsruhe, Hamburg, Mainz, Cologne, Bremen, Freiburg) where there are Sinti social workers or teachers who try to improve the education of the children but these efforts are isolated and lacking in continuity – there is no co-ordination between them either at regional or national level. It would be desirable if this co-ordination could be organised by the Gypsies themselves with support from the local authorities.

Most Gypsy children start school later than their non-Gypsy contemporaries and they often finish by going to special schools. This is very much in keeping with the attitude of the Sinti towards their children and towards education and training in general. The children remain children for longer. Discipline, routine, the ability to be quiet, to learn abstract facts – these are things which differ in the daily life of a Sinti child from that of another child. The teachers do not know about the way of life of these children and so misunderstandings arise. The children cease to want to go to school. Many children end up in special schools for the handicapped. Many parents prefer to send their children to special schools as it isn't such a serious matter if they are absent, and this makes it easier for the family to travel. This vicious circle shows how necessary it is for there to be real communication between the school and the Sinti enabling them to make better use of what the schools have to offer and so that the schools can respond better to the needs of the Sinti. Until now this kind of communication has been only rudimentary and intermittent.

Some parents have given up travelling so that their children can go to school. Among those who do go regularly, some young men succeed in finishing the primary stage of school (at sixteen) and then take an apprenticeship. The problem then is – do they renounce their Sinti identity? The young men who receive no training for work find themselves in the world of work in which the traditional skills of the Sinti are rapidly losing their importance.

Among the girls a certain number finish primary education at the age of sixteen but I do not know of any case in which a girl has started, let alone finished, any vocational training. They are more strongly bound to the family tradition and so the girls stay at home waiting for a young man to come and marry them. Later, however, when they themselves are young mothers they wish their daughters to have a better kind of life than they themselves have had.

Action-research

In the Federal German Republic there is no overview of action-research in this field. Initiatives are intermittent and casual. They are as follows:

■ In Munich an initiative of the Social Department. There has been basic literacy tuition and support for individual children since 1978. Since 1988 there has been a house called "The school for Sinti adults and children" where it is possible to give basic literacy classes to the adults and to do some supportive work with the children at the same time.

■ At Karlsruhe an initiative of the Sinti Association. A teacher, formerly unemployed but now paid by the town of Karlsruhe and by the Employment Agency, works with the children and establishes contacts between parents and teachers.

■ At Bremen, 1986-90, a model project paid for by the federal and regional governments. The project worked with children and teachers and organised in-service training for teachers.

■ At Mainz, Hamburg, Freiburg, Cologne and elsewhere there are other projects but I have no detailed information on these.

It is necessary to create some posts so as to guarantee some continuity of work in this sphere because up to now the various schemes have been due to the efforts of particular individuals. Where there is continuous encouragement, attendance at school is more regular and more success follows. The problem is assimilation. How much do the Sinti wish to be assimilated?

Teachers and local authorities need to be better informed about the Sinti, their lives, their history and their culture. A dialogue between them should be established.

Co-ordination

In the Federal German Republic there is a federal culture in which the states are the education authorities. As a result it is difficult to take action nationally and there is no co-ordination of initiatives in this field. Nevertheless, it is urgent to:

■ create posts for those involved with the problem of the education of Gypsy children

■ give those posts preferably to the Sinti or at least to consult the Sinti about these posts

■ create channels of communication between the scattered initiatives

■ interest teachers in the problems of the Gypsy children and give these teachers information and support.

Paper 6   Greece
Evangelos Marselos, General Secretariat of Public Education

The Greek Government's interest in the needs of Gypsies started in the 1980s. An essential first step was the legislation passed in 1978 which gave Greek naturalisation rights to Gypsies who previously had been registered as 'of unknown origin', effectively making them stateless.

1979 saw a move towards the primary education of nomadic Gypsy children recently settled from Western Attica and supported by the Save the Children Fund. A parallel initiative was begun by the Bishop of Florina, supporting the integration of Gypsies of this region through Christianisation and settlement. Also in 1979, the Young People's Department (DFA) of the Ministry of National Education and Religions (MENR) included Gypsies amongst the social groups targeted for integration. After the participation of the author at the Third World Congress of the Romany Union, the Young People's Department (DFA) decided on the creation of a Centre for Development proposed by the Panhellenic Association of Greek Gypsies (APAG).

In 1982, the DFA set up a working group to examine the problem of illiteracy. During the years 1981-84 attention was directed towards the promotion of literacy and the General Secretariat of State Education (SGEP) became part of the Ministry of Culture and Science (MSC). 1984 saw the start of a developmental pilot project for Gypsies planned by the Centre of Study and Personal Education (CEEP/KEMEA) which set up a working group supported by the SGEP in two communities of settled Gypsies: Ayia Varvara (Attica) and Kato Achaaya (Achaie). Although the original aim had been the professional training of thirty Gypsies to become trainers themselves in the future, the action-research which followed had indicated that the main aim of the project ought to be the promotion of literacy. The three-year pilot project supported by the European Social Fund of the European Community (the Evaluation Report was published in a Greek version) had been overtaken by reality. The few initiatives begun within the State Education system had resulted in more than 100 initiatives across the country's thirty-two regions. The objective of projects within the Gypsy communities is to achieve universal social reintegration "in the sense of participation and of respect for Gypsy culture". The efforts towards literacy amongst adults led the SGEP towards an unusual role through its declared aim of intervention in the school education system focused on support for Gypsy children at school. This aim has now become central.

In 1987 Regional Colleges for Teachers of Gypsies were set up and focused on:

- the production of teaching materials
- the production of a documentary film *Roma*
- a study to find a solution to the problems of schooling for Gypsies commissioned by the Education Ministry.

The intervention of the State in the Public Education System occurred through a structure at national level as illustrated in Diagram 1.

Diagram 1
Greek State
Education System

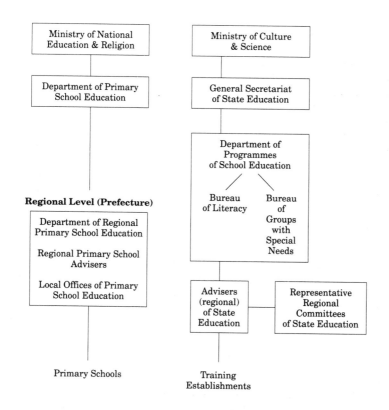

In 1987 the Bureau of Literacy of the General Secretariat of State Education proposed action-research at regional level, co-ordinated as follows:

Diagram 2

Despite rapid development up to last year, the plan for Gypsy Education risks losing ground and effectiveness if the present climate of political indecision does not change.

There is still minimal participation of Gypsies themselves in running these projects.

Our objectives are still far from being attained despite the efforts of many teachers and the positive support of all political parties. However, during the last two or three years, the growth of interest in Gypsies and concern for their problems has begun a movement for change which is irreversible.

Research has been commissioned by Further Education Colleges and various Universities: Education Departments at Athens, the Anthropology Department of the Aegean and the School of Social Work at Patras.

I would now like to make some comments on pan European aspects of gypsy and traveller education. Seminars which have been held within the framework of the Council of Europe and the Commission of the European Communities have already demonstrated the importance of networking between the different parties concerned with the education of Gypsies and Travellers in all countries. Through political initiatives and the promotion of multicultural education, Gypsies, a truly international people, can become, rather than a problem for their host countries, a bond between them. Humanitarian values, which we all seek to further, must not ignore the rights of Gypsy people. Their participation in matters at European level must also be accompanied by participation within each of the member countries. The participation and representation of Gypsies in such initiatives will be a measure of their success and a means of evaluating our efforts so that Gypsies are no more 'the problem' or the objects of research but become active participants in making decisions about their own destiny.

What is needed is the development of new attitudes on the part of European States and all non-Gypsy bodies. Gypsies will then see if our declared democratic and progressive principles are valid.

Action-research is the kind of research which can make science benefit society. It must be a synthesis between formal technocracy and empty academ-ism, social ideology and positivist rationalism. I believe that it was Schiller who said that the evil of humanity lies in the fact that "half of the people act without thinking and the other half think without acting". Action-research is the synthesis of these two opposites.

The researcher must not be an observer isolated from reality who calculates parameters formally like a mathematician. In real life, in interpret-ing reality, it is better to describe things qualitatively. It is better not to observe social factors cold-bloodedly because in the effort of remaining 'objective', there is a danger of becoming inhuman and, therefore, unreal.

The action-researcher is not engaged in science solely for his or her own career but is always conscious of an over-riding responsibility, not towards an elite of intellectuals but towards life and the society which he or she is investigating. He or she must be always conscious that, although studying people who are non-literate, he or she must retain respect for them. The pursuit of science is not an objective in itself; the ultimate goal is always to advance the human condition.

Action-research must combine personal study with collective collabora-tion. The methods employed must not be rigid and academic but must continually be reconciled with social reality: they must be flexible but aware of the fundamental principles which safeguard the deductive processes which link theory and practice.

The results of research must remain open to evaluation and comparative examination. To work at local level, 'on the ground', is vital. Collaboration between a variety of Centres of Research and other concerned individuals is of central importance to the realisation of the objectives of action-research.

But the central criterion determining the effectiveness of action-research as a scientific methodology lies, I believe, not so much in obeying formal rules but in holding a dialectic perspective and internalising its philosophical principles and values. In fact, in a society in constant change it is necessary to grasp and to value the essential elements of everyday life and to order them systematically so that relevant solutions can be found. Inevitably there exist socio-political goals even behind 'neutral' sciences. If he or she adopts a narrow-minded approach the activist researcher cannot perform his or her true role.

Paper 7   Ireland: Some Factual Information
Sheila Nunan, Association for Teachers of Travelling People

The National Situation

Where figures are only approximate this is indicated with an asterix.

Population Structure

Number of Travellers living in Ireland	15,000 – 20,000
Number of Travelling people under 15	8,000*
Number of Travelling people under 25	13,000*
Number of Travelling people over 55	716*

Distribution Pattern

Almost 53 per cent of the population live around the four major cities:

Dublin	23%	3,500
Galway	13%	2,200
Limerick	9%	1,300
Cork	8%	1,200

Accommodation Pattern

Permanent housing	50%
Official caravan sites	25%
Unofficial sites	25%

The Travelling community, while a distinct community in its own right, shares the same language as the settled Irish population (English). Its members also share the same religion as the majority of the settled Irish community (Roman Catholic). The term 'Traveller' is the preferred name of the members of that community.

Educational Provision for Travelling Children

Number of children of 4-5 years		7,300 (approx.)

School Enrolment Statistics:

4-8 years	40%
8-12 years	44%
12+	16%

Number of pupils in special classes:

Class size 1:15	(30%)	2,000

Number of pupils partly integrated but given additional assistance:

Class size 1:35/40	(36%)	1,500

Number of children integrated in ordinary classes:

Class size 1:35/40	(34%)	1,350

Additional Provision
Transport costs, where necessary, are 98 per cent paid by the Department of Education. Special classes for Travellers in primary schools receive the same student grant as other special classes.

570 children attending forty-one pre-schools throughout the country. These schools are 98 per cent grant-aided by the Department of Education.

For children over twelve years of age there are ten Special Training Centres financed by the Department of Education and the Vocational Educational Authority (a second and third level autonomous educational authority).

Attainment Levels
While attainment/academic levels have risen over the last few years Travelling children are not yet achieving the same standards of literacy and numeracy as the average school-going child. There are many reasons for this. Patterns of attendance are a major problem. The average attendance for the mainstream population is 95 per cent. Health and environmental difficulties have a negative effect on learning. While many teachers have found, through trial and error, suitable teaching methods and materials there is no specific pre-service or in-service training for teachers of Travellers. A curriculum for Travelling children was devised in 1985 on a trial basis but was rejected by teachers because it was not appropriate. The principal demand is for adequate in-service training and appropriate and adequate classroom resources. There is a complete lack of curricular material based on aspects of Traveller culture and lifestyle.

Co-ordination
Official / State Structures
Primary education in Ireland is managed by denominational bodies and administered centrally by the Department of Education. There are no regional education authorities at primary level. Initiatives are taken at local level and are sanctioned by the Department. In the case of setting up a provision for Travellers, information is gathered at local level, e.g. numbers of children and their perceived needs. A request is then made for resources and forwarded to the Department of Education for approval.

The main difficulty with this system is that it depends on the interest of local people to represent the Travellers. In an area where the attitude is hostile, the Travellers' needs may not be represented. The Department of

Education works through a School Inspectorate. Each inspector is responsible for a region and also has responsibility for the Travelling children attending school in that region. The Inspectorate does not have a function where children are outside the school system. Overall responsibility for Traveller education at primary level lies with a Chief Inspector.

Visiting Teacher Service
Because of the special needs of the Travelling community in 1982 the Department of Education also appointed six visiting teachers in four areas of high Traveller population. These teachers act as co-ordinators in their regions. They liaise between homes, schools, social services and the Department of Education to encourage greater participation of Travelling children in school. Each visiting teacher has approximately 200 families in his or her region. The teachers are not attached to any one school and are responsible to the Chief Inspector. The establishment of the visiting teacher service has greatly improved the access to schooling in the areas in which it operates and the transfer of children from one school to next. It also has facilitated greater parent consultation and provides a good support service for teachers.

Other Co-ordination Agencies
The National Council for Travelling People, a voluntary agency, employs a National Co-ordinator for Traveller education. She has responsibility for children between four to fifteen years of age. The National Co-ordinator liaises with local voluntary groups, schools, the Department of Education and the visiting teacher service and promotes the development of educational provision. The National Co-ordinator reports annually to the National Council.

Teacher Co-ordination
The Association of Teachers of Travelling People is open to all teachers and others working in the area of Traveller education. The current membership of 150 is largely made up of personnel involved in primary education. It organises two general meetings yearly and has regional representatives who organise regional meetings between the general meetings. The Association is currently working towards creating a network of pre-school personnel who will examine the areas of curriculum, training and parent participation in pre-schools. The Association publishes two annual newsletters and depends entirely on voluntary membership fees which limits the extent of its work.

General Comment
While there is considerable contact between the partners in Traveller education there is room for much improvement in the area of co-ordination. There is a need for clear Departmental policy in relation to educational provision for Travellers. The last policy document was written in 1970 and a lot of thinking has changed since then. A new policy document should take into account the opinions of teacher organisations, the visiting teacher service, parents and the national co-ordinator. There is also a need for the Department to engage in on-going evaluation of the educational provision particularly in relation to special class provision. An updated policy document would be a useful framework for evaluation. The extension of the visiting teacher service would also be a practical step towards greater co-ordination and within it the development of more structured parent consultations.

Paper 8 The Concept of Action-research in Education
in Ireland
*Mairin Kenny, Dublin Travellers Education and
Development Group (DTEDG)*

Action-research programmes in Ireland in the area of schooling are best
exemplified by three projects. There are two at pre-school/primary level
assisted by the Van Leer Foundation: one in inner-city Dublin and one in an
Irish-speaking rural area in the West; the third comprises a set of alternative
educational experiments for alienated youth called Youth Encounter Projects.
The three are characterised by intensive planning, on-going monitoring and
published evaluations. Parental/community involvement is sought and
developed through the work of home-school liaison personnel and community
and social workers. Also involved are personnel from the Educational Research
Centres. The involved partners work as teams; the latest developments in
pedagogic methods and materials are drawn on, and these are modified or new
ones developed, to match the particular circumstances of the projects.
   Theoretical findings as well as materials and methods thus developed and
tested are disseminated to wider groups of teachers through seminars and in-
service courses. This action-research in relation to schooling for the disadvantaged and ethnic groups involves the Government Department of Education
which sanctions and funds it. Its inspectorate is involved in the planning,
operation and evaluation of these projects and in the dissemination of the
findings.
   When it comes to Traveller schooling the situation is different. There is
research and there is action which is often innovative. However, the two exist
separately. Both have developed in relative isolation from developments in the
wider field of research and of action, and of action-research in education in
Ireland. Most of the research in the area of Traveller children in schools
remains on University shelves and the teachers do not know about it; that
which is well known is outdated in terms of its theoretical framework. The
teachers develop, in response to their own situations, innovative practices

which they judge to be appropriate. Thanks to their efforts and to the Travellers who voice their criticisms of practices relating to their children in schools, the forms of provision for Traveller children have become more and more flexible: this is very good. However, not all the innovations are enlightened. Some forms of provision offered to Traveller children with the aim of facilitating their progress towards integration in schools have, in fact, ensured their segregation: for example, the special classes/special teachers as they function in certain schools. Where this is the outcome, one must consider whether the form of provision itself is the cause of the problem or whether it is due to its unsuitability or misuse at local level.

It is a question of conceptualisation and evaluation. The concept of a pilot or research project is never invoked in relation to school provision for Traveller children. The inspectors of the Department of Education, who should evaluate and observe innovative concepts in practice, do not do so. They visit the classes for Traveller children certainly, and make their reports, but the work of both inspectors and teachers in these situations goes on without the benefit of the kind of well-researched framework it needs. The varied forms of special provision for Traveller children which have developed must be considered as pilot projects and given supports within a serious and rigorous framework.

The Dublin Travellers Education and Development Group
There is a voluntary group which tries to work within an action-research framework: it is the Dublin Travellers Education and Development Group (DTEDG) and I have been a member since its formation in 1983. Although this Group works primarily in the field of adult and community education, not schooling, the two areas of education do impinge on each other. Also, I would suggest that an examination of the Group's methods could be useful in relation to our task here; we are all involved in formal education of some sort. I will give a brief account here of the history and projects of the Group; a fuller account can be found in John O'Connell's presentation which he gave at the Benidorm Conference – mine is drawn from that.

The DTEDG, an organisation comprised of Travellers and settled people, was set up by a group of professionals from different disciplines who, in dialogue with Travellers, set out to examine their situation. The Group decided to search for alternative approaches to work with Travellers based on principles of self-determination and on the premise that no lasting progress could be made unless Travellers themselves were involved in all stages of the process. Some members of the Group had previously worked abroad and brought with them a keen awareness of the value of inter-cultural dialogue. The Group promoted the view that Travellers are an ethnic group with a right to develop their own distinctive way of life. Some insights and methods which have been developed in work with oppressed groups in other cultures were adopted and applied (e.g. Freire's pedagogy). The Group's projects are developed within this framework of analysis and methodology. There are three main aspects to these projects.

Direct Work with Travellers Themselves
This work was undertaken with young adults and women and consisted of education, training and community work. As this work progressed it became clear how necessary it was to respond to the situation which existed: widespread prejudice towards Travellers and lack of information about them.

Raising Awareness and Combating Prejudice
A programme was set up to organise (for the settled community) adult education courses, conferences and seminars, visits to schools and the use of media. Recognition and acceptance of Travellers' cultural identity was promoted and efforts were made to break down barriers of suspicion and fear. We also engaged in networking and campaigning with others who share our vision.

The main aim of the courses was to develop a critical awareness of Irish society and an analysis of the Travellers' situation in order to create the conditions for Travellers to take more control of their lives. As a result of these courses a number of programmes have been set up with Travellers employed as full-time workers, such as youth and community work programmes, an enterprise programme and a women's programme.

Research, Policy Formation and Publications.
This has not received the attention it requires due to lack of finance, resources and staffing. Most of the time, energy and resources were spent on organising and running courses for young adult Travellers and for Traveller women. However, some progress has been made and in the coming year it is hoped to develop this further.

One important part of this work is done continuously: the courses and work programmes are monitored carefully throughout and evaluated regularly by the staff and management with outside consultants. Staff and management work as a team with a common ideology; everyone is involved in the process of identification, planning, monitoring and evaluation of projects.

The work with the adult Travellers, with the settled population and the analysis of projects and of the Irish situation have all led the Group to formulate policy in relation to the school system in Ireland and its role in relation to Traveller children. This is described in the following paper.

Paper 9   Action-research and the Schooling of Traveller
Children in Ireland
*Mairin Kenny, Dublin Travellers Education and Development
Group (DTEDG)*

The analysis which I will present in this paper is based on two areas of
experience and reflection. I have been a member of a small independent group,
the Dublin Travellers Education and Development Group (DTEDG), since it
was first established. I believe that a major part of the difficulty in relation to
instigating action-research in Traveller schooling lies in the neglect of the area
of conceptualisation and analysis. I have also been a teacher of Traveller
children for thirteen years and as such I was involved in preparing a draft
curriculum for Traveller children. I am also currently engaged in a doctoral
research project, the subject of which is the schooling of Travellers aged twelve
and above.

For the DTEDG, analysis and action go together. Briefly, as a reminder,
the three aspects of our work are:
■ direct work with Travellers consisting of education, training and community
work
■ educational activities with the settled community, networking with others
who have a common vision and campaigning
■ research, policy formation and publications.

Traveller Identity and Activities
Before I go on to speak of schools and our educational policy, I will outline one
piece of analysis which is basic to all our action and research: it concerns the
issue of Traveller identity and attitudes towards this issue. What follows here
on this subject is drawn from John O'Connell's presentation given in Benidorm
(1989).

We analysed the existing approaches to work with Travellers and the
philosophies underlying them because we felt it was important to clarify ideas
and perceptions about Travellers, both our own and those of other people.

From written and spoken statements about Travellers and from actual work being done we identified a set of perceptions and images.

Travellers Are the Same as Anybody Else
While this view reflects a positive attitude to Travellers as equal citizens, it denies their distinct cultural identity.

Travellers as Social Misfits and Deviants
This view arises from an analysis of society which views individuals and groups who deviate from mainstream society as the problem.

A Sub-culture of Poverty
While accepting that Travellers have a distinct culture, this view suggests that it persists only because of poverty. It does not explain the Travellers' language, nomadism and dynamism.

The Romantic View
The idea of "those colourful Travellers wandering the rainbows of Ireland" presents them as exotic nomads who come from an idyllic and carefree past. Such exoticisation is insulting and racist.

An Ethnic Group
This view is based on the notion that Travellers can be considered an ethnic group because they regard themselves and are regarded by others as a distinct community by virtue of the following characteristics:
■ they have a long shared history which, even though largely unresearched, can be traced back for centuries
■ they have their own values, customs, lifestyle and traditions associated with nomadism
■ they come from a small number of ancestors and, although different families are associated with different parts of the country, one becomes a Traveller not just by choice but by birth
■ they have their own language called Cant, Gammon or Shelta and are also recognisable by their accents and use of language
■ they have an oral tradition rich in folklore and also have a distinctive style of singing
■ the majority adhere to a form of popular religiosity in the Roman Catholic tradition
■ they are a small minority group (approximately 0.5 per cent of the population) who have a common experience of oppression and discrimination down through the years.
    A final, useful comment on the notion of ethnicity: "Ethnicity is a subjective experience of what you are in relationship to being part of a group... It follows from that that ethnicity isn't the property of an individual; it is partly a sense of collective identity. Ethnicity is not a fixed property of people. So Travellers' ethnicity doesn't mean that every day of their lives and in everything they do they should go about proclaiming that they are Travellers and must behave like that. In invoking their own identity and asserting that they are an ethnic group Travellers don't have to prove it 24 hours of the day". (Dr. Charles Husband, in a lecture on Racism and Ethnicity, Dublin 1989)
    A minority working with Travellers supported this perception of

Travellers as an ethnic group but it was not sufficiently accepted to influence policies on the overall direction of work with Travellers. The Report of the Travelling People Review Body, published by the government in 1983, stated that while there had been "some academic debate on the question whether Travellers comprise a distinct culture, an ethnic group or... sub-culture of poverty" there was no agreement among researchers "as to the origins of Travellers or their status as a group". The Report stated that it was not within the terms of reference of the Review Body to resolve the issue. The task of the Review Body was to "review current policies and services for the Travelling People and to make recommendations to improve the existing situation". What this position assumes, wrongly in our view, is that the question of identity is an academic one with little relevance for the concrete situation. As I said earlier, the importance of theory is underestimated.

The DTEDG and the Education of Travellers

Insight, of course, comes from analysis of action as well as from theory. I will speak here of aspects of our projects relevant to the topic of this seminar. Although the Group is primarily engaged with adults, Traveller and settled, schools do impinge. Traveller adults are concerned about their children and the issue of schools has entered our work in other ways also. The following are some examples:

■ we run regular evening courses for involved personnel, including teachers, in which current research on Travellers is presented and discussed

■ a theatre-in-education group, called Team Theatre, has worked with the adult Travellers on the leadership courses, exploring in drama issues about Traveller culture and Traveller-settled relations. A young Traveller member of the DTEDG joined Team Theatre as an actor and this year's drama-in-education project presented in schools by Team Theatre is the product of work with the DTEDG

■ Traveller trainees from the Group also visit secondary schools to discuss Traveller issues with students and teachers.

Arising from the analysis of experience gained in developing and putting into operation the courses, dramas and visits of which I have spoken already, and from insights thrown up by research, we are currently preparing an information pack on Travellers for use in schools. We have also developed a module for inclusion in teacher-training courses next year and made a submission to the Government Curriculum Review Board on Travellers and the Curriculum.

Research and Practice into Traveller Schooling

At a purely theoretical level there are a number of M.A. theses, most of them unknown in teacher circles, on Travellers and on Traveller education. Most of the research was done in the sixties and treats the Travellers as a sub-culture of poverty. In all these works there is no rigorous analysis of Travellers and their schooling in the context of the structures of the dominant settled Irish society and of its school system. Likewise, from the other side: sociological and educational research into the dominant society does not include Travellers. The left hand does not know what the right hand does.

Yet school provision for Travellers in Ireland is very innovative. The question is: on what basis and to what effect? To ascertain this, we need to look at policy and practice.

Policy Framework
The policy framework for all the provision which my colleague has outlined is to be found in the First and Second Government Commission Reports (1963 and 1983) and in the Department of Education's Report (1970). In the 1970 document Travellers are presented as needing compensatory education to facilitate their passage into integration and ultimate absorption. No new policy document has been produced. Since then special facilities have proliferated and diversified. This development, and the level of take-up and of need, has been documented triennially by the National co-ordinator. However, all this educational documentation amounts to very little and it is unanalytical and conceptually inadequate. As the language used about Travellers changed over the years, internal contradictions have crept in. For example, in the first Report (1963) nothing of value in their way of life is identified and in the second Report (1983) they have a 'unique culture' but the conception of Travellers-as-problem still persists.

Practice
In fact, policy in relation to practice is developed, neither in research documents nor in policy documents, but orally at meetings of Travellers and their teachers. Since Ireland is a small country, most teachers of Travellers know each other as they attend meetings and courses, organised by their Association or by the Department and so new ideas are disseminated orally. There have also been local initiatives: the Navan Committee for Travellers, in conjunction with teachers and with development education workers, published a resource book on Travellers for use in mainstream schools; other groups have made videos which are useful in work with Traveller children and adults locally; health education videos have been produced; the Irish branch of Barnardo's Preschool Association has compiled a toy library as a resource for Traveller preschools and individual teachers pass around materials they have devised.

In short, one can attribute changes both in policy and in practice to Travellers and their teachers who have spoken about their experience. The Department has indeed listened to them and the result has been the encouragement of flexibility in terms of the teaching methods used.

Action-research
However, nobody is allocated to structure this rich interaction, to analyse innovative practice within a rigorous conceptual framework and sort out the good from the bad. The ad hoc growth of insight and varied practice, born of a process of accretion and omission in response to immediate needs and to incidental encounter with new ideas, lends itself to the development of internal contradictions. This is true of developments over the years in both policy documents and in practice.

There has been one formal action-research project. Thanks to teacher pressure, the Department of Education did set up a small sub-committee which produced a Draft Curriculum for Travellers in 1984. As a member of that committee for a time, I have to say that the final document reflected little or nothing of teachers' experience. It was pedagogically dated and inadequate and did not reflect Traveller culture. On these grounds teachers, through their Association, formally rejected it, and this rejection has been accepted by the Department as valid.

A Current Research Project
I am currently engaged in research into the resistance practices of Traveller children aged twelve and above in school. This is leading to a study of the nature of school provision in the Junior Training Centres. These centres are an example of the diversity and innovativeness in Irish Traveller education. They are unique in the Irish school system: they are separate from mainstream post-primary schools and the curriculum followed in them is devised by the teachers. Although many of them are excellent there are clearly questions about structure, curriculum, aims and practices which must be addressed. The centres have not been evaluated by any education authority but they are increasing in number. There are now twelve. Four are in Dublin, the rest distributed through Ireland and they cater for about 300 Traveller children aged twelve and above.

I have spent a year as participant observer in these centres and I have interviewed pupils and teachers in all of them. I wish to ascertain what the pupils resist and why: what are they protecting and what are they rejecting in this resistance? I believe that their action reveals something about how Travellers construct their identity as an ethnic group but also something about how this group perceives the educational system as represented in the policy and practice of the personnel in these centres. Although this is an academic research project, I intend to report back to involved personnel and hope to provide useful insights and evaluations.

Travellers and the Curriculum
The DTEDG's submission on the Curriculum and Travellers referred to earlier is based on discussion with Travellers and on the findings of Liégeois' Report on School Provision, as well as on our own analysis of research and of experience in our projects with both Travellers and the Curriculum.

As indicated earlier, research and action in the area of Traveller schooling are isolated from each other and both are isolated from developments in the mainstream. Therefore, our submission is specifically entitled *Travellers and the Curriculum*, not *The Curriculum for Travellers*. We believe that the curriculum for all children should be multi-cultural and present the culture and history and socio-economic position of Travellers as an integral part of study of Irish society. In fact, because the present curriculum is mono-cultural it ignores other ethnic groups in Ireland also such as the Jews and the Gaeltacht people. All groups, Travellers included, do surface in partial ways in certain subject areas but the multi-cultural framework is absent.

We believe the development of this kind of framework is the correct starting point because it is arguably racist to be concerned about Travellers in the curriculum only when Travellers are present. The issue of Travellers in school, and the schooling of Travellers, tends to be dealt with separately from all other school issues and it must be thoroughly integrated. In an integrated, multi-cultural curricular context, fuller treatment of areas of Traveller culture and experience could be engaged in when Travellers are in the class. It would no longer be a matter of Travellers vanishing from the curriculum when they are absent from the classroom or of offensive material about Travellers, such as one gets in some children's rhymes, being taught if Travellers are not present and becoming problematic only when Travellers are present. In such a framework any special provision deemed necessary is appropriately situated and developed.

This framework is not only necessary at primary and secondary level: we assert the need for a multi-cultural framework for all teacher-training within which a module on Travellers would be an obligatory part of the course. This should include an analysis of the socio-political aspect of the Traveller's situation and correct identification of the roots of many of the Traveller children's difficulties born, not of their innate inadequacies, but of an actively maintained exclusive society. The module must, therefore, include training in racism awareness and anti-racist practice. Multi-culturalism must include or be accompanied by confrontation of the exclusion practices of the dominant society, particularly as they can be engaged in, often unconsciously and subtly, within the classroom. Similar in-service training should be provided.

In Conclusion

The response to the call for action-research in the area of Traveller schooling must, in our opinion, be at two levels: theory and practice and the two are, of course, interrelated.

Theory

In order to avoid being ghettoised and/or producing ghettoisation, action-research in this area must be preceded by an integrative move towards multi-culturalism, both at the level of theory and of practice.

Practice

In a multi-cultural framework, and as part of the process of developing it, we need systematically to collect and evaluate current developments in insight and practice. These should be returned through in-service training, in developed and conceptually sound form, to the teachers. Even in a small country like Ireland, such teachers feel isolated in their attempts to develop forms of schooling which are more integrated and more appropriate both for the Traveller children and for the settled.

As indicated earlier, the DTEDG is already working on some of the proposals referred to in its submission:

■ we engage in discussions with Travellers about schools and about their hopes for their children

■ the Group has prepared a module, based on the analyses I have outlined, for inclusion in teacher-training courses, starting in the coming year; members of the Group contribute regularly to in-service courses for professionals involved with Travellers

■ we are preparing an information pack, which can be used in schools and with study groups, Traveller or settled. The pack will contain information sheets, instructions and suggestions for group sessions along the lines of those developed in our own training courses.

Finally, the responsibility for putting this work on a serious and co-ordinated basis lies with the Department of Education. Resources must be committed to this task; unless the Department accepts this responsibility the present situation will persist. Both Travellers and settled children will suffer in the process. The teachers, who work without such support will be blamed and racism, where it exists in Irish schools, will remain effectively unchallenged.

Paper 10   Italy: General Information and Action-research

Mirella Karpati, Centre for Gypsy Studies.

Based on information from several Italian regions we can estimate fairly accurately that the number of Travellers in Italy is between 70,000 and 80,000, about 0.14 per cent of the population.

The oldest and largest group is the Rom from southern Italy. In former times tinmen, blacksmiths or horse dealers, they are now general tradesmen, especially the Rom from the Abruzzi, and their standard of living is adequate except for pockets of extreme poverty as, for example, in Calabria. Formerly they led a semi-nomadic life but now they have become settled. Their language, based on Indian and Greek, is characterised by the number of words borrowed from Italian. They probably arrived by sea direct from the Byzantine Empire towards the end of the fourteenth century.

A second large group, which has existed for centuries in Italy, is the Sinti who are also present in Austria, Germany and France where they are also called Manouche. Their language is characterised by various words borrowed from German. They live mainly in the north of Italy. They were habitual participants in fairground shows and today still work in fairgrounds and women augment the family income by hawking. These activities make it imperative to travel but in winter they tend to spend quite a while in large towns. For them the question of stopping places is very important as is the matter of sites which the municipal authorities are obliged to provide by law (337/1968) for circus and fairground people and which are rarely available to the Sinti, given the competition from these large commercial enterprises.

This century, historical events have caused fresh immigration. In the early 1900s the Rom Vlax (Kalderasha, Lovara, Tchourara) arrived from Romania where they had escaped from slavery. Although they travel a lot in large convoys, they also tend to buy houses which they live in from time to time.

The alteration of frontiers after World War I led to the inclusion of the Estrekharja Sinti from Austria, the Krassarja Sinti from Karst, who were musicians and the Slovenian and Istrian Rom who were horse dealers. These Rom increased in numbers during World War II as a number of families fled from Slovenia and Croatia to Italy to escape massacre by the Ustashas, the Croatian fascists. Originally nomads, they now tend to settle in country districts, sometimes buying abandoned farms and take up animal husbandry or become scrap merchants. Their language is close to the Gypsy dialects of the Balkans.

Since the 1960s there has been a considerable immigration of the Rom from Yugoslavia. These are Dassikane Rom from Serbia (who are orthodox Christians) and Khorakane Rom from Bosnia, Macedonia, Cerna Gora and Kosova (Muslim). To these should be added the Rudari of Rumanian origin and a few families of Rom Lovara from Poland. This immigration has increased in recent years as some, who, having tried their luck in France and Germany and been rejected by the authorities of those countries, have come to Italy. If they find a place where they are allowed to stay, the Yugoslavian Rom build huts. They maintain close links with Yugoslavia, go there frequently to visit relations and to buy horses and other property with the proceeds from their time in Italy. They also take their dead back for burial and their young men do their military service there. Their way of life, the use of children for begging and thieving, and the fact that they are foreigners, have occasionally provoked outbreaks of violence against them in several Italian towns, especially Rome, where there are almost 3,000 of them.

It should be emphasised that the Khorakhanian Rom, despite the conditions of marginalisation in which they live, are developing some interesting cultural activities. The Rasim Sejdic Association in Rome has organised sporting activities such as marathons, football and chess tournaments with the local people and their amateur theatrical group has put on shows, not only in Rome but also at the recent Festival of Nations at Lugano in Switzerland.

The young Rom from the Abruzzi are also in the process of setting up a cultural association called Tem Romano (Gypsy World) and in Bolzano there is an association called Sintengro Drom – The Sinti Road.

Finally, there are in Italy, Travellers who are not Gypsies. They are the Caminanti of Sicily – pedlars who speak a dialect of their own. The spread of the Pentecostal movement, which gave rise to the 'Evangelical Gypsy Mission', has brought to Italy a certain number of Lovara families of French nationality who have settled in Milan. Also of French nationality are the five families of the Kaulja – North African Rom – who live in Rome.

I should also like to draw attention to what I consider is an important development which may have an outstanding part to play in the education of the younger generation – namely, the progressive reduction in the nomadic quality of their lives, due on the one hand to the difficulty of finding stopping places and, on the other, the increase in the availability of motor vehicles.

Although regional regulations and, more recently, the Ministry of the Interior provide for the allocation of funds for the creation of sites for Travellers, municipal authorities always encounter difficulties – the opposition of the townsfolk who are unwilling to have Gypsies as neighbours. For these reasons, Gypsy families stop where they can find a place to stay either buying houses or land, or requesting low rent municipal housing, or finding a permanent place on a site which becomes their home.

The motor vehicle, for its part, makes rapid movement possible whether for business or for making contact with other groups, while part of the family stays 'at home'. Gypsies are no longer the nomads they once were.

Action-research

From the pedagogical point of view the teaching process itself can be looked upon as action-research; in the primary school teaching is generally organised in 'units' focusing on particular parts of the syllabus. The syllabus links learning in the different subject disciplines. The 'units' correspond to some degree to Decroly's 'centres of interest'. Although they allow for the fact that they are dealing with children who have their own interests, motivations and experiences, they nevertheless overcome the risk of being fragmentary or haphazard because they fit into the succession of stages becoming a 'continuum'. In other words, they fit into the programme which every teacher draws up at the beginning of the school year thus providing a specific content for the programmes drawn up by the Ministry of Public Instruction with a definite subject matter suitable for a particular class.

To sum up: the units are aimed at certain levels of performance in relation to the memorising and understanding of fixed subject matter; the ground covered follows a route chosen by the teacher and evaluation is to do with the mastery of knowledge and skills (tests).

On the other hand, the teaching process can be an open-ended experience which may be modified by the interaction of those taking part. First among these are the pupils engaged in research activities or team work. These may lead in the long term to higher levels of achievement, whether convergent (analysis and synthesis) or divergent (imagination and creativity). Consequently, evaluation will require open and complicated means of assessment. The aims remain those set out in ministerial programmes for 'cultural literacy', that is to say, "the acquisition of all the fundamental types of language and an elementary level of mastery of the concepts essential for the understanding of the world about us".

During the school year 1988/89 plans were drawn up for a better education for Traveller children. These projects are presented in the supplement at the end of the following chapter on co-ordination. They were carried out by experts or specialised organisations, co-ordinated for the Opera Nomadi du Lazio by Grazia Capitani, Aurora Mereu and Antonia Rullo.

What I aim to do here is to describe the main features. We started from several basic ideas, namely: the quasi-ineffectiveness of support teachers, the isolation of Gypsy children when placed in a class and the difficulty of deciding what ground to cover. Support teachers usually take a Gypsy child out of the class in order to give him some individual tuition which often consists of simple drawing exercises which never get near the level of actual writing, that is, the written expression of a thought. There is hardly ever any co-ordination between the class teacher and the support teacher. Furthermore, this separation of the child ends up by producing a sort of stigmatisation of him in the eyes of the other pupils ("he's dim") and increase his sense of isolation. Enquiries (e.g. by sociogrammes) have revealed that the Gypsy child 'doesn't exist' for his classmates – nobody considers him as a possible partner in either school or out-of-school activities. All this constitutes a serious obstacle both in socialisation and learning, the two mainsprings of the education process. Indeed, after a long struggle, we have succeeded in securing for Gypsy children the right of entry to school, we are still a long way from guaranteeing them the right to a complete education and it is in this respect that we must devise new methods.

Finally, we considered the results of earlier research, in which Gypsy children produced positive results in language work. We therefore chose expressive activities of various kinds with all the pupils involved in the experiment and, when possible, included some adult Travellers as well. Our aim was threefold:

- The acquisition of new languages
- A long-term improvement in communication skills
- Training in 'social poise': in meeting other people, cultivating the feeling of 'belonging', going beyond self or immediate group.

Evaluation is positive. We are convinced we have started along the right track but also that we have only taken our first steps along it. A careful analysis of our procedures, our deviations from the planned course and the results obtained will enable us to adjust subsequent projects. Teachers are the first to say, "What's missing is the money!"

Informing Teachers and Other Personnel

In Rome, in the past, the Opera Mundi Nomadi of Lazio concentrated its information dissemination on the support teachers. After a three-fifths of a day seminar at the beginning of the school year there followed a monthly one-day study for reflection and evaluation throughout the school year. From 1987 onwards we considered involving the whole school along with other interested parties. With the agreement of the Provveditore agli studi (regional inspector) we organised study days for the staffs of primary and secondary schools of the first and second levels and in schools attended by the 330 Gypsy children who were being followed up by the Opera Nomadi team. The aim of these study days for all teachers was to increase knowledge of the cultural heritage of Gypsy children (their attitudes, view of the world, models of behaviour and values) so that teaching and the educational process should not be superimposed, one on top of the other, but complement one another. In addition, meetings and debates were organised in the school districts with those responsible for administration in the 'boroughs'. (Rome is divided into twenty 'boroughs', each with a deputy-mayor and its own health service unit). They are closely connected and share a common responsibility for education, housing and health.

The results of the kind of approach we have described are not yet able to be evaluated in view of the fact that no concrete developments, beyond simple declarations of principle, have yet taken place. Nevertheless, some school teachers have organised research projects with their pupils, collections of documentation, visits to sites where Gypsies live and interviews with their parents – in short, a considerable learning activity, echoes of which appear in class diaries and little books made by pupils.

Paper 11   Italy: Co-ordination
Secondo Massano, Headteacher of a Primary School

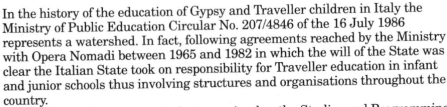

In the history of the education of Gypsy and Traveller children in Italy the Ministry of Public Education Circular No. 207/4846 of the 16 July 1986 represents a watershed. In fact, following agreements reached by the Ministry with Opera Nomadi between 1965 and 1982 in which the will of the State was clear the Italian State took on responsibility for Traveller education in infant and junior schools thus involving structures and organisations throughout the country.

Moreover, in response to the same circular, the Studies and Programming Department of the Ministry of Public Education decided on its own initiative to collect information concerning:

■ the whereabouts of Gypsies throughout the country
■ possible ways of integrating them into the school system, the use of support staff and a final evaluation
■ whether or not suggestions and proposals should emanate from the Administration.

Co-ordination at Provincial Level
Still acting on the Ministerial Circular already mentioned, the plan since 1986 has been to establish a centre in each Local Education Office for persons interested in making schools available to Travellers. These Centres would be equipped to ascertain local demand in agreement with other interested organisations and other Education Offices in the district. Advice was given that use should also be made of the resources already provided by the State administration for the handicapped, the disadvantaged and the geographically isolated. The tasks of local co-ordination are:

■ educational provision as of right, with support, even on sites
■ provision for study (co-operation required from the local authorities and the

social and health services)
■ acceptance of voluntary help
■ liaison with Gypsies' own groups and associations
■ the organisation of adult literacy courses
■ keeping teachers, heads of schools and inspectors informed.

Local Co-ordination
Local organisations (schools) are invited to prepare a variety of strategies.

Regional Co-ordination
This has not been planned or envisaged. In the absence of specific instructions, regional co-ordination could be achieved by those regions which have already made regulations for the support of Traveller culture including full-time education of Gypsies and Travellers.

Achievements
Measures are more or less in place at provincial level, thanks to the sympathy and availability of personnel from within the administration and from outside.
The National Curriculum Development Council, when consulted, proved reluctant to consider the problems of widely scattered pupils and the education of foreigners from countries outside the European Community.

Objective Considerations
The welcome interest shown by the Minister of Public Instruction raised our hopes since it indicated his acceptance of the proposals and past research of Opera Nomadi. Despite this, the Opera Nomadi Association has found that at both local and regional level it has had to continue to emphasise the need for effective co-ordination (nationally and locall) of the relevant State school personnel (eleven persons covering the country), in line with a plan of action presented annually to the Ministry of Public Education.
The main points of the plan are:
■ contacts with Provincial Education Offices
■ contacts with the main education institutions
■ activities promoting inspiration, information and support of teachers
■ contact with local authorities and district institutions
■ monitoring and evaluation of the effects of the current regulations concerning schooling
■ periodical bulletin of statistics concerning the education of Traveller children in Italy
■ information and liaison with schools with the help of the bulletin *Romano Lil Scuola*; activities in support of Assistance Educative (a voluntary body) and the organisation of district educational meetings.

Evaluation of Co-ordination Activities
I am both the head of a primary school in Turin and responsible at national level for the Opera Nomadi Association. I am, therefore, aware of both progress and its absence in the education of Gypsy and Traveller children in Italy.
Although the Minister was, of course, aware of the long involvement of Opera Nomadi in helping to promote the education of Gypsies in state schools I had to make personal contact with him to remind him of:
■ the research commissioned by the Minister of Public Instruction and present

independent enquiries which were largely covered by circular 207/86 (itself a fundamental document in the struggle for the education of Gypsies but difficult to apply in real situations)
■ the dissemination of information achieved by meeting all over the country, yearly for primary schoolteachers, and in 1985 and 1986, for directors of primary schools and secondary schools as well. Since 1988 this activity has lapsed
■ the regular presence of Opera Nomadi in European congresses in order to present an account of the attendance of Traveller children at school in Italy
■ the information and documentation supplied to scholastic institutions, cultural centres, local authorities, especially by means of the review Lacio Drom from the Centro Studi Zingari (Centre for Gypsy Studies) which is linked by its articles of association with Opera Nomadi.
    Continuing our dialogue with the Minister, we requested:
■ the involvement of the General Administration of the Ministry of Public Instruction (infant, junior and secondary) in putting into effect Ministerial Circular Min.207/86
■ the adaptation of schools in line with the recommendations of the European Commission and in particular:
■ flexibility of structures and rules including preparatory schools and professional workshops on sites
■ research (knowledge of elements and of experiments, studies and teaching aids of use in the education of Gypsies) and action (pilot projects at various levels for information, technical help, encouragement and support in areas specially targeted)
■ the necessity of considering problems of multi-culturality which also affect Italian schools that are open to foreign pupils and not only Gypsies.
    The Minister was also reminded that although in the past Gypsy children had been admitted to primary school as of right, in these days it is not possible to dispense with basic, professional preparation. Yet that is what we are still waiting for.

History, Roles, Difficulties and Functions of a National Association
Opera Nomadi, at first a regional association for the education of gypsy and Traveller children in the Trentino Alto Adige (1963), became a national association in 1965 and acquired legal status in 1970. At present, it is composed of twenty one territorial sections and seven groups of collaborators.
    The Association was born as a result of the conviction that it was essential for a voluntary group to take steps to bring Gypsies and other Travellers or groups of nomadic origin out of the situation of marginalisation to which they had been relegated, and to create in the national community an understanding of, and welcome for, those who are different.
    Generally Opera Nomadi acts as a mediator between the public authorities and Gypsy groups, watching over their rights and intervening specifically to avoid them being put at a disadvantage. Priority is given to the following sectors: environment, school, language, entertainment, cultural information and activities.
    In the field of school education a convention for the establishment and functioning of special schools for Gypsy pupils (Lacio drom school) was signed in 1965/66 by the Minister of Public Instruction and Opera Nomadi. This convention was renewed annually from 1971 to 1981 with the intention of

preparing for the integration of Gypsy pupils into mainstream classes, along with qualified support staff. Since 1982 a new Convention has required that Gypsy pupils should be included in mainstream classes with support staff provided in the ratio of 1:6. The convention also included:
■ a subsidy to Opera Nomadi for its help with educational work in schools
■ the development, in collaboration with the Centro Studi Zingari, of annual training courses authorised and financed by the Minister for teachers of classes into which Gypsies are placed
■ the co-ordination of the service by the working group already planned for the integration of handicapped pupils, a group operated by the provincial education office.

The convention of 24 February 1982 has now been superseded by the new law 270/82. However, it was possible to retain several features in some projects on teaching and learning strategies for pupils with learning difficulties and needing specific help. Opera Nomadi too, at this juncture, continued to assist teachers in the interpretation and application of law 270/82 in order to advance the education of Gypsies and other nomads.

Establishing Priorities and Co-ordinating New Projects

Despite the picture we have drawn there has been progress. Never the less, it is important that the system gives reassurance, encouragement and support so that the programme can continue.

Experiments are being carried out in some areas: there are working groups in schools, working groups in school districts, working groups in provincial education offices and there are already working groups among local organisations (in communes and neighbourhoods).

In some places proposals have been made to employ supplementary teachers in schools for Gypsy pupils and for exchanges with colleagues and with Gypsy families and for a teacher to be employed at district level where there are a considerable number of Gypsies; for social activities, the dissemination of information, the management of information banks and contact with local organisations; for a teacher to be employed at provincial level for liaison with teachers in the districts and schools, the gathering and cataloguing of teaching aids and methods, the distribution of materials for liaison: books, bulletins, bibliographies and the preparation of periodic meetings.

At the Curriculum Development Council of the Ministry of Public Instruction great importance is attached to the institution of a National Centre which would follow the movement and distribution of schoolchildren and the socio-cultural disadvantage of Gypsies. The Centre would gather and make known the results of research into educational projects and experiments, relationships with local authority services, Gypsies' own voluntary associations and other voluntary bodies. The centre should also be in touch with similar centres in the other countries of the European Community.

Reports of Practical Learning Projects
Laboratory of Theatrical Production and Psychoscenic Techniques
Carried out by Laura Costa. Teachers collaborated for teaching linguistic and grapho-pictural expression. Co-ordinator: Aurora Mereu. Class: Khorakhane children. Duration: Seven months (two hours twice a week). Participants: three primary school classes, including ten Gypsy pupils; some adult Gypsies, attending a professional course for scene-builders.

Aims
To help children, both Gypsy and non-Gypsy, to know and socialise in a world which they have to accept and in which they will have to put up with the uncertainties and confusion of adults and the selfishness and indifference of the group to which they belong. We have tried to transform their aggressive energy into something useful and to change bitterness into hope, irascibility and rage into trust of those around them. We have tried to develop in their hearts the conviction that bad temper, opposition, scorn 'a priori', and self-destruction can be overturned and transformed into a desire to meet people and know them, by developing better forms of relationship. We are convinced that, above all, it is necessary to know oneself but also other people, and to love them.

Methodology
We played, improvised, danced, created little dramas from everyday life, as well as imaginary situations, to bring us all together in the realm of the imagination and goodwill, since in the past ill will had left no possibility of our understanding one another. We worked with the body, endeavouring to use it and its life as a means of expressing recognition and love, and not as a mere object. With this aim, we used psychomotor exercises, the cultivation of a sense of rhythm, dramatic improvisations, seeking to widen more and more the level of body-consciousness and so foster a less traumatising integration and better levels of achievement.

Evaluation
During the first year of experiment, I set myself no immediate goal but sought to establish a climate which one could call 'of the here and now'. I concentrated on helping the children to acquire the first fundamental motor capacities and a certain level of muscle tone, considering this an essential pre-condition for further progress. The children themselves chose the timing, emphasising their demands, pointing out possibilities and deficiencies, their desires and dreams, the gaps due to lack of family training, their aspirations and their limits.

We worked with this vibrant, living material, balancing the technical demands with sensitivity and the materialising of ideas with pure creativity. Little by little an atmosphere of co-operation was created and we were able to consider the possibility of a final performance. This we built up by putting together several improvisations, particularly those in which pupils could recognise themselves. From this there developed what might be called a fantasy danced and recited by the children, representing the victory of a single common will over the separate, egotistic wills of a collection of human beings.

Today, the children who took part in this psychoscenic activity have all got an idea of what constitutes co-operative work, a way of living together, not only on the physical plane but also in the devotion to the idea of getting to know and respect one another. The experience of seven months working together has helped motivate them and give a meaning to their participation in the life of the school.

Innovation
This work with the body encouraged physical contact among the children as it was essential in the improvisations for them to touch one another, whereas in class the separation between Gypsies and non-Gypsies was complete – and not

only physically but psychologically as well. This activity helped to break down barriers and produced approaches on the affective plane. The presence in the school of adult Gypsies engaged in a teaching workshop helped to create a positive image in the eyes of both the non-Gypsies (teachers, pupils and parents) and also the Gypsy pupils themselves who were proud to present their parents as experts in a productive activity like carpentry and joinery.

Change the Context and Get a Warmer Welcome

Carried out by teachers, prepared and led by the coordinator, Antonia Rullo. Aimed at: the Rom children from the Abruzzi attending primary school No.143, duration the whole school year 1988-89. Participants: members of the adult literacy class for Gypsy women (eleven Romnia from the Abruzzi and two Sicilian Camminanti), four primary classes, a group of non-Gypsy parents.

Aims

■ to achieve for Gypsy children improved collaboration from the school
■ to verify the hypothesis that to encourage integration, it is necessary to concentrate instead on the contexts in which differences occur rather than focusing attention on differences
■ to increase knowledge of Gypsy culture with a view to mutual enrichment
■ involvement of both Gypsy and non-Gypsy parents in the educational itinerary.

Methodology

Various sub-groups were organised according to individuals' interests in specific areas (history, language, tradition, social cohesion and forms of self-defence) and exchanges of information between Gypsy and non-Gypsy, both adults and children, also took place.

Evaluation

Results should be considered on two levels. For children and adult Gypsies the goals achieved are a realisation, especially by the young, of their cultural identity of which some elements had been lost and also the motivation to learn the instruments of the non-Gypsy culture.

For the children and adult non-Gypsies an undertaking to become promoters of a better knowledge of Gypsy culture in schools as a means of overcoming the fears aroused by a stereotype of those that are different, a realisation of the limited acceptance of others and a determination to foster the values which bring about equality.

Innovation

In drawing up the programme of welcome we stopped concentrating on the difference in cultures and concentrated instead on the contexts in which differences occur. Adult Gypsies and non-Gypsies alike were involved in the educational 'itinerary' of their children. Traveller culture has been included in the teaching programme.

Musical Education

Carried out by Co-operative Donna Olimpia, co-ordinator M. Grazia Capitani; aimed at Knovakhane children; duration two months; participants: the pupils of six classes (3rd and 4th year) of primary school No.135.

Objectives
- intellectual development: music exercises and develops capacities for thought
- emotional development: music gives the experience of a whole series of emotions which refine the listener's sensibility
- social development: music as a means of communication
- the general aim was to stimulate auditory perception beyond the everyday passive non-discriminatory level.

Methodology
One and a half hours per week for each class. A final concert, linked with an illustrative lesson, to ensure a better understanding of the piece: its period in history, the composer's intentions and the instruments used. The exploration became a piece of listening research: we considered the sounds of the experience, the sounds were reproduced graphically, showing their duration and their pauses. We used the commonest instruments and composed simple sequences of notes on instruments made by the children out of 'junk' materials.

Evaluation
Through listening to, recognising and understanding the environment of sound around them, the pupils were enabled to live through the stages of a process giving them the ability to orientate themselves in the real world and create within themselves an image of it.

A Teaching-Learning Experiment
in the Field of Psychometry and Expressiveness
Carried out by The Institute of Orthophonology (Dr. Bianchi), co-ordinator Grazia Capitani; aimed at Rudari and Rom children from the Abruzzi, aged four to seven; duration the whole school year 1988-89; participants: the pupils of seven classes of the primary school and two classes of the infant school.

Objectives
To increase the value placed on both verbal language and body language and to overcome several problematic situations due to the extreme variations of individual levels to start with. To help children to live in harmony, determined to discover the possibilities of using the body as a means of communication, expression and acquisition of knowledge.

Methodology
The work took place in three phases:
- we asked the teachers to write a description of each child's history and home background and point out everything that could be important in understanding the child
- investigations to enable the drawing up of a psychomotor profile of each child (Vayer's test), lateralisation, rhythm, perceptive and spatial organisation (Santucci's test), figurative synthesis (cubes of Khos) and classification. We also applied projective tests (Wartegg, Luscher), sociograms and gave drawing tests (drawing of a house, a human face, the family, a beautiful place, an ugly place)
- verbalisation and graphic transposition of the psychomotor activity already performed; games with the object of discovering the body and valuing the way of life of the children.

Evaluation

In the area of psychomotricity there are no significant differences between Gypsy and non-Gypsy children, except under the heading 'postural control', which requires great attention to be paid to the body.

In the grapho-perceptive area the Gypsy children are inferior in the reproduction of abstract forms but normal in the reproduction of concrete objects and familiar situations.

In the psychological area it is impossible to generalise but it is, nevertheless, important to emphasise the fact that in Gypsy children the feeling of belonging to their group is much stronger than it is in others.

As for merging with the class groups, we discovered that the Gypsy children are not considered in either a positive or a negative sense.

In the third phase, the Gypsy children gave positive results in the games and rhythmic exercises. The graphic exercises gave very interesting results. This led to their being thought of in a favourable light by their companions and increased their own self-confidence.

Innovation

The psychological investigations were only the starting point for a teaching/learning activity designed, not to discover shortcomings, but to allow the Gypsy children to express all their potential and to participate actively in the life of the group in the school.

Paper 12   The Netherlands: Secondary Education for Children of Gypsies and Travellers

Gerrit Peterink, National Co-ordinator and Head of the Catholic Pedagogical Centre

The general situation in the Netherlands and in particular the organisation of co-ordination was the subject of a long presentation by Harry Hutjens at the Summer University held in Montauban, France in July 1988. His presentation was published in the report *Gypsy Children at School: The Training of Teachers and Other Personnel* (Council of Europe, document DECS/EGT(88)42). This publication forms part of the required preparatory reading for this meeting (see Appendix 1) and was distributed in French and English by the Council of Europe. This paper is concerned with secondary education of gypsies and Travellers in the Netherlands.

Historical Background

In the 1960s all sites, both large and small, situated at the edge of towns and villages were closed down and centralised. Large sites were set up with sometimes more than 100 places. They provided good facilities such as social welfare, schools, club buildings, scrap areas, sports accommodation and an outbuilding with a toilet and shower for every Traveller family. As a result more than fifty site schools came into existence providing complete education.

In 1975 the site school was the centre for all educational activities for the children of Travellers and Gypsies aged three to sixteen. Very few children attended mainstream secondary schools. Even then, however, a start had been made in the decentralisation process as these sites did not live up to expectations and led to the inhabitants becoming more and more isolated. The closure of these sites also resulted in a reduction in the number of site schools. In 1985 there were twenty five schools left, in 1987 there were fifteen and in 1988 only eight remained. In 1982 the Catholic Pedagogical Centre, in co-operation with the Christian and General Pedagogical Centre, started to look into this situation and as a result increasing numbers of children now attend

Diagram 1

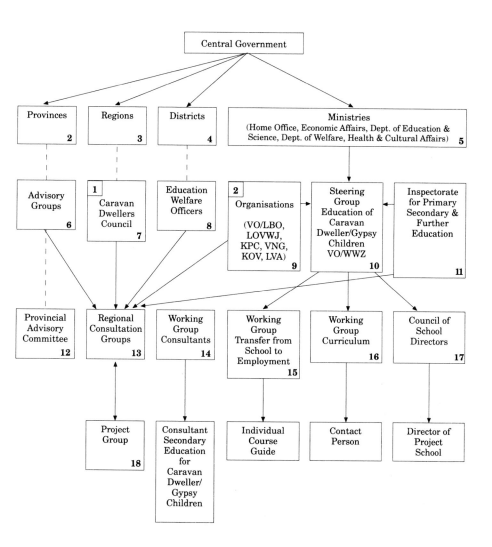

Notes

1   Holland has Caravan Dweller Councils in most provinces. Members of these councils are representatives of the caravan dweller community and the gypsy community as well as people working with these communities and people working in local/central government. Representatives of the gypsy community are a recent addition (1990) to these councils.

2   The abbreviations for the names of organisations indicate the organisations mentioned below under representatives in the Community for Secondary Education to children of caravan dwellers and gypsies (VO/WWZ).

mainstream schools. At that time Ria Timmermans and Gerrit Peterink carried out a national survey into the educational situation. From this it became clear that about 7 per cent of all students aged thirteen to sixteen attended a mainstream secondary school.

From this survey it also became clear that a structural, rigidly organised national approach was advisable in order to change the mentality of both parents and children with respect to the usefulness of school attendance.

Organisation

In 1982 the Committee for the Secondary Education of Children of Caravan Dwellers and Gypsies (VO/WWZ) was set up. Gerrit Peterink was the chairman. The aims can be summarised as follows:
■ to increase school attendance
■ to promote regular attendance
■ to support qualified school leavers and those children dropping out of school.

Diagram 1 is a mixture of the existing structure and the structure laid down in a policy document of the Ministry of Education and Science to be implemented from September 1989. The VO/WWZ committee will then be known as the OWWZ Steering Group as the work not only involves secondary education but also primary education and links up with the job market.

The Steering Group, which meets five times a year, consists of representatives from:
■ the Ministry of Education and Science (box 5)
■ Department of Health (box 5)
■ the Inspectorate for Primary and Secondary Education (box 5)
■ VO/LBO (Schools for Secondary Education)
■ welfare agencies
■ VNG (the Vereniging Nederlandse Gemeenten, Association of Dutch Municipalities)
■ KOV, the trade unions
■ LVLA (Schools and the National Association of Civil Servants concerned with Compulsory Education)
■ LOVWJ (the National Organisation for the Education of Young Workers)
■ KPC (the Catholic Pedagogical Centre).

At regional and departmental level Regional Co-operative Groups (RSVs) were set up (box 13). They meet twice a year but each has a project group to deal with day to day matters (box 13). All groups concerned with the education and welfare of Travellers and Gypsies are represented in an RSV.

In 1985, with a great deal of difficulty, we obtained a subsidy from the government and started three projects in the following regions:
■ at Amersfoort, a separate group for Traveller boys at the Amerij School. The group is now fully integrated
■ at Almelo, with boys and girls of Travellers integrated in the St. Paul School
■ at Someren, a separate group for Gypsy girls in the Waterdael School. Gypsy boys have also been admitted since 1987. Integration proceeds slowly.

In 1986, six more projects were added: Groninged, province of Friesland, Zwolle, Arnhem, Nieuwegein (foreign Gypsies) and Dordrecht and then in 1988 Breda and the Veenendaal region. In this way, more than 500 pupils have been reached. There are about 1,650 Traveller and Gypsy pupils aged thirteen to sixteen, mostly living on sites consisting of up to fifteen caravans, in practically every town and village in the Netherlands.

Working Group of Consultants (See diagram 1, box 15)
Every region has a full-time consultant who does not do any teaching and who works according to a handbook for consultants which is used throughout the Netherlands. These consultants are usually attached to schools for lower vocational education or general secondary education. From here they can reach other schools in the area that have children from our target group. The consultants meet on a monthly basis for talks, training, professionalisation and mutual support. Every year three conferences or workshops are organised. A total of eighty-three educational institutions with 568 pupils aged thirteen to sixteen of all denominations participate in the projects.

Meeting of Directors (See box 17)
The directors of the schools concerned in every region meet once every two months. They discuss matters mainly relating to policy. Feedback from these meetings is passed on to the VO/WWZ Committee. Recently they decided that every project should be supplied with an advanced computer to provide them with easy access to data concerning registration, reports and evaluations and to make co-ordination easier.

Working Group for Programme Development (See box 16)
This working group consists of teachers from the project areas. It meets six times a year and is headed by the Catholic Pedagogical Centre. It has produced a handbook *Over the Barrier* for use by schools or teachers coming into contact with our target group for the first time.

Working Group on School / Work Links (See box 15)
The first qualified students have just left school and need support in their choice of further education or work. It is practically impossible for them to make a living in the Netherlands in the traditional trades such as dealing in scrap, dealing in cars, etc. as the laws relating to waste disposal and the environment no longer allow this. About 90 per cent of the Traveller and Gypsy population is unemployed, classed as unemployable by the Department of Employment and living on social security. An employment consultant has been appointed in the Arnhem region. He works in close co-operation with the education consultant. His role is to help pupils in the transition from school to work.

Reporting and Evaluation
In order to gain a better insight into the situation, and to be accountable to the Regional Co-operative Groups (RSV), the VO/WWZ and the Ministry of Education and Science, each consultant's work is organised according to content, organisation and structure based on the following:
■ Daily register completed by the consultant
■ Register of pupils' absences completed by consultants and schools
■ Reports by the consultants and RSV
■ Evaluation-reports issued by the Catholic Pedagogical Centre
Further details of each of these is given below.

Daily Register
Each day five activities of about an hour and a half are registered. The reason for the activity, the school or institution visited and the problem areas are written down by

means of codes (see below). The processing of this data is completely automated. KPC and all of the consultants have access to computers.

Diagram 2
Daily Register:
example of
weekly form

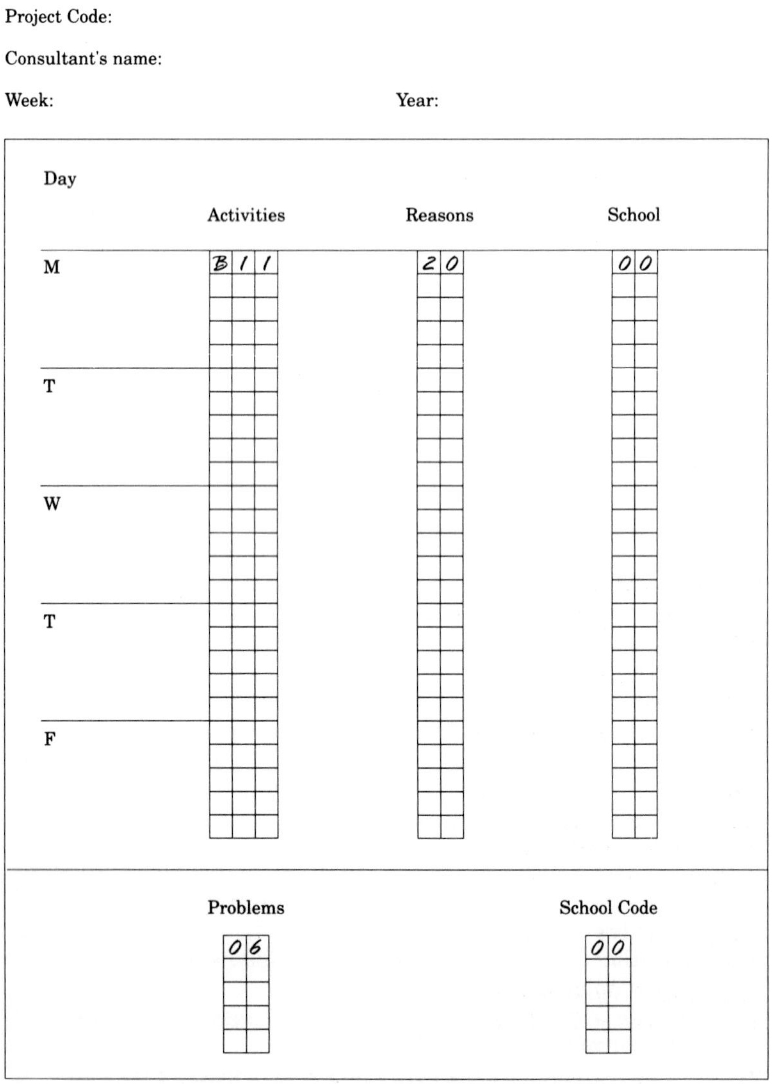

Project Code:

Consultant's name:

Week: Year:

Day	Activities	Reasons	School
M	B I I	2 0	0 0
T			
W			
T			
F			

Problems	School Code
0 6	0 0

A. Content
A.1   Classroom
       A11: organisation
       A12: adaptation

A.2   Lessons (aim, objective, materials etc.)
       A21: orientation
       A22: purchases
       A23: preparation
       A24: adaptation
       A25: timetabling
       A26: testing, written and oral

A.3   Lessons to pupils
       A31: assistance or teaching
       A32: substitution for other teachers
       A33: present at lessons
       A34: preparing lessons

B. Organisation
B.1   Contact with parents
       B11: visits to caravan, home or boat
       B12: by telephone
       B13: parents visit school
       B14: parents' evening
       B15: parents' day/afternoon
       B16: parents' committee

B.2   Contact with students
       B21: with target group pupils
       B22: with other pupils
       B23: with both
       B24: assistance with homework
       B25: contact with ex-pupils

B.3   Contact with project teachers
       B31: with an individual teacher
       B32: with project team
       B33: with form teacher

B.4   Contact with non-project teachers
       B41: with an individual teacher
       B42: with form teacher
       B43: with teaching team

B.5   Contact with school management/board etc.
       B51: management
       B52: board
       B53: educational support staff

B.6   Out of school activities
      B61: preparation
      B62: attendance

C. Structure
C.1   Administrative and organisational activities
      C11: project report (internal)
      C12: project report (external)
      C13: preparing/reporting meetings
      C14: preparing/reporting workshop
      C15: designing models/filling in forms/making summaries etc.

C.2   Contacts with external schools
      C21: primary school
      C22: secondary school
      C23: special school
      C24: site school
      C25: partial education
      C26: other VO/WWZ project schools
      C27: other schools

C.3   Contacts with outside agencies
      C31: municipality: civil servant dealing with compulsory education
      C32: municipality: others
      C33: welfare work
      C34: national pedagogical centres/educational guidance centre
          LPC/OBD
      C35: Ministry of Education and Science/Department of Health
      C36: province/provincial centre
      C37: other agencies

C.4   School/work transition
      C41: talks about work experience/work
      C42: preparation for work experience/work
      C43: supervision of work experience/work
      C44: visit to work experience placement
      C45: projects

C.5   Structural co-ordination
      C51: Regional Co-operative Group (RSV)
      C52: RSV project group
      C53: consultants' meeting
      C54: other VO/WWZ meeting
      C55: conference/working visit
      C56: professionalisation for consultant

Reasons/Cause for Activity
      01: planned visit/meeting/activity
      02: as a result of an incident
      03: to give advice
      04: to get advice

05: to make an appointment
06: to give support
07: as a result of non-attendance
08: as a result of an application for exemption from compulsory
    education
09: registration of future pupils
10: transfer of pupil
11: meeting about state of affairs
12: as a result of sickness of teacher
13: as a result of sickness of pupil
14: introduction
15: observation
16: transfer
17: organising transport
18: setting up/implementation of project
19: by invitation
20: to support parents
21: to support teacher(s)

Main Problem Areas
01: non-attendance
02: absenteeism/dropping out/not enrolling
03: clan formation at school
04: bad conduct
05: late entry/not completing
06: motivation of the pupils
07: early holidays
08: didactical problems
09: contact with parents
10: involvement of parents
11: finances
12: link up between first and second phase
13: link up school - school
14: reduction in non-teaching periods in secondary education
15: discouragement of those involved
16: transport
17: instability of the project (one day everything goes right, the next
    everything goes wrong)
18: regionalisation of the project
19: stagnation of the integration
20: decentralisation of the caravan site
21: link up school - work
22: lack of co-operation from external bodies
23: attractiveness of the educational centre and/or other projects
(e.g. learning opportunities at the work place)

Registration of Pupils and Absences
All pupils in the project areas are registered. In order to safeguard their
privacy their names and forenames are known only to the consultants and the
schools. In the central register, which is kept by one of the consultants, only
the codes are known. Collective lists only are used for the purpose of reports

and evaluation. A card (see below) is kept in the computer for every pupil.

Main menu: VO/WWZ

T. create card
W. remove card
V. amend card
P. data to printer
S. stop, return to DOS
D. return to dBase III+

Option (enter letter)

---

surname: forename:

date of birth: place:

culture (G/T):   male/female: code:

0 = none
1 = site school
2 = primary school (special)
3 = primary school
4 = cultural training centre
5 = secondary school (special)
6 = symbiosis
7 = secondary school
8 = special support group

phase (primary/secondary):

type of school:

name of school:

class:

Reports
A list of resolutions is sent to the evaluator after every meeting. Extensive reports are produced of conferences and workshops. These can later be ordered from KPC by anyone interested.

Evaluation Reports
Evaluation reports are produced once every six months. Once a year all projects formulate their aims according to a single, pre-programmed model which gives an indication of how these aims can be realised by means of a time plan. The evaluator gives an indication of the extent to which results have been achieved based on the registers and reports. He also points out the main problem areas and compares the projects with each other.

Results

School Attendance

As mentioned earlier, at the outset of the project school attendance was about 7 per cent. Through the hard work of the consultants many pupils aged twelve to sixteen have been tracked down in the regions, have been motivated to go to school and have been supported in this. The following overview shows the results for the academic years 1986-87, 1987-88 and 1988-89. In these years, the number of pupils attending school went up from 7 per cent to 91 per cent.

Diagram 3
Absence catagorised as: due
to sickness, authorised and
non-authorised (total
average per project over
three months).

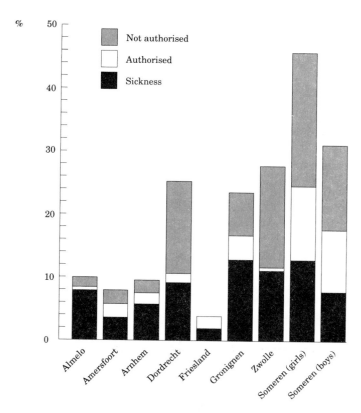

Overview of absenteeism

Consultants' Daily Record
This example of a record is for the academic year 1987-88. The various activities listed in the record can be found on the form Record of Activities (Diagram 4).

The activities are grouped in the following manner:

■ A1 to A3 Curricular work
■ B1 to B6 Organisational work
■ 1 to C5 Structural work.
The two sets of figures, one for Gypsy and one for Caravan Dweller children, indicate a noticeable difference in time spent on the various types of activities.

Diagram 4
Record of Activities

Code	Activity	Caravan Dwellers	Gypsies	Remarks
A11 to A34	teaching and in class support	1.7%	5.8%	caravan dwellers integrated gypsies separated
B21 to B26	other contact with pupils	8.3%	1.4%	
B11 to B16	contact with parents/ site visits	14.8%	12.6%	
B31 to B43	contact with teachers	9.1%	14.1%	
B51 to B53	contact with school management/board	4.5%	5.5%	
B61 to B62	out of school activities	1.6%	2.0%	
C21 to C27	administrative/ organisational activities	21.6%	19.7%	
C31 to C37	contacts with external schools/agencies	21.1%	11.0%	most gypsy pupils usually attend the same school
C41 to C45	supporting transfer from school to employment	3.1%	0%	not relevant at the moment for gypsy pupils
C51 to C56	structural consultation; Regional Consultation Group, Project Group, conferences, study visits, professional training	13.2%	26.0%	gypsy children require much more support

Making the Transition from School to Employment

Dutch children usually attend primary school from the age of four until the age of eleven. Primary schools are organised in 8 groups for each year. Pupils in group 6 would normally be about nine years old, in group 7 they would be ten years old and in group 8 they would be eleven years old.

Secondary school is organised in classes for each year with the number of classes depending on the type of secondary education. The Netherlands has several types of secondary education (MAVO, HAVO and VWO). The future career of pupils depends in part on which school they attend. For example, a pupil attending a VWO school will be able to go to University but a pupil attending a MAVO school is far more likely to leave school at the age of sixteen to take a job. Education is compulsory until the age of sixteen.

We have opted for an individual approach in helping parents and students since we believe that staying together as a group in further education or employment can have a number of negative results. We call this individual approach 'individual course guidance'.

Diagram 5
Individual Course Guidance
Structure for caravan
Dweller/Gypsy Children:
a special support scheme to
ease the transfer from
primary to secondary
education

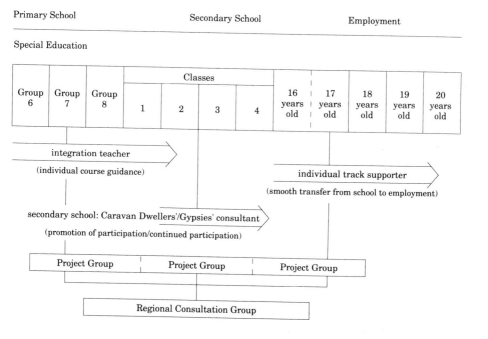

A special scheme has been developed for caravan dwellers and gypsy children (see Diagram 5) which covers the last three years of primary education, secondary education and assistance in seeking work up to the age of twenty. In primary education, the supervision is still done by the 'integration teachers' in some places. They used to be teachers at site schools but after the closure of these schools they were given the opportunity to continue their work for another three years at various schools (with a particular emphasis on didactic work).

During these three years or at their end their the work is handed over to a VO/WWZ consultant who, in close co-operation with the individual course supervisor (employment consultant), makes the link to the job market. An employment consultant has been appointed to work on a pilot project in Arnhem under a special arrangement designed to reduce unemployment among the Dutch population.

Present and Future Government Policy

The political parties in the Netherlands are unanimous in their opinion that the system used in the pilot projects should be continued and expanded. Previous Ministers of Education have repeatedly said that the changeover from site schools to regular schools should take place on a neutral budget. The implementation of this is laid down in a policy document. In this there is mention of a national network of Regional Consultation Groups each having to design their own plan, analogous to existing projects, in which they state how they want to realise primary education, secondary education and the transfer between school/work and further education. The plans should be submitted to the national Steering Group OWWZ (Education and Employment for Children of Travellers and Gypsies) which is to be set up. This OWWZ steering group replaces the VO/WWZ committee and will be set up on 1 August 1989. It will have to advise the Minister.

The Catholic Pedagogical Centre takes care of the administration, setting up of plans, co-ordination, evaluation and complete support/supervision. The academic year 1989-90 will be a transitional period in which to draw up plans, to assess and to allocate the areas. In the years 1990-94 the national network will be phased out, followed by an overall evaluation in 1994. Central to this policy are the position of the consultant, the co-operation of schools and institutions in a Regional Consultation Group and the co-ordinating task of the Catholic Pedagogical Centre.

Paper 13 Portugal: General Information
Maria de Lurdes Almeida Gil da Silva, Co-ordinator of the
National Project to Support the Schooling of Gypsy Children

There are approximately 20,000 Portuguese Gypsies, 0.2 per cent of the total population or, in other words, roughly one Gypsy per 500 inhabitants.

Geographical distribution is not uniform. The maximum concentration can be found in the Lisbon district where about 6,000 Gypsies are settled. In second place come the districts of Porto and Sebutal, each with about 1,500 to 2,000 Gypsies. These are areas of dense population suitable for their work as travelling traders. There are about 1,500 Gypsies in the neighbouring border districts and the tourist districts such as the Algarve (see map 1).

The living conditions of the Portuguese Gypsies are, in general, very poor and help from Social Services is often required. Trading is the preferred form of employment. The majority are illegally working as travelling traders. Those who have a legal trade prefer working in markets. There are some families who possess a traditional, commercial establishment, most often dealing in carpets. The richest families have bought their own houses. The others, the vast majority, experience bad living conditions. Approximately 70 per cent of the Gypsy population lives in extreme poverty in 'shanty towns' on the outskirts of towns, in a collection of huts without essential sanitary facilities.

In co-operation with the Fundo de Fomento de Habitação some district councils have provided housing for Gypsies but at a very slow pace. It is, therefore, necessary to make a bigger investment in this sector to abolish the 'shanty towns' which are also inhabited by other Portuguese people and immigrants from Cap-Vert. This is a problem of national proportions which must be solved soon.

The majority of Gypsies belongs to the Gitan group. There is also a group of Rom Kalderash but numbers are dwindling to about 0.5 per cent. These Rom engage in metal crafts especially coppersmithing. They speak Calo and Portuguese and many of them also speak Castilian due to the frequent evictions in Spain.

Gradually they have lost their fundamental characteristic of nomadism. The majority lives a sedentary existence in bad conditions, as I explained earlier, and has begun to travel only in the fair season from spring to the end of autumn. Seasonal travel is one of the reasons for school absence which worries teachers.

Almost 90 per cent of the adult Gypsy population is illiterate. This indicates the urgent need for measures which will facilitate the education of Gypsy children in schools. Such an education must value and respect their socio-cultural characteristics. The Gypsy children attend school in mixed classes. Support for children with learning difficulties is the same for all children and does not take into account the specific problems experienced by Gypsies. Consequently, the Department for Primary and Secondary Education initiated a support project in 1987-88. I am responsible for this support project for the education of Gypsy children.

As a first step we devised a national questionnaire to gain an insight into the situation (see map 2). We have established that there are 4,082 registered pupils which represents only 30 per cent of the children of school age. There are some districts where none of the Gypsy children of school age attends school. This disinterest on the part of parents partly corresponds to the level of illiteracy but at the same time it must be acknowledged that there is a fear of loss of cultural identity and a possibly justifiable resentment of Gypsies towards educational institutions for this reason.

We have also noticed a high educational failure rate amongst Gypsy children: 50 per cent at primary and 47 per cent at secondary level. Because of this situation we have started a national programme of further training for teachers. This training focuses specifically on Gypsy culture and its character-istics. The aim is to motivate teachers to introduce the necessary reforms and educational innovations by transforming the school into a place where all pupils can feel at home. We felt that one of the causes of continual absenteeism among Gypsy pupils was that school held little attraction for them because it was seen to be – and, in fact, is – totally divorced from their culture. There is, therefore, a great need for multi-cultural education. The teacher has to understand the specific nature of Gypsy culture and the complications this will cause for pupils from this cultural group.

We consider this a priority in the training of teachers but it is also necessary to identify other aspects to ensure that teachers are technically well-prepared and that the quality of teaching and the performance of teachers reflects the inter-cultural. The characteristic cohesion and the preservation of the cultural models of this ethnic group are factors in the difficulties experi-enced in education, even if an inter-cultural approach is taken, and, as such, must be taken into account. The cycles of segregation and forced assimilation have left deep scars on the collective memory which are difficult to erase. They make communication between school and the Gypsy community essential. Adequately trained and professionally suitable teachers are needed to establish this communication. At the moment, we are carrying out a pilot project in stages which has the characteristics of action-research.

Action-research

We consider Jean-Pierre Liégeois' suggestion that we start our work here by considering the nature of action-research very well timed since it will give us a starting-point for the development of theory in this area.

The expression 'action-research' combines two concepts which should be united. In our view the need to discover a model which will integrate the constituent parts into a vast and co-ordinated piece of work is more important than a change of name. As a starting-point we can consider three components of this model:

Diagram 1

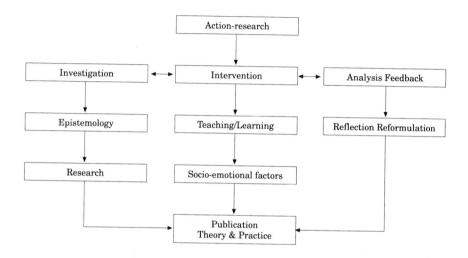

It goes without saying that this proposal must be considered as a starting point for the conceptualisation of the desired definition.

Within the concept of action-research a vast number of other notions and concepts is hidden. Therefore, when we consider the daily inter-cultural activities of a teacher, we will also find the trainer, the co-ordinator and, above all, the child. It is within this dichotomy of teacher/child, trainer/trainee and co-ordinator/project that the concept of action-research is contained. In the specific area of intervention in these elements of the teaching process the very act of teaching becomes an investigation. The way to research is through activities. It is a dynamic process and leads to innovation. By reconsidering each of the proposed models the groups will be predisposed to choose one or more of the components.

In the end one has to underline the fundamental importance of including action-research in the further training of teachers and in self-training. In my view action-research is the practical use (action) of the experience and knowledge acquired in teaching activities which, in their turn and in addition to the teaching provided for the pupil, also constitute a new source of knowledge for the teacher (research). There is a reciprocal mechanism, therefore, in which the teacher educates the pupil and the pupil, albeit indirectly, educates the teacher.

In our view, pedagogical research is a good method of further teacher-training in which self-training also has an important role. We consider it an excellent means of achieving the desired modifications of educational structures especially as they affect the education of Gypsy children. Pedagogical research can give a greater power to adapt, greater flexibility and the empowerment to respond adequately to the needs of the Gypsy world. Action-research also relates to the production of educational materials, a fundamental support for teaching/learning.

At the moment, other initiatives are being undertaken in Portugal by Pastoral Work with Gypsies and The Santa Casa da Misericórdia de Lisbon. These projects are mainly interested in nursery schools and in leisure activities and have made remarkable progress in the area of action-research. In addition, we have been able to select two schools on the basis of the interest and the professional suitability of the teachers, social environment, difficulties in settling Gypsy children into school and their subsequent lack of achievement and we have initiated action-research pilot projects. These projects have been supported by the recently founded Human Rights Committee in Education and Pastoral Work with Gypsies. The projects involve teamwork which will benefit from the considerations and conclusions of our work here. This working seminar is thus very timely from our point of view.

Co-ordination

Co-ordination is another fundamental aspect of projects with shared objectives and, perhaps, the most difficult given the involvement of various institutions which, of course, renders agreement more problematic.

In our view, co-ordination at a national level would be desirable involving the co-ordinators of the representative institutions in Portugal. These institutions in their turn must allow decentralisation to regional co-ordination, which then must decentralise to create local co-ordination. These local groups are closest to the client group and, therefore, best equipped to evaluate and propose the essential measures. This is the only means of finding adequate answers to the specific problems of each locality.

It is the only way for co-ordination to acquire the permanent feedback needed to make it operational and objective. Otherwise, one risks working in isolation without liaison with other groups or, worse, with a co-ordination which does not fundamentally serve the individuals concerned.

It does not sound an easy task to obtain a consensus but, if we succeed in identifying the common strand needed to galvanise both statutory and private organisations, the freeing of the logjam will be certain to follow. One has to realise that much work has already been done in this area. After defining the abilities and limitations of all those involved, we can innovate with more confidence and with the prospect of a greater degree of success.

Diagram 2
Education of
Gypsy Children
(school year
1987/88).

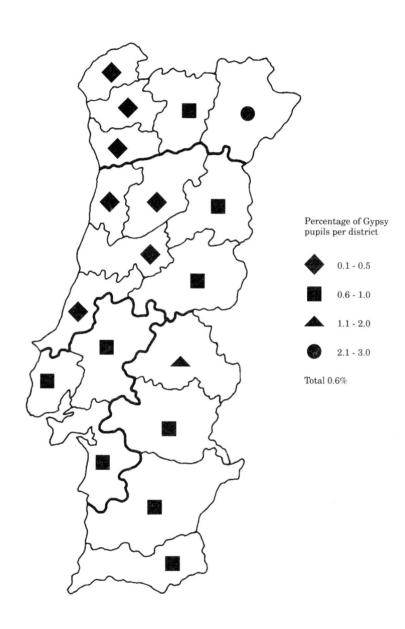

Percentage of Gypsy
pupils per district

◆ 0.1 - 0.5

■ 0.6 - 1.0

▲ 1.1 - 2.0

● 2.1 - 3.0

Total 0.6%

Diagram 3
Geographical
distribution of
the Gypsy
population.

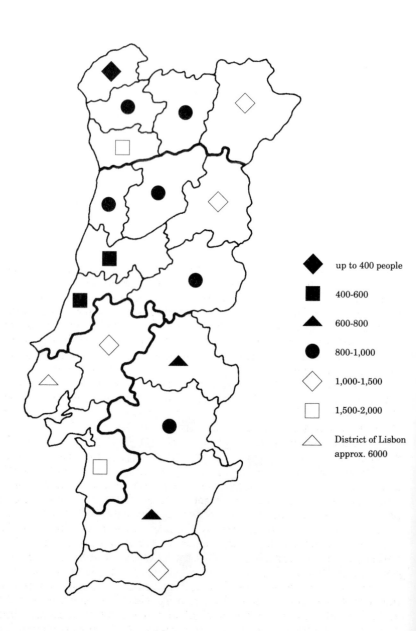

up to 400 people

400-600

600-800

800-1,000

1,000-1,500

1,500-2,000

District of Lisbon
approx. 6000

Paper 14 Case Study of a School

Rosa Maria Almeida de Medeiros, Primary Teacher.

The Curraleira primary school is situated in a deprived area of Lisbon. 50 per cent of the parents are from Lisbon and the other 50 per cent form part of a population which consists of people from various regions in Portugal, African countries where Portuguese is spoken, Indians and Gypsies. The illiteracy rate among parents of pupils attending the school in 1986-87 was 30 per cent for fathers and 46 per cent for mothers. The socio-economical level is low and many of the families live in shacks. The majority of the population has non-qualified employment. The Gypsies are often travelling traders.

The educational team in the school is relatively new. It promotes cultural activities, contacts with different ideas and a canteen as central to the life of the school. By analysing the failure and absenteeism observed in the period 1983-88 in stages, several conclusions could be drawn.

Absenteeism reduced substantially in the 1984-85 school year. The reasons for this decrease are partly intervention by organisations who developed work with Gypsies and partly the intervention of the school doctor at the request of the Teachers' Committee. However, the reduction in absenteeism coincided with an increase in the number of children failing academically probably caused by the lack of response by the school to the particular problems experienced by the Gypsy children who started attending. The educational team attributed this failure to the difficult behaviour of the pupils and requested psychological support from the Directorate of Educational Services for Primary/Secondary Schools to resolve these behavioural problems.

During the 1985-86 school year, the educational team organised a meeting of teachers, social workers and Gypsies to raise awareness of Gypsy and other cultures. As a result of this initiative, a better understanding and acceptance of different cultures were achieved. A greater number of Gypsy pupils enrolled in school.

During the 1986-87 school year, a psychologist came to the school to study the causes of academic failure with the teachers. This led the team to reconsider its teaching practice and pupil/teacher relationships have developed positively.

At the end of the year, the teachers asked the Further Education College for a further training project which started in 1987. This was based on the perspective of a balance between teaching practice and the socio-cultural reality of the borough and of an intensification of the relationship between school and borough. It is an action-research project structured by quarterly plenary meetings for planning and evaluation and incorporates various methods such as workshops and small training sessions adapted to the needs of the groups. An arts project also operates in the school. That year, the number of school failures dropped but the degree of absenteeism remained stable.

In the current year (1989), the training project by the Further Education College and the arts project training sessions have continued. The school has received subsidies for the children's canteen as this is integrated into the total programme for the promotion of school success. Leisure time workshops (e.g. woodwork, weaving, sports) have functioned for a few months. It is in this current year that the Education of Gypsy Children project started. My school benefits from this training work.

Diversified training has caused a change in the teachers' practice which now matches local needs and recognises the importance of different activities which contribute to easing difficult situations. The teachers have gained a better understanding of Gypsy culture. This year the results have not been evaluated.

My work is integral to the school's project to which I have contributed the idea of applying an inter-cultural approach. I have defined the problem as the existence of children from different ethnic backgrounds in a class. I would argue that absenteeism is provoked by the imposition by schools of socio-cultural, ethno-centric values on ethnic minority children.

My class consists of twenty-one pupils in the first year of primary school (six year olds) among whom there are three children of African parents, one of Indian parents and four Gypsies. Daniel, a six year old, is a lively Gypsy child. I saw him for the first time in the Gypsy area of town during the first week of term when the school organised a visit to study the local environment. Antonio, a seven year old, is repeating the first year. He is a calm if somewhat defensive child. During the year he has been absent whenever his family needed him and he often arrived late, especially in the first few months of the school year. Carina is a very happy, agile child who sees herself as the youngest of the class. She lives in a shack opposite the school. Her parents sell ready-made clothes in the covered market in a shopping centre. The girl insists that her father does not work and that only her mother and the shop girls attend the shop. Her older sister, Isabel, a ten year old, is also in my class. She attended a special needs class for four years but did not do well there and her absences from school had increased. She is the eldest of the children and is responsible for the housework and the care of the younger children. She was delicate before she arrived in my class but this year she has started to develop.

As a theory I have suggested that an inter-cultural approach can alleviate cultural domination of minorities by recognising and observing the complex interactions in the class and by all the social participants (parents, pupils and teachers) having knowledge of the different cultures present.

I suggest the following strategies for effective intervention:
■ the study of a particular topic by all the pupils in the class
■ organisation of work areas and time to encompass changes (leisure time/ systematic studying time) and organisation of workshops
■ project work, e.g. The Fair – in a play, the difference in interpretation of the term 'fair' for Gypsy children (selling) and non-Gypsies (a place where you can have fun) was expressed. The two images formed the basis of the activity for the class. Knowledge of different cultures was elaborated in workbooks
■ free texts which provide a global method for the teaching of reading and writing skills using the child's own expressions
■ groupwork, with some individual work on learning and on behaviour, e.g. Antonio, the Gypsy boy who always arrives late. The other pupils wrote him a letter to invite him to come to school. He did so because he felt he was important in the class
■ class discussion – this has proved necessary to resolve some problems in the class, rethinking of the class, its organisation, the daily teaching, discussion of themes
■ the 'talking wall' newspaper.

Evaluation of the Process
This indicated that the rejection of ethnic minority children had crept into the 'What I Don't Like' heading of the talking wall. Demands for punishment of the Gypsy children were numerous. The global results of the work show that the Gypsies brought their culture to add to the cultures of the other children, that all the children discussed Gypsy/non-Gypsy relations in class and identified a culture clash. There was no absenteeism.

The success of the Gypsy children can be found in all three learning levels. The youngest of the Gypsies has become more and more independent. The oldest, who had not done well until recently, obtains better results now because she feels motivated and valued by her relationship with the class. The child who was often absent now attends because of the intervention of his friends. The methods used have motivated the Gypsy children.

In my view there is an urgent need for:
■ the establishment of a centre for Gypsy studies
■ the enrichment of teacher-training by contributions from interested educationists, sociologists and anthropologists
■ the development of new initiatives.

I believe that the bringing together of interested professionals in intercultural theme groups within all areas of work would help develop both theory and practice.

Paper 15   Spain: A Brief Critical Analysis of the Schooling
Situation of the Gypsy Community
Concepción Gozalo Yagües, Educational Psychologist

**The School System in the Context of the Spanish State, Constitution,
Democracy and Rights**
In December 1978, after the national referendum Spain became a state where
constitutional, social and democratic rights existed.

The written constitution, confirmed by the Spanish citizens, establishes
the general principles underpinning the norms according to which Spanish
society should function, norms which place specific responsibilities on the
public authorities. All this rests on a legal recognition of an historical reality, a
pluri-cultural society, which in practice is not respected by the public authorities. Thus one speaks for the first time of historic nationalities, of co-official
languages of the Spanish state, although these are limited to the territory in
which they are spoken. The Gypsy language ('a chipi calli') is not officially
recognised because those who speak it have no demarcated territory.

The fundamental principles on which the Spanish state is based are:
justice, liberty, participation, pluralism, equality of individuals and the groups
to which they belong, democratic co-existence and the predominance of the law
as the expression of sovereignty and of the popular will.

Constitutional principles define the 'should be' of a pluralist society which
does not yet exist in Spain. In article 3.3 the Constitution recognises the
richness of Spanish cultural diversity and proclaims that the cultures and
traditional languages and institutions which form its common heritage will be
the object of special respect and protection. The implications for the education
system are obvious. Compulsory, free education is proclaimed. Education is
regarded as an instrument to be used consciously to prepare citizens for a
pluralist society, multi-cultural and inter-cultural, where the different majority
and minority cultures live together (and not simply co-exist). Such an education gives to each individual the right to receive from society a training which

makes possible the full development of his or her personality and opens its doors to diversity, not only quantitatively but qualitatively. It accepts differences (of language, culture and traditions) and respects them, values them and encourages them across the education system. This is an education, therefore, which is differentiated and differentiating rather than the standardised education of the past: an education which demands the participation of every individual and social group affected by the school community so that it can function effectively and make possible a political structure which ceases to be purely a mechanism for the indoctrination and submission of the pupil to the rules of the dominant society (devaluing, subduing or annulling that which is different in the classroom and in the streets).

The Schooling Situation of the Gypsy Community in Spain

The last decade, 1978-88, has seen a marked advance in the schooling of Gypsy children in Spain: more Gypsies have been welcomed into school in the course of this short period of time than in the whole previous history of Gypsies in the Iberian Peninsula.

However, it must not be forgotten that (according to the education authorities) one quarter of Gypsy children do not attend school and the drop-out rate is very high at all ages, although particularly high from the age of eleven (before the end of compulsory schooling). There is a high percentage of school failure (failure to progress to the next year group), absenteeism is high and affects all ages and entry into school of Gypsy boys and girls is often late and always later than the average in Spanish society. The enormous percentage of illiterate adults among Gypsies (85 per cent according to Unesco figures) does nothing to encourage parental awareness of the need for schooling and this impedes the schooling of the children. The school is not ready and does not seem to wish to be ready to develop what the Gypsy children need – individual, specific and differentiated treatment which is at the same time inter-cultural.

Moreover there is inequality of opportunity in access to schooling. I must stress the importance of the lack of institutional attention to pre-school provision. There is no preventative or corrective action taken in the face of the instability, inequalities, rejections and failures of the children who originate from the most underprivileged sectors of society. There is also inequality of opportunity in the educational process, because from the pedagogical point of view teaching and instruction methods are scandalously inadequate and there is a lack of differentiation and adaptation of programmes of study and methods suited to the interests, lives, values and particular features of the Gypsy community. From a social perspective, the Gypsy child in school experiences the educational process of non-Gypsy society. The absence of a favourable climate, as much institutional as social, is a determining factor in variables such as satisfaction, motivation, attitude, receptivity, outcomes, learning. Nor is there equality of opportunity in participation in educational and social 'success'. In the context which we have described, the extension of democracy and free schooling to the whole of Spanish society without discrimination of any kind has not proved to be a successful framework for the Gypsy minority. Access to schooling is contributing to an increase in the figures for school failure and in practice, in schools where integrated schooling is allowed, the presence of Gypsy children in class has been seen by some parents and teachers as the cause of increased school failures among non-Gypsy children. There are many teachers who are professionally incapable of understanding and combating the failure of the education system. On the other hand, it is certainly comforting to state that there are professionals who have a true vocation, although this is often institutionally and structurally unsupported.

This distressing and intolerable situation being suffered by the Gypsy community has not been created in the education system. The situation of inferiority in which Gypsy children find themselves in school is a reflection of the conditions of life suffered by a large proportion of the Gypsy community on a permanent basis in Spanish society in general. What happens in school is explained by what happens outside, in the daily life of Spanish society. The educational sub-system depends on a context of interaction between demography, environment, level of instruction, attitudes, professional activity. Education cannot hope to achieve its objectives if it works in isolation.

The Minister of Education initiated a project specifically to support settled Gypsies, consisting of a programme of compensatory action. The project, which for its time presented certain advanced ideas (the education system had not been mobilised for a long time), was very limited although in some places it had a consolidating effect on the schooling of Gypsy children. The evaluation of this programme has not been made public. Why?

The Minister of Education has not officially created training courses for teachers and other professionals concerned in the Gypsy situation. There are periodic meetings between these professionals but permanent public training programmes are needed for concerned teachers.

Teachers in compensatory education must no longer be marginalised. The training and information courses which are necessary for the education of Gypsy children and adults must be attended by all schools and teachers involved, not just some, otherwise discrimination and rejection can sometimes occur within the educational framework itself. This can create unproductive differences and points of friction.

Help, assistance, training and informing of teachers should be universal rather than focussed on minorities, including one group and excluding others.

The starting point must be an inter-cultural and pluri-cultural philosophy (campaign in depth to raise awareness).

Other Priorities

■ The development of pedagogical materials: books, audio-visual materials, methods and strategies which are concerned with diversity and the socio-cultural adaptation of the children who co-exist in the class

■ adaptation of school timetables with flexible time periods for teaching, flexible daily working hours. This type of flexibility would allow a better adjustment of children and families to school

■ the creation of an assessment system which is always positive in relation to the children's work, to give value to their work and to their personal and intellectual efforts in adapting to school

■ the observation of and positive attitude towards all the elements which arise in a cyclical process of action-research

■ monitoring the care of the child and the equality of the opportunities in school and throughout his or her school career

■ exchange of experience and research in the school context facilitated by appropriate personnel and systems.

Action-research

I understand by this term a method of working which reunites theory and practice in one whole activity, ideas put into practice, a process of analysis, understanding, reflection, elaboration, testing, evaluation and assessment of practice. Action-research includes strategies in which one wishes to combine tentative theories, working practices, the partners involved, professionals (researchers, teachers...) in order to understand what is happening in the classroom, or in defined situations, and what needs to be done to change it. It is research into and action upon situations or contexts perceived as posing a problem.

Who Does the Research?
Research that is participatory (teachers, parents, pupils, researchers) and democratic (common decision making) which requires the participation of the different individuals concerned in and concerned about the problems or the situation.

How is the Research Done?
Action-research is a cyclical process of study in depth which requires flexibility in planning. The superimposing of action and reflection allows changes in planning to be based on critical and reflective analysis of working practice.

Diagram 1

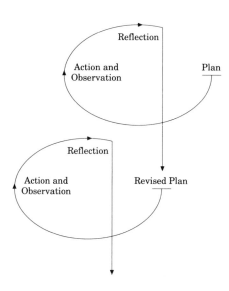

Some techniques of collection of the qualitative ethnographic information which may be used are: participant observation, diary, notes taken at the time of observation and combining different sources of information. Action-research is a process of access to reality. Procedures of negotiation make the principle of democratic research possible. Action-research is consistent with a concept of education which takes into account human reality in personal, moral, ethical and expressive terms and which at the same time is socially committed. Theory is seen as a process which emerges from a reflective dialogue between those involved.

Questions for Consideration
How can education contribute to social change? How can action-research contribute to the solutions of the universal problems affecting schooling?

Paper 16 Spain: Some Facts Concerning the Situation in
Andalucia
Martirio Muñoz Enrique, Headteacher

My report will try to describe the situation of the Gypsy community in
Andalucia. It is more a reflection than a series of facts. We work with the
Gypsy community but, since our activities have not been the subject of any
research, we lack facts.

The Gypsy Communities in Andalucia
Of the 14 million Gypsies in Europe, half a million live in Spain and half of
these in Andalucia. The Gypsy community is not a compact and homogeneous
whole but varies according to origin, economic and social position, stability of
accommodation.

Environment
The Gypsy population is traditionally found in out-lying districts which usually
lack a service infrastructure: water, electricity, road systems, sewerage and
drainage. Accommodation is often in caves dug out of the hillside and shanty
towns (43 per cent). In Granada the Gypsies live in four storey apartment
blocks. The number of Gypsy families who live in Granada is upwards of 650,
that is 3,700 people. This represents 1.5 per cent of the population. In nearby
villages, such as Afarte, they make up 10 per cent of the population. Several
families share the same accommodation in order to avoid being 'isolated' in
other districts. The average number of persons per household is six.

Employment
According to a study by the Andalucian government, 61 per cent of heads of
family are on the dole. Given the nature of their employment (some are
flamenco artists, some are tourist guides, others collect cardboard and iron, the
women sell heather or take to begging with their children) it follows that their

sources of fixed income are insecure. Drug trafficking is increasing among the Gypsy population, especially the young. This type of commerce appears particularly in urban areas. In general the type of work is a function of the economic activity particular to each area.

Illiteracy

Nearly half of the Gypsy population over forty years old are illiterate. Illiteracy is more widespread among women. Many remember having attended school and having learned to read and write but since they have not been in the habit of practising these skills they find it difficult to maintain them. At present there are some Schools for Adults where Gypsies go in particular to obtain their driving licences and the women take courses in, for example, cutting out and making of clothing.

Schooling

In general Gypsies are interested in non-Gypsy education, although among the older people one often hears it said that since they will not become doctors or solicitors it is sufficient to know how to read and write. The stability of accommodation of the Gypsy community in Andalucia is favourable to regular schooling. However, according to Andalucian government statistics, 53 per cent of Gypsy children of school age (between the ages of six and fourteen) do not attend school.

The types of school attended by the children are either mainstream schools or 'bridge-schools' (schools for Gypsies) which are tending to disappear in a move towards integration.

Schooling is not well-established, that is: those children who go to school do not attend very regularly, absenteeism is high, the Spanish language is barely mastered and the children are not integrated into classes which correspond to their age.

These facts serve as an excuse and make integration difficult in mainstream classes. Sometimes the Gypsy children, although 'integrated' in mainstream schooling, are enrolled in special classes.

Reasons for Difficulties in Schooling and Low Level of Achievement

■ The Gypsy people, as an ethnic minority, has its own culture, its own manner of being, of interpreting reality and of organising itself according to its own hierachy of values.

■ Our modern world has a written culture which conditions the intellectual structure of the mind.

■ The Gypsy world identifies itself with an orally transmitted culture which structures its thought according to the spoken word.

Present Projects

Mainstream education forms part of a specially organised compensatory education scheme whose objective is to compensate for inequalities. Its aims are to improve socialisation and encourage educational outcomes that are more useful in terms of future employment.

Needs

The Gypsies need to learn to live and co-exist with the world which surrounds them rather than to achieve certain levels of qualifications. The training they need must take account of their unfavourable situation. It must adapt itself in response to their specific needs.

There is a need to work with adults in parallel manner in order to avoid the situation where the Gypsy child is faced by a different set of values throughout his schooling to those transmitted in his family groups. There is a strong relationship between the high level of illiteracy, the amount of schooling and the underestimation of the school.

There is a need for greater flexibility in the educational system, which is very bureaucratic and excessively rigid (timetables, ages, understanding) and does not take into account the inequalities or the particular characteristics of the Gypsy people. The teacher who is going to work with Gypsies should make the effort to reflect on and understand the Gypsy world and its customs.

Instruments of reflection and instruction must be created to form a coherent and adapted programme which would cover areas such as the history, language, rites and customs of this people. Co-ordination would avoid waste of energy and money.

Paper 17 Spain: The Association of Teachers and Gypsies

Maria Assumpció Casas and Angel Marzo Guarinas,
Association of Teachers and Gypsies

During the school year 1979-80 a group of teachers in Aragon decided to contact other teachers in regions close to them to discuss the question of the education of Gypsy children. These contacts proved as useful in answering the need to exchange experiences and research in their common field of work as they were in filling gaps that the different administrations lacked the knowledge to fill. Apart from establishing that the Gypsies' educational situation was deplorable they tried to intervene in the educational system in such a way that assimilation on the part of the dominant/majority culture would be avoided, offering instead tools for development in present day society. It was in this way that they agreed to work, to remedy the historic situation of segregation and inequality which operated so severely against the Gypsy people.

From these beginnings were born the contacts which resulted in 'Days for Teachers' at Huesca in 1980, which, in the years to follow, were to become the pivot of this project for co-ordination and promotion of education. Since 1982 the Teachers' Days have taken place in a different region each September to strengthen action in the districts, each time giving a warmer welcome to new teachers. They have been held in Huesca (1980), Saragossa (1982), Valencia (1983), Bilbao (1984), Granada (1985), Madrid (1986), Badalona (1987) and La Coruna (1988). This year (1989) the Teachers' Days will take place once more in Saragossa.

Teachers' Days are opportunities for synthesis and the birth of new ideas. Theoretical and practical matters are discussed, proposals made to the administration and new initiatives are publicised. They are organised by the different Collectives which, year after year, develop and strengthen themselves in each area.

In the course of the third Teachers' Days the participation extended beyond the strictly educational field through the inclusion of several categories of professionals working with the Gypsy population. In this way we have been able to advance towards reflection and interdisciplinary projects. At the end of the fifth Teachers' Days it was decided to form a National Association of Teachers and Gypsies which provides technical support to the activities of the Collectives.

At present (1989) the Association is not only concerned with the preparation of the annual Teachers' Days but with supporting and following up projects, combined action and exchanges and, depending on specific situations during the school year, promoting new contacts. During the sixth Days some conclusions were drafted in the form of recommendations on the education of Gypsies which form the idealogical base of the Collectives. It was then that a minimal organisational structure was created: this functions during the whole school year and co-ordinates and monitors the initiatives of the different Collectives.

In any case, the day to day activity takes place in the establishments where the professionals work, in the neighbourhoods and the communities where work is developed and it is the Collectives of the different regions who make themselves responsible for pushing on the work. A particular kind of will and sensibility are drawn on to ensure that the taking of decisions affecting the Gypsy community is carried out in such a way that those concerned, the Gypsies, take part in the process. This works effectively when permanent contact and collaboration are maintained between Gypsy associations and competent people in each district or in each group. This has been equally welcomed in the Association by Gypsy professionals from different fields in relation to education and community development.

The Objects of the Collectives

The Collectives of teachers and Gypsies try to get together educationists who work with the marginalised Gypsy population so that they can reflect together on the problems specific to this field. This platform provides possibilities for improvement, co-ordination, professional exchanges and a source of documentation.

The general aims are to organise and direct all types of activities in the field of education, culture and social work in connection with professionals who work with Gypsies and who are concerned with the promotion of this community, and to back up research, further training and meetings of professionals who work in this field.

In order to clarify the aims of the Collectives so that priorities may be established the following specific objectives are defined:

- to contribute to reducing the marginalisation and underdevelopment to which Gypsies are subject and to furnish the conditions which will allow them to live their lives according to their own customs, language and traditions
- to promote a social climate which will permit the consideration of specific Gypsy culture as a question of cultural difference, not in terms of conflict and deviance as it is at present
- to promote the improved training of professionals working with Gypsies in the cultural field and in social work in order to make possible integration into the present day wider society
- to support research in order to promote action on awareness-raising and information on the subject of the Gypsy question
- to arrive at sufficient understanding of the Gypsy situation at national and

international level, not only in quantitative but in qualitative terms, so that it is possible to produce as complete as possible a diagnostic base on the subject of the different situations in which Gypsies find themselves and thus to have a wide bank of information which can serve as a base for future action and projects
■ to offer a service of documentation, information and resources in the domain of the Gypsy question to all associations and to professionals who work in this field.

Organisational Structures
In order to achieve its objectives, the Association, as the focus for the co-ordination of the Collectives, rests on an internal structure within which the different activities are linked. The Days lie at the centre of the organisation; the Assembly, being the executive organ, meets during the course of the days.

Diagram 1
The Management Structure
of the Association

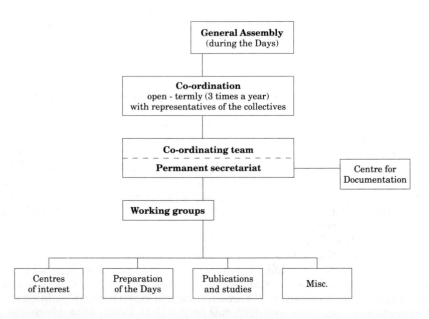

The structure of the Days is determined by several methods of work and participation: working groups which debate the different themes studied during the course of the school year so conclusions may be reached, conferences and round tables on the central theme, exchanges of experiences, exhibitions and cultural activities and a general assembly where approval is sought for conclusions arrived at and decisions on future action.

As well as the Days there is a general co-ordination group with representatives from all the Collectives. This is open in character, making it possible for all those groups and individuals who took part in the days to participate if they so wish.

The establishment of this co-ordination group takes place at the days and during the first meeting the date of the following meeting is decided. The function of the group is to organise and put into practice the decisions taken by the Assembly. There is also a permanent secretariat which deals with information, maintains contacts, sends out notices for meetings, obtains subscriptions, and (in accordance with the responsibilities laid on it by the Assembly and by the co-ordination group and the working groups) requests interviews with the administration. The address of this secretariat is: calle Lele del Pozo 20, 28018 Madrid. Telephone: 91/785-10-28.

A co-ordinating team, composed of representatives of the different Collectives, exists to take any essential decisions between meetings of the co-ordination groups. If the decision is an important one this team will call a meeting of all the co-ordination groups.

At present (1989) there is also a documentation centre which is supported by the co-ordinating team and is in direct contact with the permanent secretariat. This centre publishes a bulletin.

Finally, there are the working groups on concrete themes where the work is co-ordinated and the impetus given to the Association's projects and the projects of the Collectives e.g. the Centres of Interest Group. Committees are formed to deal with particular matters which may arise: for example, the preparation of a publication, the request for a study, contacts with the administration, etc.

Some of the activities carried out are:

■ the establishment of working groups whose members come from different autonomous communities (co-existence of non-Gypsy and Gypsy children, social assistance in the Gypsy quarters, adult participation, social and professional development)

■ a variety of general meetings for project co-ordinators

■ the setting up of an active documentation centre

■ permanent courses on the development of programmes, of Centres of Interest in general basic education in order to put forward curriculum content in tune with the relevant local social environment

■ documentation of the Gypsies' social and educational situation

■ publication in the *Cuardernos de Pedagogia* (Pedagogic Notebooks) of facts relating to the social and educational situation of Gypsies and collaboration with other publications (*Guix, Nevipens Romani*, etc.)

■ further elaboration of this documentation by including the conclusions and information arising from different days

■ the annual organisation of the Days

■ carrying out a study within the framework of the research led by the Commission of European Communities on the education of Gypsy and Traveller children in Spain and Portugal

■ the production of three issues of an information bulletin.

United Kingdom: Introduction

The United Kingdom presentation was co-ordinated by the authors of Papers 18-21 with input at two preparatory meetings from:

Ann Bagehot, Save the Children Fund, UK Department (SCF)
Bubbles Brazil, Advisory Council for the Education for Romany and other Travellers (ACERT) and
Paul Johnson, National Association of Teachers of Travellers (NATT)

Three types of action-research were identified by the UK participants:

Observational Research
A professional researcher/academic joins in the 'everydayness' of a working situation for her own purpose

Participant Observation
The researcher goes into a working situation, joining in the work instigated by those normally involved, often focusing on her own questions but frequently, too, on a shared focus. The observations once made may be reflected on only by the researcher or in collaboration with others who may or may not include those normally involved

Research Carried Out and Controlled by the One Normally Involved in the Work Situation Being Examined
Someone working unaccompanied or in collaboration with one or two chosen colleagues, whether professional or not. Frequently the focus for such research is arrived at as a result of unfocused recording, using diary records, a 'running' audio or video recording or a combination of two of these

We also think that pre-action studies or surveys are important. It is necessary that the initiative for making such studies be taken and supported by those who have the power to effect improvements based on the results of the study.

There is a single list of references for all four papers at the end of the final paper.

Paper 18   United Kingdom: Gypsies and Travellers in the
United Kingdom
Nathan Lee, National Gypsy Education Council (NGEC)

Numbers

It is estimated that there are about 100,000 Gypsies and Travellers in the UK. Of these some 45,000-50,000 are nomadic or semi-nomadic. This includes those living on official Gypsy sites within the nomadic category as these families are in reality semi-nomadic. There are about 48,000-50,000 sedentary or housed Gypsies/Travellers.

The numbers of Gypsies/Travellers in each category fluctuates owing to some slight seasonal migratory movement during the times of certain fairs and festivals, for example, Epsom Derby and Appleby Horse Fair, and also when seasonal work is available. These figures are also hard to evaluate precisely owing to the numbers of families, predominantly newly arrived Irish Travellers, who, owing to the harsh legislation in the UK concerning unauthorised encampments, are often forced into local authority homeless family accommodation, bed and breakfast or hostels.

Whilst these are my own figures, they tally with all known estimates made in recent years including those in the research carried out by Acton and Kenrick for the Commission of the European Communities in the framework of the study published by Liégeois in 1986 (1). However, I am sure that these figures can be said to be grossly understated as no account in recent times is taken of the many Gypsy families who have settled in housing, many for as long as five or six generations. These people have merged in with the Gauje population in their style of housing and in the work they take up. Their children go to school like everyone else and while it would be untruthful to say they had become assimilated completely, they are indeed so well integrated with the host society as to be, as it were, 'invisible'. Many hold responsible positions or are professionals; some work in education and some are in entertainment. The majority of these people try to hide their being Gypsy from their neighbours and colleagues, not from any shame of their racial origins, but because of the negative image and pejorative connotations the very word 'Gypsy' arouses in the mind of the average British Gauje.

I know of many cases where a Gypsy has lost his job or failed to get one when it has become known that he is a Gypsy. Is it any surprise that such people choose to keep their ethnic origins hidden?

We hope in the near future to have better data on the Gypsy/Traveller population in the UK as the Department of the Environment (DOE) has commissioned research projects (14), not only on population figures but also to investigate the methods used by local authorities to collect these figures. The last published DOE figures (January 1989) show 33 per cent of caravans in England on unauthorised stopping places. Many estimate the percentage on unauthorised sites to be nearer 40 per cent.

Following a discussion which I had with the London Race and Housing Research Unit a pilot research project was set up to survey sites in five London Boroughs. The effectiveness of education and health services in relation to site provision was also studied (2).

Gypsy/Traveller Language in the United Kingdom

Romanichals

The largest group in the UK is the Romanichals who number around 61,000, of whom about a half may be classed as nomadic, or, when living on authorised sites, as semi-nomadic; roughly half the Romanichals are sedentary.

All Romanichals speak English although their English is strongly influenced by regional dialects. The Romanes they speak is known as Anglo-Romani, known in Romanes as 'poggadi-jib' – literally 'broken tongue'. It is a highly creolised language consisting of between three and eight hundred words of Romani origin used with both slang and English vocabulary in a largely English grammatical context.

Perhaps between 500 and 800 hundred Romanichals, for the most part descended from Welsh Gypsies, speak an inflected form of Romanes, using correct gender endings and a Romani grammar similar to the Welsh Kale. The Romanichals can be found throughout the United Kingdom and there are some in Eire.

Kale

Welsh Kale are a comparatively small group numbering about 2,000. Data on this group are not readily available but it is believed that the large majority of them are sedentary. Identifying the Kale is fairly difficult because of their intermarriage with other groups, mainly Romanichals and quite often with Irish Minceirs, making recognition of individuals as Kale difficult. Kale speak Welsh, English and a Romanes which is inflected and purer than that of the Romanichals; their Romanes has been likened to the Manouche dialect spoken in Brittany. Some Gypsyologists believe that this pure form of Romanes has ceased to exist in the UK but this is not true and there are still many people who speak this language. The greater part of the Kale are to be found in North Wales with some in South Wales but rarely in the South of England.

Scottish Travellers

Scottish Travellers, or 'Tinklers' as they are sometimes called in their native land, number around 19,000 of whom just over two thirds are estimated to be *better education* [handwritten]

sedentary. I believe the high proportion of settlement amongst this group stems from a time some years ago when the children of Scottish Travellers were compelled to attend school for several months in each year. During the winter the families would settle in houses for the months of mandatory schooling. This freed them for the more lucrative summer months when agricultural work was more readily available. Many families would keep the house during the summer months. From that it was a short step to permanent settlement.

The majority of Scottish Travellers speak English although a small number in the highland regions and outlying islands speak only Scots Gaelic. The Scottish Traveller language is known as Cant; it is different from the Cant of Irish Travellers although there are some similarities between the two. The majority of Scottish Travellers speak some Anglo-Romanes. The further south in Scotland they come from, the more Romani words are used. There is much intermarriage between Scottish Travellers and English, Welsh Romanichals and Irish Travellers. Scottish Travellers are found throughout the United Kingdom and many make regular visits to the Irish Republic.

Irish Travellers

Irish Travellers, or, in their own tongue, 'Minceirs', number around 15,000 in the UK although these figures can vary almost daily. Amongst all UK Gypsies/ Travellers the Irish Travellers seem the most highly mobile section and subject to more frequent change than any other group. In the mid 1980s we have seen an increase in immigration from the Irish Republic. I would estimate that two thirds of Irish Travellers are sedentary but again this seems to change constantly with Travellers being forced into bed and breakfast accommodation and often soon forced out again by prejudice.

Irish Travellers speak English and a good number speak at least a little Anglo-Romanes. Their own language is known as Shelta or Gammon and has a long history, dating back to medieval Ireland's monastic orders and travelling tradesmen. Irish Travellers, in those days known as Tinkers, are the first recorded travelling people in the UK, pre-dating the Romani Gypsies by at least a hundred years.

Irish Travellers are found throughout Scotland, Wales and England, mainly in and around the big cities. In fact they seem to be the most urban of all the nomadic groups in the UK. This is mainly because of the trades they follow – building, road resurfacing, antique and carpet dealing.

Other Groups

There are also a number of other small groups of non-UK origin which together total about 3,000: Rom, or Vlax speaking groups, Kalderash, Machvaya, emigrants from the United States and Canada, the Romungri and Boyash from Hungary. These groups are for the most part sedentary, living in and around London. I have also met Bosnian Gypsies, Belgian Yenish and Spanish Gypsies travelling in the UK during the late 1980s.

The UK has seen, in the early 1970s, the emergence of new nomadic groups often known as New Age Travellers. These groups are not linked with the other groups already mentioned. The Department of the Environment does not include them in the official caravan count but, nevertheless, some of them have taken places in some authorised sites even though there are not enough places for Gypsies and Travellers.

Gypsies/Travellers and their Education

The most important initiatives began at the end of the 1960s. There were isolated efforts before then such as that of Trinity Cooper, a Gypsy girl, who in 1811, through her own persistence won school places for herself and her two brothers, and those of George Smith in 1883 and a local education authority which, in 1924, built a school in the midst of the wooden cabins which, deep in woodland, constituted an authorised winter encampment.

Many sincere, concerned and hardworking people spent many unrewarding hours striving to ensure that Gypsy/Traveller children received an education. These people came from all walks of life but were mainly teachers, local authority officers, health workers or social workers. I feel it was because of their professions that they were initially viewed by the Gypsies with some suspicion. All professional people were viewed as local authority officers and as such, had, up to that time, been seen as anti-Gypsy. Indeed, some social workers and health visitors were seen as being instrumental in the removing of Gypsy/Traveller children into care. Some of these children never saw their families again. As this compulsory removal of children was not on the scale of, say, the Swiss Pro Juventute organisation, it has not been so well documented. Nevertheless, the Gypsies remembered, and, coupled with stories from friends and relatives from Europe of how such people as Eva Justin, Dr Rutter and Dr Arnold had 'befriended' the Sinti of Germany prior to the holocaust, they were rightly suspicious. However, once these barriers began to be broken down, things progressed.

The initial breakthrough came from teachers working in mobile or on-site schools who were known by the Gypsies/Travellers and there was increasing interest in education among the newly politicised Gypsies/Travellers coming into Gypsy civil rights movements. At the onset of such politically motivated initiatives education was not seen as the greatest priority as it was felt that until adequate site provision was available there was no chance of staying in any one place long enough to attend school.

The 1968 Caravan Sites Act made it a duty for local authorities to provide stopping places for nomadic Gypsies and Travellers. This act was not implemented until 1970 and, although programmes of site provision were started, the figures for Gypsies/Travellers given by local authorities were so low that even now, twenty one years after the act, at least 40 per cent of the Gypsies/Travellers in UK have no legal place to stay. One aspect of the 1968 Act that is seen as ultra repressive by all concerned is the granting to authorities of Designation Orders. These orders give the right to all local authorities which have satisfied the government that they have made enough sites, to evict all families which do not have places on authorised sites. In this way local authority areas, one after another, have acquired no-go status. Some authorities were actually granted designation with no site provision whatsoever. This law changed camping on unauthorised sites from a civil offence to a criminal one, linked to higher fines or even the risk of prison; the eviction process is also more rapid.

The 1944 Education Act made local authorities responsible for the education of all children and parents responsible for sending their children to school. This law did not help Gypsies/Travellers to benefit from their educational rights. Often children were refused places in schools and then their parents would be threatened with prosecution for not sending their children to school. Often the Education Act became a tool to be used by those who wanted families to move out of the area.

However, during the 1980s, Gypsies and Travellers have become aware of an increasing need for education. The main reasons appear to be:

- the lack of traditional opportunities such as agricultural work or the old trades such as tin smithing and lace and peg making
- the newer trades of building and motor repairs require the ability to read plans and manuals and to write estimates and receipts
- increased mechanisation, the change from horses to motor vehicles requires literacy skills for the driving licence test and the completing of tax and insurance forms
- the need for everyone to read and write in order to deal with printed matter of all kinds. (In the 1980s forms must be completed to obtain all public services, health, employment, social security, education)
- there is also the desire to protect the privacy of personal letters and documents
- most parents who have seen the good work done in the civil rights field by both Gypsy and non-Gypsy activists, realise that without an educated generation to follow us we could lose what little has been gained.

Finally, I am convinced that we need education if we are to have self-determination. For, in a society which has historically denied us education, the first reason given for not recognising our needs is that we are ignorant.

Illiteracy should not be confused with ignorance. Illiteracy can be made to disappear – and I believe that that will be done.

Paper 19   United Kingdom: Educational Provision for Gypsy and Traveller Children in the UK

Sally Naylor, National Association of Teachers of Travellers

The 1944 and 1988 Education Acts apply only to England and Wales although they influence legislation and practice in Scotland and Northern Ireland. This paper is mainly concerned with England and coverage is in no way complete because of constraints of time and resources.

Background

Every child has the right to full time education. This is guaranteed under the Education Acts. The Department of Education and Science (DES) Circular 1/81 states that local education authorities have a duty to provide education for "... all children residing in their area. The duty thus embraces in particular travelling children, including gypsies ..." (3).

Responsibility for the aims, objectives, content and organisation of education was delegated to Local Education Authorities (LEAs), guided and monitored by central government. The Education Reform Act 1988 changes much of this but I will return to this later.

Because of this delegation of responsibility to local authorities and the need for policies and priorities to be voted on by elected members at a local level, there is a wide variety in the details of educational provision for all children and an even greater variety in specific provision to support the education of Traveller and Gypsy children. Educational structures, conditions of work and teachers' positions on the pay scales vary according to LEAs.

There are 104 local education authorities in England and Wales. No publication gives detailed information on the extent and type of differently organised provision for supporting the education of Gypsy and Traveller children, or guidance on the advantages and disadvantages of different types of provision in differing circumstances, or any evaluation of quality or effective-ness. Local authority levels of commitment range from teams of teachers working from resource centres to no specific provision at all.

The most recent officially published estimate of numbers is contained in Her Majesty's Inspectorate (HMI) Discussion Paper *The Education of Travellers' Children*, 1983 (4). "... evidence gathered by HM Inspectors suggested that as few as 40-50 per cent of primary age children of Travelling families attend school and those attending regularly are but a small proportion of the total." (4). This estimate almost certainly refers to the situation in 1980. We have come a long way since then. This year, 1989, there will be a Department of Education and Science Draft Circular on Traveller education (5) detailing the procedures for obtaining specific funding and indicating provision which would be considered as good practice.

Funding has been based on the No-Area Pool – the source of financing particular provision for children of no fixed abode – the children of service personnel, circus and fairground children, Gypsy and Traveller children. All authorities pay into this Pool and those actually providing education for these groups are entitled to claim on it.

Many local authorities do not claim. Gypsy and Traveller communities are the object of extreme levels of hostility and prejudice. Many local councillors and some MPs attract votes by publicly supporting prejudice. Even when 75 per cent of the expense incurred can be reclaimed (and some expenditure is reclaimable at 100 per cent) there is often lack of political will to take the necessary positive action.

The Swann Report (1985), *Education for All – The Report of the Committee of Inquiry into the Education of Children from Ethnic Minority Groups* (6), points out that the situation of Gypsy and Traveller children "... illustrates to an extreme degree the experience of prejudice and alienation which faces many other ethnic minority children."

The Education Reform Act 1988

In April 1990 the current funding (No-Area Pool) will be replaced by a central government grant administered through the Department of Education and Science. Bids, supported by detailed plans, will have to be made in advance. It seems that expenditure will be considered relating to fields of work not covered in the past, such as specific in-service education of teachers and school personnel, adult and pre-school provision. However, the percentage of expenditure may well be less and there will need to be more positive planning by local authorities. In the face of so much change within the education system in a very short time, there is a danger that Traveller education will be even lower on the list of priorities and suffer accordingly.

The Education Reform Act 1988 will have major and far-reaching effects on all aspects of education. The potential of the Act is tremendous. It clearly states what every child is entitled to in education. However it was written for the majority of children and there are large areas of concern for many children. Individual schools and their governors will have more autonomy, local education authorities less power. There will be greater parental influence in the governing of schools, and it is possible, in the context of lack of information and prejudice in the general public, that this could result in more rejections of Gypsy/Traveller applications for admission.

A National Curriculum of core subjects is to be introduced; attainment targets are to be linked to national testing at seven, eleven, fourteen and sixteen and test results published. While the emphasis on continuous positive recording of the achievements of individual children both in and out of school should be of benefit to Gypsy and Traveller children, there could be a narrowing of the curriculum aimed at achieving high test scores. Over reliance on test results could damage the learning environment.

It is impossible to predict the full effect of such wide ranging changes as those which will come from the Education Reform Act 1988 but parents, Traveller education teams and professional and other voluntary bodies working in the field will need to be vigilant.

General Factors Influencing the Learning Environment

There are two other elements which seriously influence the learning environment of Gypsy and Traveller pupils.

The Grave Lack of Authorised Caravan Sites

The Department of the Environment estimates that twenty years after the Act requiring local authorities to provide sites, 33 per cent of caravans in England have no authorised stopping places. It is accepted that this is an underestimate. This 33 per cent is a national average. In some areas up to 90 per cent of the children to be catered for may live on unauthorised sites.

This lack of authorised caravan sites adds to difficulties in obtaining access to schools thereby adding to the problems caused by lack of continuity and sometimes making any schooling impossible.

The Lack of Respect accorded to Gypsy/Traveller Communities

This is most clearly demonstrated by the choices made of locations for sites and the poor quality of most of those which do exist.

"As long as the relations between Gypsies and Travellers and the communities surrounding them remain conflictual, the relations of Gypsy and Traveller parents – and pupils – with the school will remain largely determined by the negative tone of these relations... In this situation... the school has an important role to play in educating both communities towards mutual understanding and respect."(7)

Positive Trends

In the absence, since 1983, of an official national picture of Traveller education I can give only a personal view of trends. This is based on the written information sent to me by members of the National Association of Teachers of Travellers (NATT) in preparation for the Carcassonne Seminar, information gained from personal contacts with practising teachers and others at national and regional courses and meetings, and my own experience within the local authority where I teach.

An increasing number of local authorities are being made aware of the need to take positive steps to overcome the difficulties Traveller and Gypsy children may encounter. There are at least fifteen teams of teachers (three or more people) employed by local education authorities and more are in the process of being established. Some include other professionals – for example, education welfare officers.

In the three years, 1986-1989, three new local authority teams have been set up by different local education authorities. In each case there was prior involvement by HM Inspectorate, input from teachers, other professionals and voluntary bodies and, in advance of decision taking, surveys of the need to be addressed.

Here is an example of the structure of one of these teams: six peripatetic teachers assigned to different administrative areas within a county, answering to the inspector for multi-cultural education. Two specialist education welfare officers are part of the team. The teachers support up to thirty schools each and 60 per cent of their time must be spent teaching. Any extra teaching or welfare support must be negotiated separately with the relevant administrative office, depending on particular needs.

Although I can give no supporting figures there are other clear trends in the field of Gypsy/Traveller education:

■ more children are attending under-five provision

■ more children aged five to eleven are attending school for longer periods of time

■ more children aged eleven to sixteen are attending school

■ more children are taking public examinations

■ more adults and young adults are taking part in literacy courses, skills training and community education

■ more children from unauthorised, and therefore insecure, stopping places are attending primary schools; a few are attending secondary schools.

■ more secondary school teachers are having to find flexible approaches to the varying needs of children who do not find the curriculum relevant. This also benefits Gypsy and Traveller children

■ more children are being supported in their classroom situation rather than being withdrawn for individual or group teaching. The extra teaching support also benefits other children in class

■ Traveller and Gypsy issues are increasingly included in wider multi-cultural issues. Many teachers now believe that books aimed at one particular ethnic group are no longer appropriate and that all children should be offered a range of books which reflect a wide variety of cultural and social backgrounds.

More and more teachers use teaching methods based on the theories of Frank Smith (7) which emphasise the role of the teachers in helping children to become autonomous learners. Learning is supported where children feel at ease in their school, valued as individuals and free to make mistakes and learn from them. This approach is advocated by more and more teacher trainers and practised in more and more schools benefiting all children and especially Gypsy and Traveller children. Reading methods based on this approach emphasise the process of learning and lead to the use of a wide variety of books which are small samples of literature, interesting for both child and teacher to read together again and again. Children are helped from the beginning to read books that interest them, including stories of their own or those made by other members of the class, using the language chosen by the child. Thus children's abilities as storytellers are encouraged and celebrated. These methods are on the increase in the United Kingdom.

Co-ordination is both increasing and improving through participation in meetings, courses and the informal exchange of information through the network of teachers and others.

There is an increasing incidence of litigation. The ethnic status of Gypsies was confirmed by the High Court in July 1988. More and more cases are being brought by and on behalf of Gypsies and Travellers relating to site provision. We have yet to see the first litigation in the field of education.

Paper 20   United Kingdom: Co-ordination
Mary Waterson, Advisory Council for the Education of Romany and other Travellers (ACERT)

National Co-ordination

Co-ordination began in 1970. For the first time a member of Her Majesty's Inspectorate (HMI) was given responsibility for the oversight of Gypsy/Traveller education.

In 1973 the Inspector having that responsibility organised on behalf of the Department of Education and Science its first short course on Gypsy/Traveller education. These courses now take place every other year and each one lasts for five days. Places may be requested by anyone concerned in the education of Gypsies and Travellers – teachers, administrators, social workers and health workers, members of voluntary organisations and, on occasion, there have been individual police officers and bailiffs. A limited number of Gypsies/Travellers is invited.

These courses give rise to a number of different forms of co-ordination, for example, networking, i.e. meetings with colleagues which facilitate exchanges of ideas on strategies, methods and resources. One of the most precious and long lasting of resources obtained is the list of all those who have participated in the course, their roles and their addresses. Another benefit of such courses is the series of lectures on topics of current importance.

A report of course proceedings was published until 1982; this is no longer produced. The chief disadvantages of the report were that before it was published it had to be submitted to the DES for approval so the lapse of time which occurred before it was actually published was too long. However, that report was a means of disseminating ideas.

During the 1986 short course a group of thirty five teachers discussed "professional needs and proposals for the future". This resulted in a document – the *Post Chester Proposals* (1986) (9) which, five months later, was published jointly by the National Association of Teachers and Travellers (NATT) and the

Advisory Council for the Education of Romany and other Travellers (ACERT). This document was circulated to: all members of NATT, all local education authorities, all concerned government departments, all political parties, all professional associations of teachers, the Commission for Racial Equality, religious bodies and other interested organisations. There was little response. The National Union of Teachers produced a policy document (10) and a press statement. It is regrettable that the principal education journal accorded it merely five lines single column.

NATT and ACERT also collaborated in formulating a questionnaire which went to all local authorities in order to discover how local authority policy and practice accorded with the *Post Chester Proposals*. Proof was obtained of serious nation-wide disparities.

National Co-ordination at Government Department Level

Meetings have taken place from time to time between different government departments and HMI. The results of these meetings are not made known.

From time to time meetings have taken place at the Department of Education and Science with civil servants responsible for multi-cultural education, one or two Education Inspectors (HMI), representatives of the Advisory Council for the Education of Romany and other Travellers (ACERT), the National Association of Teachers of Travellers (NATT), the National Gypsy Education Council (NGEC), and Save the Children Fund UK Department, Traveller Information Unit (SCF). At one of these meetings the idea of a national or regional record system for Gypsy/Traveller education was discussed. A pilot scheme has been proposed for a single region.

Contacts exist, personal rather than official, between HMI in England and Wales and those in Scotland. Education is administered separately in Scotland and in Northern Ireland. Information which circulates between England and the other countries of the United Kingdom is limited.

Co-ordination Between National Organisations

The National Association of Teachers of Travellers (NATT)
The National Gypsy Education Council (NGEC)
The Save the Children Fund, UK Department (SCF Travellers' Information Unit)
Advisory Council for the Education of Romany and other Travellers (ACERT).

These organisations provide information and support to their own members, answer enquiries from innumerable sources and have a very important lobbying function particularly in times of change.

Regional Co-ordination

Two or more local authorities may make joint demands to the Department of Education and Science for the funds necessary to set up a regional course lasting two or more days.

There are other regional conferences and courses, often held termly and funded for the most part by participating LEAs, in: London, West Midlands, North of England, North West England, Greater Manchester, Yorkshire, Hertfordshire and Buckinghamshire, Essex/Norfolk/Suffolk, East Anglia, Oxfordshire/Berkshire, South West England/South Wales. Most of these conferences are due to teacher demand.

Co-ordination Operated by Local Authorities

There are three regions where co-ordination has existed over very many years, the structure differing in each case.

West Midlands

The West Midlands Education Service for Travelling Children started operating in 1975 – the result of co-ordination between eleven local education authorities (see Paper 21). This service is led by a permanent co-ordinator.

East Anglia

The Regional Consultative Group for Traveller Education, based at the Cambridge Institute of Education and formed in 1978, brought together an education officer and a teacher from each of seven local authorities. In 1989 it includes eight local authorities. The level of enthusiasm among the administrators varies with the local authority. To this structure was added a termly meeting of teachers from all eight authorities. These teachers planned their own programme of in-service training for the years 1988-90 (see page 144).

Once a term there are two multi-disciplinary meetings which cover more or less the same region. They are both due to demands made by those working in the field.

In June 1989 the East Anglian Regional Advisory Council for Further Education established a Travellers Staff Development Group for those working in adult and community education.

The dissemination of pedagogical and administrative information and practice throughout the region is supported by these interconnected meetings.

Inner London

The Inner London Education Authority (ILEA) covers thirteen inner London Boroughs. On the one hand there are liaison teachers who work with families living on authorised sites and the schools where their children are enrolled. On the other hand there is a team of seven teachers with two education social workers who work across the thirteen local authorities, arranging places in school wherever that is possible for the hundreds of children whose families are unable to obtain pitches on authorised sites. Established in 1975 this team can also provide some educational contact for children for whom there are no school places locally and for those being moved on so fast that it is impractical to offer places in school. One of the team's excellent publications *Travellers and Education in Inner London* (1989) (11) describes their service and the context in which it works. All the teacher members of this team have equal status.

There is a need to evaluate these different structures and make recommendations for the future.

The Way Forward

Department of Education and Science Short Courses should make greater demands on the participants before, during and after the course. There should be a required reading list, structured preparation and follow-up.

Education is organised at local authority level. It is important that all specific provision for the education of Gypsies/Travellers is completely integrated within the structure of the education service which caters for all children, otherwise the quality of the service could depend on individuals. The service could disappear if, or when, an individual changes employment.

Research: now is the time to evaluate the many different approaches to ensuring full access to mainstream education for Gypsy/Traveller children (see note on action-research in the introduction to the UK papers) and to make recommendations for the future.

Priorities and Proposals for the Future

Gypsies/Travellers need information on rights and duties where education is concerned; for example, what to do when there is difficulty in obtaining school places.

As with other ethnic minority groups there is a need for serious initiatives which will increase participation by Gypsies/Travellers in all levels of the education service, as well as their involvement in the management of the schools attended by their own children.

At both national and local government levels positive co-ordinated action must be taken to reduce prejudice in education,and in education administration (cf Resolution 125 (1981) from that year's Conference of European Local and Regional Authorities) (12).

This is particularly necessary in mono-cultural schools and areas. It is equally important that Gypsies/Travellers do not become marginalised within this field. The Committee of Ministers – Council of Europe – Recommendation No. R (85)7 in Appendix 5.1 iii (13) could provide the baseline for this work "... future teachers should, for example, ... learn to identify and combat all forms of discrimination in schools and society and be encouraged to confront and overcome their own prejudices."

There should be direction to local authority inspectorates to support them in their duty to co-ordinate and make known inter-cultural literature and resources, specifically including items which will inform and interest both teachers and students. The Gypsy/Traveller communities need to be involved in this work.

It is essential that local education authorities receive specific directions from the Department of Education and Science on their duties under the Education Acts in respect of the education of Gypsy/Traveller children. To ensure this we recommend that:

■ there be named persons at all levels, including at the Department of Education and Science

■ information be sent annually from the Department of Education and Science to Local Education Authorities detailing their duties regarding the education of Gypsy and Traveller children and the procedures for obtaining specific funding

■ similar information should be sent by Local Education Authorities to schools detailing lines of communication and additional resources available.

The Department of Education and Science must demand the percentages of Gypsy/Traveller children of different age levels who actually go to each school; in that way good practice can be identified and emulated. It must be insisted that all local education authorities make an evaluation of their actual provision for the education of Gypsies and Travellers.

We have an example from one local authority where, during the last three years (1986-1989), the number of Gypsies/Travellers going to secondary school has increased by 550 per cent. Although the actual numbers are comparatively small, this progress is typical of authorities where appropriate support is ensured. Similar figures must exist elsewhere but they are neither collated nor published.

The National Association of Teachers of Travellers (NATT) and the concerned voluntary organisations are independent of local authorities. The importance of their role should be recognised and their work encouraged and supported.

It is impolitic for a teacher, being the employee of a local authority, to draw attention to that authority's neglect of its duty. Information made available to the non-statutory organisations can be acted upon while maintaining the anonymity of the source. These organisations can also draw the attention of Inspectors of Education (HMI) to cases of negligence and in this way HMI are able to take steps to improve the situation (see page 138).

UK Co-ordination

Structured co-ordination is needed between England, Wales, Scotland and Northern Ireland aiming at the establishment of a UK policy for Gypsy/Traveller education and co-ordinated exchange of information. Developments in parts of Wales are known only through the voluntary organisations' network (see example below). In Scotland, in 1985, the Secretary of State for Scotland called for an initiative in co-ordination based on a College of Education. The results so far are not widely known: these should be evaluated and made available throughout the UK. Links with Northern Ireland are mainly personal ones made through the Department of Education and Science Short Courses.

European Co-ordination

It becomes increasingly clear that the best hope for the advancement of human rights in the years to come lies in the influence that can be brought to bear by Europe and the legislation which will affect us all. The banning of corporal punishment in UK schools was made possible only when cases were referred to Europe. The European resolution on Gypsy/Traveller education adopted in May 1989 (Appendix 2) will need all possible backing from Brussels if it is to be effective in the UK.

United Nations

Once the United Nations Draft Convention on the Rights of the Child has been adopted, this too should be invoked on behalf of Gypsy/Traveller children.

An Example of Co-ordination between National Organisations and Local Authority Officers

This is the story of collaboration involving two national voluntary organisations, a doctor, a health visitor, some education officers and teachers. It illustrates a situation which is no longer typical in the United Kingdom and the progress which can be achieved even in the face of political antagonism.

The story unrolls in Wales; it underlines the need for support from independent sources for employees of local authorities.

1977

There were forty one caravans on three unauthorised stopping places, all threatened with eviction. Two teachers were appointed to provide education for the Traveller children on those sites. The local authority provided an ex-school meals van adapted for the purpose but poorly equipped. In September the National Gypsy Council called a conference at Swansea University and in the same month an anti-Gypsy group held a meeting at a school.

1978
The BBC made a video on the situation showing the living conditions for the Travellers and the hostility of the Gauje. This video was shown at the Department of Education and Science Short Course on Traveller Education in July. For most of the participants it was the first time they had had any information on Travellers in Swansea.

1979
A hundred caravans threatened by eviction.

1979 – 1982
No information.

1982
Two teachers were appointed to be responsible for the education of all the Traveller children whose ages ranged from three and a half to sixteen. The local education authority allocated a classroom, separate from the rest of the school, at the head of a long stone staircase. The toilets were below, on the other side of a small playground. One of the teachers wrote that after Christmas the cold became insupportable and that all the children stopped coming. Officially, the classes went on until the summer of 1985.

1985
The local education authority was operating an 'open door' policy: if a family could find places in a school – that was fine, if not – that was just too bad.
And there were still no authorised stopping places.

1986
In June 1986 James Gilheaney took the County to the High Court. At that time, in Briton Ferry, not far from Swansea, there were many caravans stopping on a disused industrial area, all threatened by eviction. The judge decided that the local authority did not have the right to carry out the evictions because the county had no sites and that there was no possibility of the families finding authorised stopping places. The local education authority ignored the presence of the Traveller children and their need for education. The hostility to the Travellers was frightening. There was an anti-Gypsy committee and demonstrations in which posters were carried bearing slogans against the placing of Gypsy children in the local schools. The Secretary of State for Wales ordered the County of West Glamorgan to provide sufficient authorised sites to accommodate sixty caravans.

1987
Because of the 1986 judgement the families could not officially be threatened with eviction. Some families in Swansea tried to enrol their children in school. When the families gave their address to the head they were refused places. Then, at last, came the collaboration. The Travellers' doctor telephoned the local education department. Each time she spoke with different people, each time she received different information. She wrote to the education department but received no response. Being a member of the local branch of Save the Children Fund (SCF) she asked for their support and also contacted the Advisory Council for the Education of Romany and other Travellers (ACERT).

Letters were written and telephone calls made. However, the children stayed without schooling for four months. At that time Peter Gilheaney, one of the Travellers, asked the BBC to make a video on their situation. Peter and Margaret Gilheaney and their children had appeared in the 1978 video: they appeared in the 1987 one – still waiting for a site to be built by the local authority although they had now been provided with a communal tap.

The BBC TV team invited the local education department to take part but they did not wish to and because of this ACERT provided input on the steps to take to obtain school places. This participation in the video provided opportunities for discussions between ACERT and the Travellers and between ACERT and the education adviser who had been given the task of reactivating special classes which, in 1987, had as their aim the placing of the children in ordinary schools. Information and relevant publications were provided. The children were offered segregated education in the rooms which had been used five years earlier. They were not allowed to play or to eat with the other children; there were even complaints because the Travellers used the same dining room as the others.

1987-1988 – winter
ACERT drew the attention of the Education Inspectorate to the poor educational environment. A member of the inspectorate visited the school and there were some changes.

1988
Officers of ACERT and SCF arranged separate meetings with education officers, a head of a school where the Traveller children had been integrated, Traveller families and members of Swansea SHELTER and SCF. ACERT put the education adviser and the teachers working with the Traveller children in contact with their opposite numbers in an English county which was within easy reach. The contact led to a visit to see how another county organised education provision for Gypsies and Travellers and the resources they had available. The visitors considered they might well be able to use the ideas in their own county.

The two teachers also took part in the 1988 Department of Education and Science Short Course and returned home full of enthusiasm and ideas for the future.

1988-1989
The two teachers worked within the framework of multi-cultural education in West Glamorgan. They set up exhibitions both in schools and out. They brought together collections of books and other materials to both sensitize and inform their colleagues with regard to Gypsies/Travellers and, in particular, on questions raised by the Education Reform Act 1988. They made presentations for INSET (in-service training for teachers). They established an adult literacy group which met in the evening.

1989
The Traveller children in the segregated classes were permitted to play and to eat with all the other children in the school. The education authority had plans to organise a conference for the whole of Wales, in the autumn, on the education of Gypsies/Travellers. The locations for a few authorised sites were chosen.

The teachers identified thirty schools around those locations and organised discussions with each headteacher.

The history recorded up to this point is based on a draft text submitted by ACERT to the education authority. The authority provided additional information and this has been included.

According to the Travellers' doctor, now in retirement, the situation after the local elections in May 1989 gave rise to serious concern. Two county councillors were elected on an anti-Gypsy platform. Still more children were enrolled in the segregated classes. Some schools now dared to state that they were not obliged to take Traveller children. Other schools, which had welcomed them without any recourse to special classes, could not understand why some of their colleagues were refusing the Traveller children.

The story of Swansea was chosen to illustrate the difficulties which can be encountered by education administrators and Travellers in obtaining education for Traveller children when the lack of authorised sites foments such serious hostility towards Gypsy/Traveller communities. How can advances be made when local councillors, who need to win votes, must be the ones to decide on the provision of sites and, consequently, access to school?

Paper 21   An Example of Regional Co-ordination
Mike Baldwin, West Midlands Education Service for
Travelling Children (WMESTC)

The West Midlands Education Service for Travelling Children
On behalf of the eleven participating local education authorities the Service co-ordinates, monitors, advises, supervises and assists the educational provision for children from Travelling communities throughout the West Midlands region.

The Service operates:

■ a pupil record transfer system to ensure that the childrens' educational records follow the children as they change schools and local authority area

■ a system for monitoring records ensuring that the individual children make progress in school and that the schools receive practical advice on the education of Travelling children

■ an advisory welfare service for the benefit of the Travelling families and the local authority social welfare service

■ a pool of specially trained teachers experienced in teaching communication skills and who are familiar with the lifestyles of the Travelling communities

■ four minibuses and four mobile classroom units to provide immediate assistance to schools registering Travelling children but experiencing transport or space difficulties

■ an advisory education service through the pool of advisory teachers, under the direction of the Senior Advisory Teacher, to assist schools in meeting the needs of Traveller children

■ a resources centre containing appropriate and tested materials for use with Travelling children

■ a library/archive for use by teachers and students (visitors are most welcome)

■ an in-service training programme for school staff, welfare staff and students involved with Travelling families to promote awareness of Traveller culture and lifestyles, positive attitudes towards the children and an understanding of their educational needs.

Planning for Success and Continuity – Resources
In order to assist Traveller children towards being confident and successful learners the Service has concentrated on developing and providing resource materials to encourage their positive self-image and also to support a more positive understanding of Traveller lifestyles amongst all children.
The materials developed range from:
■ wooden toys
■ matching, sequencing and jigsaw items using photographs taken within the Traveller communities
■ materials for project work
■ wooden inset scenes for language extension
■ pre-literacy and numeracy booklets
■ a phonic programme
■ reading books and an introductory reading and writing programme *The Literacy Trail*.
The Literacy Trail is intended to give some structured support and continuity to Traveller children's early reading experiences as they move between schools, local authorities and regions. It is not intended to provide their sole reading and language experience. As with all children they should be given access to a wide variety of books, reading materials and language experiences. A display and master copy of *The Literacy Trail* and other materials are also available for sale outside the West Midlands region (price list on request).

The Children of Fairground Families
In the spring when the children leave the schools where they have spent the autumn and winter, the Service provides them with folders of work for the summer. We discuss the work with their parents who will be giving support to the children during the summer. In these folders work based on the lifestyle of the children is also included. The folders are designed individually for the children and are not available for sale. Nevertheless, the Service is prepared to pool its ideas and to provide examples of such work to those teachers interested in the development of this type of folder for the use of the children of fairground families.

The Partnership Project
The Partnership Project is the result of co-operation between the Save the Children Fund (SCF), the West Midlands Education Service for Travelling Children and the Walsall Health Authority. These three agencies agreed to share their experience, expertise and resources to the benefit of Travellers and Gypsies in the West Midlands region. The aims of the project are:
■ to improve Travellers' knowledge of services and their access to them
■ to increase inter-disciplinary initiatives and co-operation to the benefit of Travelling families – with a focus on under-fives and their parents
■ to increase mutual respect and tolerance between Travelling families and the rest of the community.
Walsall Health Authority employs a Health Visitor with a special responsibility to work with Traveller families on health promotion and illness prevention. Most of her work is with babies and toddlers but the role extends

beyond that in an attempt to meet as many needs of the whole family as possible.

The Health Visitor's responsibilities include developing immunization programmes, monitoring child development and improving links between families and the health services. Walsall is one of a few areas in the UK piloting the provision of client-held health records for Gypsy and Traveller families. Co-operative working between Education, Health and Voluntary Agencies can facilitate initiatives such as:

- health education programmes in school
- women's health groups
- informing others of the health care needs of Gypsies and Travellers.
- The National Health Service is available for everyone and should always be sensitive to the needs of the individual.

Save the Children Fund (SCF) is an international organisation based on a Charter for the Rights of the Child. Children, young people and their families are always involved in planning the kind of programmes they need. The Fund has accepted that there is a strong and unanswerable case for continuing to work with Gypsies and other Travellers. There can be no doubt that these communities are generally disadvantaged and are discriminated against on grounds of both race and their nomadic lifestyle. Many of the Rights of the Child are infringed and SCF's work with Gypsies and other Travellers should, in particular, uphold their rights to:

- equality regardless of race and ethnicity
- follow a nomadic way of life
- appropriate educational provision.

The Partnership Project is being monitored and evaluated externally through a Higher Education establishment. The final evaluation report will be submitted at the end of 1989 and the project will be altered, extended, reduced or refocused following the results of the evaluation report. Some examples of initiatives carried out within the framework of the Project are given below.

Nursery Provision

In an attempt to encourage Gypsy children into a nursery class, a teenage Gypsy girl, from the same site as the little ones, with some primary and a little secondary experience, was engaged as an assistant in the nursery class and paid by the Project. She was also encouraged and supported into formalising her child care skills into Nursery Nurse training. She is currently being supported through her training. Her skill and influence in the nursery class resulted in the regular participation of Gypsy children.

Client-held Health Records for Travellers

Inter-authority co-operation: the Project has demonstrated through its inter-agency links the lack of continuity in health care to mobile families. As a result of the development of health links with families and a greater awareness of the needs of the client group, the participating authority has initiated client-held health records for Gypsy/Traveller families whilst also taking positive steps to develop health links and co-operation between authorities to improve continuity of health care.

Women's Group
The Project facilitates meetings of women from the Gypsy site who want to get together for health education and leisure interests. The group has greatly assisted in developing the confidence of individuals and women are now participating in adult education and leisure groups outside the weekly meetings.

Links with Other Agencies
The Project is being successful in proving that improvements in delivery of professional services within a particular discipline can make measurable differences to families' opportunities when they have access to the collective effects of co-ordinated inter-agency good practice.

Some Examples of Action-Research by the WMESTC
Record Card Survey
In August 1988 the administrative staff of the West Midlands Education Service for Travelling Children conducted a survey on the effective use of their Educational Record Card System. They took a random sample of 100 primary education record cards and asked four basic questions to examine whether the record card had operated as intended:
1. Was the correct procedure followed by the school, the service, the family?
2. Were the administrative sections responded to?
3. Was the medical information section responded to?
4. Were the education sections responded to?
    There was no attempt in this analysis to measure the responses in a qualitative way. Questions 1, 2 and 4 obtained 74 per cent positive responses. Question 3 gave an alarmingly low response – 11 per cent. This focused the Service's efforts into improving their health network and into instigating training/awareness initiatives.

Pupil Transfer from Primary to Secondary Schools
Different styles and strategies of establishing and supporting links between primary and secondary schools have been developed in relation to transfer issues in different authorities within the region. During the final term the primary leavers' class goes to the secondary school once a week for a computer studies lesson in the computer laboratory. For one afternoon each week the teacher responsible for secondary first year children teaches in the primary school class. Each primary child shadows a secondary pupil through one school day. The secondary school pastoral care teacher visits the primary pupils in their homes. Gypsy children who miss the timetabled events in this model are guided through the programme by the support teacher. This particular school was successful in improving uptake of education at secondary level by Gypsy children. The strategies this model employs are transferable to other areas and the advisory/support teachers can be the means of taking examples of good practice from one education authority to another.

Preparing for Pre-vocational Training
The service has a number of initiatives in the early stages of development within the context of preparing for vocational training. Essentially, efforts have been focused on work-experience opportunities within the school year. It has been necessary to win the collaboration of Gypsy businessmen in being work-

experience employers in those businesses of particular interest to Gypsy pupils: scrap metal, leather, carpets, stoneware, stainless steel items for trailer living. The girls have taken particular interest in child care training until now but it is hoped to extend their areas of interest. It is too early to measure the success of these initiatives but several youngsters are now engaged in work experience which interests them.

An Example of a Co-ordinated Regional Training Programme

A representative of each of seven local education authorities (six co-ordinators of teacher teams and one administrator) met on 28 April 1988 to plan a programme concerning Traveller Education for practising teachers for 1988/89/90. Administration of the programme would be through one education authority but each authority would assume responsibility for an individual day's events.

25 May 1988: Sally Ambrose, Hertfordshire
Theme: Strategies for Supporting Schools/Children/Teachers by Examining Practice

2 November 1988: Rocky Deans, Brent
Theme: The Hidden Curriculum

8 March 1989: Lorna Bradley, Norfolk
Theme: The Impact of the Education Reform Act 1988
Education Officers attended and contributed to this day

17 May 1989: Tim Everson, Suffolk
Theme: Profiles/Testing (am) and separate groups for Primary and Secondary (pm)

8 November 1989: Sheila Forrest, Bedfordshire
Theme: The National Curriculum

2 February 1990: Jackie Nesbitt, Essex
Theme: Conditions of Service/Job Description/Working Practices

18 May 1990: Sally Ambrose, Hertfordshire
Theme: Further In-service Training for the 1990s

References
For UK Presentations, Papers 18-21

1   LIEGEOIS, Jean-Pierre. *School Provision for Gypsy and Traveller Children: a Synthesis Report.* Commission of the European Communities, 1986.

2   HYMAN, Mavis. *Sites for Travellers: a study in five London boroughs.* Runnymede Trust, 1989.

3   DEPARTMENT OF EDUCATION AND SCIENCE. Circular 1/81. DES, 1981.

4   DEPARTMENT OF EDUCATION AND SCIENCE. *The Education of Travellers' Children*. HMSO, 1983.

5   DEPARTMENT OF EDUCATION AND SCIENCE. *Draft Circular No. 10/90*.

6   DEPARTMENT OF EDUCATION AND SCIENCE. *Education for All: The Report on the Education of Children from Ethnic Minority Groups – Ch. 16*. HMSO, 1985.

7   LIEGEOIS Jean-Pierre. *School Provision for Gypsy and Traveller Children: Orientation document for reflection and for action, 1988*. Distribution in the UK by Traveller Education Service, c/o Burgess Becker CP School, Monsall Lane, Harpurhey, Manchester M9 1QE.

8   SMITH Frank. *Reading*. Cambridge University Press, 1978.

9   ACERT/NATT. *Post Chester Proposals*. ACERT, Moot House, The Stow, Harlow CM2 3AG, 1986.

10 NATIONAL UNION OF TEACHERS. *The Education of Travellers' Children*. NUT, Hamilton House, Mabledon Place, London WC1, 1987.

11 ILEA TEACHERS FOR TRAVELLERS. *Travellers and Education in Inner London*. LTET, Ilderton School, Varcoe Road, London SE16, 1989.

12 CONFERENCE OF LOCAL AND REGIONAL AUTHORITIES OF EUROPE. *Resolution 125*. 1981.

13 COUNCIL OF EUROPE COMMITTEE OF MINISTERS. *Recommendation No. R (85) 7*. 1985.

Part 3 Discussion and Proposals

Gypsies in Conference

General Statement
Soledad Dubos, Ana Gimenez, Jean-Joseph Gómez, Nathan Lee, Santino Spinelli, Sacha Zanko

We have been citizens of the countries of the European Community for five centuries. Currently in the twelve States, there are at least 1,200,000 Gypsy people, 50-60 per cent of whom are under the age of sixteen.

The administrative system is there to serve its citizens. It is responsible for the bad conditions under which our children are trying to receive an education:

■ our adolescents are at a disadvantage in society, ill-equipped in every situation

■ from the primary stages teachers must concern themselves with the long term consequences their teaching will have for the children who pass through their hands

■ the administration has complete control over human and material resources

■ it must take swift and practical action to resolve the catastrophic situation in which the Gypsy people in particular finds itself

■ it must become aware of the marginalisation and intolerance which our children are suffering

■ we have constitutional, national and European rights: these rights must not be violated.

The Teacher
It is essential that teachers respect the culture and the diversity of the groups they teach; they must welcome the children into school in a reassuring manner. Conversely, Gypsies must collaborate as support teachers in the

education of the child.

At present, the personal and professional training of teachers is insufficient to create a true, multi-cultural school environment. Thus, there is a need for Gypsies to take an active part in the content and execution of teacher training. Teachers must be chosen according to their level of awareness of and sympathy towards Gypsy culture.

The School

We must create at school an environment conducive to the co-existence and development of cultures on an equal footing. School is a micro-organism. We should learn to live together at school so that we can live together better in Gauje society. It is essential that the child is well nurtured at school. In order to achieve this the teacher must have a good knowledge of Gypsy culture.

We must create a school system adapted to our childrens' needs and establish strategies to obtain a high level of instruction:

■ the production of specific teaching materials
■ less rigid daily and yearly timetables
■ the establishment of a new assessment system appropriate to the intellectual development style of the Gypsy
■ the establishment of national and international training centres for Gypsy and Gauje teachers of a recognised competence comparable to the level of national teacher training in each country
■ school should be a place where the child can reinforce his culture, his language, his identity and the characteristics of his own ethnic group.

Language and Culture

As for matters of language, the school should place a value on the use of the spoken word as an inherent cultural means towards better communication between the different Gypsy groups. National and international authorities should take into account their principal minority which is the Gypsy minority.

Proposals

We need to encourage consultation meetings to uphold our knowledge and our identity. We need to face up to our problems and resolve them ourselves.

International Training Centre

It is vital to establish an international teacher training centre with enough competence to address the difficulties of our childrens' education in a multi-cultural setting. Gypsies would have to be consulted at every level of decision-making. In addition, co-ordination with national centres is necessary to develop an autonomous framework within which decisions would be independent, coherent and effective. The content of this training of teachers would have to be worked out for and by Gypsies. There are two priorities: the dissemination of our culture, history and language and the acquisition by our children of a very high level of learning.

This centre should have two functions, namely, specific training for Gypsy and non-Gypsy teachers and the official appointment of the teachers concerned.

Within the teacher training centre it is necessary to establish a department specialising in travelling schools. This department would have the responsibility for the setting up of a national network of peripatetic teachers responsible for the continuity of Gypsy children's learning and also oversight of the use of specific educational materials.

The training centre should train teachers to confront and overcome the situations of psychological conflict which put Gypsy children at a disadvantage and condition them in a negative way.

International Research Centre

There is an urgent need to establish an international research centre whose aim would be to master the three aspects of the life of the Gypsy (the past, the present and the future) through research, expression and dissemination. The research centre should produce and circulate materials of a pedagogical, linguistic, artistic and cultural nature. Its work would entail:

■ new editions of books which are out-of-print, the distribution of study grants and the procuration of financial support for research into our past and our language

■ publication of works by young Gypsy writers and composers to encourage them to enrich our culture

■ the circulation of resources to afford access for all our children to the works of their elders: books, video, radio, televised material.

There is also a need for a training centre for socio-educative co-operation to train young people who will then be able to establish a link between school and the family. Their brief would be to provide the means to resolve the lack of understanding which exists between school and the social environment of the Gypsy.

Final Statement

We, the Gypsies, having taken part in this Summer School, thank the organisation, the Commission for European Communities, for the opportunity it has given us to communicate, to participate and to express our work and our personal position regarding school provision for Gypsy and Traveller children in Europe. We would also like to thank Professor Liégeois and Manuska warmly for the interest and understanding they have shown to us during these few days and in their work.

We owe it to ourselves to state our opinion on this seminar. It is important to have more conventions where Gypsies and Gaujes can establish an awareness on a European scale of the problem of school provision.

A series of meetings must be set up to support and extend the work which has been achieved and to enable the ideas expressed to be put into practice. There should be a majority of Gypsies.

There should be three stages:

■ with young people who have a good awareness of the Gypsy condition who can give precise and reliable information on our experience. At this level participants would be continuously changing

■ with people who have direct contact, on an educational or social basis, with Gypsy children

■ Gypsies and specialists should get together to deepen the understanding of the situation and to find an effective method of resolving it. It is very important to establish this level to prevent people new to the situation from putting a curb on the work of the specialists.

At international gatherings we must have access to human and technical means of simultaneous translation to avoid a reduction in communication. On both a national and international level there must be more meetings and seminars on a single theme in which a majority of Gypsy professionals will promote communication, inter-disciplinary work and co-ordinated research.

A Message from Santino Spinelli

My name is Santino Spinelli and I am twenty-four years old. I am an Italian Gypsy, a Rom from the Abbruzzi region, the youngest of six children. My school experience was very positive in that I managed to get to University.

I began my studies at Lanciano; my family was able to settle here after long years of being nomadic. This was possible because here we found somewhere to live, albeit simple, and racism was less marked. Twenty years have already gone by and the process of integration of my family into Italian society has been on-going. My father passed from horse-dealing to trading in second-hand cars. Three of my five sisters have married Gaujes, only one has married a Rom. As for me, I am the director of a music school.

This process of integration has been characterised by a continuous adaptation of our culture to the reality of the Gaujes without there being a reciprocal exchange on the part of the Italians. The difficulties have been many, in particular because of the suspicion, paternalism and lack of regard shown towards the outsider. To these difficulties, my family responded with dignity and self-esteem, always demonstrating its wish for integration and its serious intentions. I also experienced these same difficulties at school. The first years were particularly difficult when I added self-exclusion to a partial marginalisation because I felt myself to be outside the school situation.

As the socio-economic situation of my family improved I joined in more in the life of the school and got on better with the other pupils. I was no longer ashamed of being poor and my school friends no longer considered me inferior.

My sense of pride has always made me want to win and I have to say that, in order to succeed, a Gypsy must make five times more effort than any other pupil. Naturally, these are the most crucial moments in the development of a Gypsy child, of a 'cavuro' who, frequently being incapable of adapting and surmounting this barrier, prefers to run back home and to lock himself into his traditions and into a hostile attitude towards Gaujes as a result of his own traumatic experiences. To avoid all that, the school should be endowed with a specialist teaching force capable of nurturing the Gypsy child, of understanding his needs, of adapting the school environment above all to his nature but also to his abilities and his behaviour in such a way as to ease his entry into school and his integration into society.

In order to safeguard and validate the linguistic and cultural heritage of the Rom we would need to draw up specialist courses such as those already in existence for French, English, etc. With these courses Gypsies would be able to become familiar with their history, their culture and their identity. In addition, they would be able to acquire the means to defend themselves against the aggression and pressures of the non-Gypsy society which from the beginning of time has imposed its way of life on the Rom without understanding the demands of the Gypsy world.

In the setting of a united Europe, characterised by a multi-cultural and democratic civilisation, the reality of the Gypsy must and can find a space where a true, intercultural exchange can take place which will be of benefit to all those who desire progress in human, social and cultural spheres.

We, the Gypsies
Pedro Amaya Muñoz, Gypsy from Can Tunis, Barcelona

Now is the time that we, the Gypsies, should be able to decide for ourselves our own business and to tackle our own problems. In order to do this, we must look after our own interests with the necessary and appropriate tools. If we need non-Gypsies, and certainly we do need them, we do not want them to colonise us nor use us as an experimental seed bed.

We, the Gypsies, are people with our own rights and our own duties: in Spain we are Spaniards; the Constitution recognises this. We are citizens by right but we must be so in fact and in truth. If non-Gypsies wish to work with us Gypsies this must be true collaboration with the development of our culture as its aim. What would the Catalans say if the Basques or the Andalusians imposed their culture on them?

We, the Gypsies, have no territory of our own but we have a culture, that is to say, a way of existence and a lifestyle like anyone else. Yet for almost 600 years we have suffered continuous oppression. It is high time that we were respected. It is also high time that the bullying stopped and that we were treated with the respect due to human beings who have hopes and aspirations, successes and also failures and who make mistakes. As individuals, almost all our negative aspects come from the non-Gypsy culture. As a people, we must get on well with others around us, Gypsies and non-Gypsies, in the widest sense: our territory is Catalonia, Spain, the whole world.

We, the Gypsies, like all citizens, need schools for our children but we do not want a school which is patronising. We want a school which understands us and recognises our culture, our roots and the way we live and view life. It is on this footing that we will be able to set to work to create an education programme which takes into account our values, our ways and our customs: an education programme adapted to our lifestyle but not inward looking. We want to gain all the good and positive aspects of the non-Gypsy culture. We do not accept a school, teachers or a programme which has been imposed upon us. We have to learn quickly but well. Non-Gypsies have books at home and at school. Non-Gypsies have some knowledge of the things their children are learning: for them nearly all doors are open. We, as Gypsies, have none of all that. We need a school which takes account of the yearly and daily timetable of each individual Gypsy group, a school which would equate us with the majority. The Constitution, the Rights of Man, afford us recognition. Education laws endorse equality of opportunity for access into further education and the work market. The curriculum and ethos of the school allow it too. Families and children must see the meaning school has for them as Gypsies at the end of the twentieth century in a Europe which aspires to unity. People tell us we have all the same rights and that there is equality of opportunity. Do they provide us with the same tools so we can take advantage of these opportunities? Does the school, in one way or another, consider the cultural experience, obviously different from the non-Gypsy one, that Gypsy children and their parents bring with them? Does the school compensate in some way or another for the lack of books in the Gypsy home?

On another plane, there is work but it is always for the non-Gypsy. There are social services and support systems but we have no access to them. School exists but it does not recognise us: we are of no consequence. The teachers think that they are the only ones who know. They think they know everything: they see us as ignorant. Indeed we are but of the non-Gypsy culture and the things they know. There is the mistake: they, the teachers of this school, the school of the dominant society, are unversed in our culture, in the things we know. The only difference between them and us is that we are ready to learn from them but they are not ready to learn from us. In the best of circumstances, it is not enough to say this: in everyday life they must come to recognise us, accept us, to value us, for what we are. Only then will each one of us be able to discover the other.

Otherwise, if you are not ready to like me, why do you make me waste so much of my time?

Reports from the Working Groups

During the first four working days, the groups (five in number) were selected in such a way as to mix the participants according to geographical origin, nationality or by status (teacher, trainer, inspector). The themes and sub-themes provided by the organisers or considered as important by the participants were dealt with in these groups. At the end of four days, each group issued a report which was immediately reproduced and distributed to all the participants.

The organisers analysed the contents of the reports of the working groups (by identifying keywords) and this analysis led to the recognition of five themes which the participants took as the basis of their discussions in the second week:

Group 1
Taking account of the Gypsy community's priorities for education – see page155

Group 2
Evaluation – see page 156

Group 3
Social and professional access for young Gypsies and Travellers – see page 167

Group 4
Inter-cultural education – see page 169

Group 5
Training – see page 172

One of the groups decided to continue to work together on their original theme:

Group 6
An example of action-research used to support an individual in a professional role – see page 173
In the final days meetings took place on the theme of co-ordination:

French Co-ordination
This was discussed by the French participants, more than half of those attending – see page 177

Co-ordination at the European Level
This was discussed by the participants from the nine states of the European Community – see page 178

Taking Account of the Gypsy Community's Own Priorities for Education (Group 1)

Maria de Lurdes Almeida Gil Da Silva (Portugal), Pedro Amaya Muñoz (Spain), Paule Baboulin (France), Elisabeth Bisot (France), Maria Teresa Codina (Spain), Eliane Franco (France), Jacqueline Imbert (France), Mirella Karpati (Italy), Lydie Recio (France), Sacha Zanko (France)

A Proposal for Action-research
Underlying this meeting is the acknowledgement that:
■ violation of Human Rights and of the Rights of the Child continues in all countries
■ that there is insufficient schooling in all the countries concerned which cannot be seen as separate from conditions of life in general
■ it is impossible at the present time to be sufficiently cogniscent of the Gypsies' requests (diversity, multiplicity of problems).

Action-research
The objective of action-research would be to bring to light the needs and expectations of Gypsies so that these can be presented at national and European level. This would be achieved by assigning principal roles to Gypsies ("Let them have their say"), by non-Gypsies being available to work according to the Gypsies' requirements and by allowing the project at all times to be very open to modification (evaluation/innovation) and to respect the Gypsies' requirements.

Proposals from the Group for Activities in the Short Term:
■ to promote during teacher and social worker training a listening attitude in teachers and social workers ("Learn from the Gypsies")
■ to raise awareness and understanding about Gypsy communities in the general public and in national and local government.

Keywords

right   integration   values

Gypsy linguistic system   families

the inter-cultural dynamic   needs

participation   attendance   associations

reciprocity   power   reading

Gypsy associations   means of expression

exchange   thought system   Gypsy expectations

Gauje expectations   space

adapted classes   change   time

organisation   consensus   contract

co-ordinated action   welcome

Evaluation (Group 2)

Mike Baldwin (United Kingdom), Benoît Gramond (France), Sylvain Poirier (France)

Among the keywords drawn up following the synthesis of the various working groups for the topic evaluation (a complete list is given at the end of this report) we opted to retain three, all associated with action-research:- follow-up, transformation and innovation. Under these three generic words there can be developed in paradigm a series as, for example:
■ follow-up/continuity, contracts, formulation of objectives
■ transformation/organisation, system of thought, reform
■ innovation/reciprocal transmission of knowledge, inter-cultural didactic tools, exchanges.
    Our findings can be presented in two quite distinct stages. These are 'follow-up' (with examples drawn from the UK and France) and 'instruments of innovation' permitting transformation.

Follow-up for Travellers in the United Kingdom
Since 1973 an office situated in Wolverhampton in the Midlands has used a system of Record Cards for Travellers in order to follow the education of young Travellers. Each young Traveller who arrives in a school receives a card which

he must give to his parents. This card shows only the child's first name, date of birth and a reference number corresponding to a file. When the family enrols the child in another school, they show the card to the principal who then telephones Wolverhampton to obtain the Educational Record Card. This document contains medical information on the child's health and notes on:
- pre-schooling
- method of reading used, level of reading reached and the 'sounds' understood
- the level attained in reading tests and the grammatical and numeracy levels reached
- a teacher's note on the scholastic needs of the child
- a social profile of the child
- if of that age, the child's route into secondary school.

When the child leaves a school, the teacher fills in the Record Card and returns it to the service which manages the Record Cards so that the latter can send the card on to a school which may later request it. This card can be sent to any school in the United Kingdom. This system is designed so as to respond quickly to the needs of young Travellers with the aim of giving them the same status as other school children.

Recommendations

Such a system, if organised and integrated with national and Community plans, would represent a noticeable improvement in educational provision for Gypsies and young Travellers. Over and above the function of follow-up, it also imposes a radical transformation in institutional functioning. As well as the administrative aspects already described, the 'pedagogy', the role of the teacher and his tasks, the objectives of the educational system, the education policy and the management of teaching posts, the place of the school in the 'housing estate' all appear in need of reform.

One Example Among Many

In the United Kingdom, information contained in the Record Card can assist in providing individual teaching corresponding to the exact needs of the child. In the Community, resources already exist in several States but they remain unco-ordinated. In Ireland, visiting teachers themselves ensure follow-up as do co-ordinators in Belgium. In the Netherlands, besides co-ordinators, an information network exists. Other countries have networks, for example, Spain and France. For the latter, institutional posts such as 'Providers in Zones of Educational Priority' could be a possible starting point.

Indeed, in the United Kingdom, posts of Advisory Teachers have been created. It is known that Travellers often move to the same place in the same season for various reasons. For young Travellers who undertake these regular moves, preparations can be made prior to their arrival in the next school.

This work also involves the preparation of teachers themselves to provide education adapted to these children and training of other teachers who, newly arriving in a school, will not have had any previous experience. The Advisory Teachers for Travellers provide this service as they either know the newly arrived families or know of them through their network of contacts with colleagues in other regions. The Advisory Teachers for Travellers can put at the disposal of those teachers involved appropriate teaching material, thus allowing for continuity of method. They can also contact other services, such as health or social services, as needed.

This form of preparatory work could be suggested to other countries in the Community.

Operational Means of Follow-up in France and Harmonisation with the European Community

Research on evaluation and follow-up is seen as a matter of urgency in France following the 'unofficial' report of the enquiry undertaken by CLIVE (Centre for Liaison and Information, Travel/School) and the analysis in the European Synthesis Report 1986 (2). A few words will remind you of the tone of this report: absence of evaluation due to lack of co-ordination between schools, the 'mosaic' of effective education impossible for teachers to manage at the time of

Diagram 1

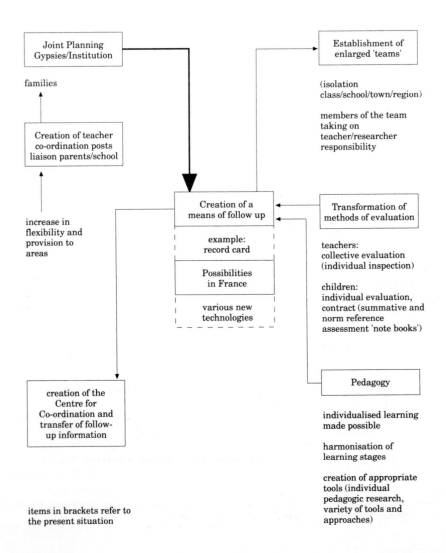

the children's arrival (contradictory or different methods), isolation of the inadequately or badly trained teacher.

Action-research aims here to create a tool adapted for teachers, parents and children to use so that the obstacles of discontinuity in space (change of school) and in time (cyclical leaving and returning at a time when the majority of the school population are 'geographically' sedentary) may be reduced as much as possible, thus leaving families facing problems of schooling the freedom of choice to 'travel'.

Evaluation and follow-up is thus present at all institutional levels but is also open to all the partners: teacher-trainers/practitioners, teachers/learners, parents/teachers, the cultural minority/the cultural majority.

Diagrams 1 and 2 suggests an approach to the subject which, although modest, indicates the lines research of this type should follow.

Diagram 2
Visualisation of
'follow-up' as in
proposals made
at Montauban in
1988 (for details
see Appendix 1)
and at this years
conference at
Carcassonne

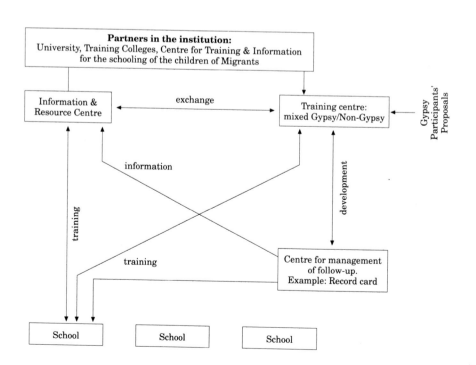

Putting Action-research into Practice
The first priority is the guarantee of total rights protecting the individual. The project, if it is undertaken, ought not to bear in any way on the private life of families or individuals. Anonymity must be guaranteed by the management system.

It is, therefore, necessary to set up meetings without delay between the institution and representatives of the Gypsies, to lay down the basis of an agreement to ascertain who should be approached with this proposal and, on a second occasion, the further action and criteria to be followed in its development.

It seems to us essential that the Minister of National Education should undertake an official national inquiry concerning the schooling of young Gypsies and Travellers. This should be as exact as possible going further than statistical data so as to index as much as is possible about methods, means, evaluation methods and reception structures. Once these facts are gathered they should be widely circulated by the National Centre of Pedagogical Documentation and its regional and departmental network.

At the same time meetings and exchanges of views at Community level should be encouraged so as not to develop a specific philosophy which ignores that of other States. These consultations ought to enrich and aid thought towards a model of harmonisation of steps without imposing strict uniformity.

Innovation for Transformation
Resources already exist in many countries but they are not all of the same type and remain largely unknown.

This first week's work made evident certain possibilities of convergent action and often even the realisation of projects, of whatever nationality , combining with others which exist elsewhere. It is necessary to state that the initials (and their concept) such as ZEP (Zone of Priority Education), or CATE (Contract for Managing the Child's Time) or aid projects regarding works such as Funds to Aid Innovation (FAI), as far as France is concerned, have their equivalents in other countries. The chance occurs then to think about these pilot projects in relation to the Community.

We now include two French examples where the projects have been supported by the administration in France.

Contract for Managing the Child's Time (CATE) in Marseilles
It has been suggested recently that elementary schools in France should partly adapt school time to the rhythms of life of the child by CATE contracts.

In Marseilles an experiment of this type will be implemented in a school which only receives settled Gypsy children. It concerns the modification of the class day:
■ the teachers receive the children between 8 and 9 am and they all breakfast together
■ the children have their midday meal together with the teachers, this time being considered as an educational activity and hence the teachers are paid
■ in the afternoon educational, artistic and sports activities are on offer under the joint responsibility of teachers and specialist presenters
■ the activities take place either in school or at the premises of the participating associations
■ the teachers are split into two teams, one team available in the school from

8am to 3pm, the other from 9 am to 4 pm, with the option of taking an immediate further paid hour for activities which overrun the timetable, for example, climbing.

The principle of managing the child's time at school can have a favourable impact in schools which generally have a structure which is too rigid for Gypsy children. The modification of links between pupils and teachers should lead to better school attendance.

Schools in Zones of Priority Education (ZEP) in Marseilles.
The Zones of Priority Education (ZEP) were created in France at the beginning of the 1980s in order to counteract scholastic failure. Teachers or headteachers were released from some of their teaching hours so as to assist those pupils experiencing difficulties. The ZEP teachers are attached to a school or several schools. With the assistance of some motivated teachers (or with the pedagogic or education team, where this exists) they can, according to need, give scholastic support, create classroom activities (gardening, photography, video, music), extend educational projects and develop co-ordination between the school and external partners.

It is often difficult to measure the impact of such work upon the life of the school and upon the learners. An annual evaluation, in the form of a survey of a marketing type, associated with a regular evaluation of the reading level of the pupils can be the means:
■ to obtain analytical information on school life, its difficulties, the social background of the pupils and their environment (exterior factors)
■ to measure the impact of a project within a certain time
■ to allow a presenter or a teacher who visits the school to get to know the determining features of the project quickly
■ to encourage (since the questionnaire would be answered throughout the school) a general debate on the work, methods and needs of the school.

The reading assessment would be undertaken at the beginning and at the end of the year in all classes using pre-planned material. This evaluation would also include an evaluation by the teachers of the project so as to suggest to the presenter any modifications necessary where objectives have not been reached.

Experimentation with this method, the personal initiative of some of the ZEP presenters, has been undertaken in Marseilles this year. A survey of this type, which Gypsy families would find readable and understandable, could be introduced to them at arranged meetings with a view to defining their expectations for their children's education and, subsequently, to improve their collaboration with the teachers.

Funds to Aid Innovation (FAI) in Herblay (Val d'Oise)
The action-research which we have made explicit during this meeting presupposes a real situation operating on different participants which involves the participants in the change of their situation.

The situation of the Jean-Jaures school group at Herblay, graphically described in the Montauban brochure (1) offers a typical action-research plan.

This year the team made a bid to the FAI for a grant for the use of new technology in the education of gypsy and traveller children. (For administrative reference see BO No. 6, 9 February 1989)). This project has been accepted and the school will receive an endowment of 15,000 francs for the purchase of material and 12,500 francs as a credit for research hours.

The Carcassonne Summer University has enlarged the frame of reference of this project since other places (in France and Italy, the schools in Turin and the Opera Nomadi association) are working on the same lines.

If, of itself, the project Funds to Aid Innovation does not fulfil all the conditions of action-research it is still one of the few resources given to teachers and institutions in France for effecting change and thus modestly supporting research and evaluation. It is thus setting itself apart from all those pedagogical innovations (Educative Action Plan, for example) limited to short term projects which in practice give only ephemeral support to teachers, children and education. It seems of interest, therefore, to give a report of the Herblay project written by Benoît Grammond, Daniel Jésu and Brigitte Cosnard, in February/March 1989.

The New Technology (video, computers and audio-visual aids)
The geographic and historic situation of the local school group, the Jean Jaurès Infant and Junior Schools, has been a paradox in that the work of the teaching team seemed to be moving in opposite directions. On the one hand, the teaching team needs to adopt an educational policy which does not exclude children on geographical and social grounds but, on the other hand, it needs to recognise these specific conditions in order to fulfil its educational role in the best possible environment.

Our borough is situated in the suburbs approximately three miles from the town centre and far from all public and socio-cultural services (library, sporting facilities, cultural centre, youth centre). The population of the Cailloux-gris borough can best be described as a mixture of the most disadvantaged socio-professional groups from the underclasses up to the middle class. To these groups a strong representation of Gypsy families and/or Traveller people are added. They are mostly settled but their specific cultural identity is evident in encounters with the Gauje.

Our non-exclusion policy requires human resources but also material resources and finance as well as extensive commitment from the school itself and from its direct partners (the local community and the region). The support of our school population for school customs and values has been a fundamental problem for the teaching team. If a minority culture is socially excluded and not taken into account, pedagogical exclusion is inevitable due to the failure of the educational institution to adapt, both in welcoming children and in the methods and content of teaching for those minorities.

This failure to adapt can be illustrated by clear and revealing statistics. Using literacy as an indicator the educational failure of our school, in spite of all our work and research, was demonstrated by a figure of 60-70 per cent non-reading children who had attended infant and junior school, albeit with repeated absenteeism which interrupted the learning process.

However, it would be too simple to identify discontinuity as the sole and unique obstacle to a good education. The teaching team has been working on this problem for many years now: it has demonstrated its adaptability by implementing structural and pedagogical changes in the school. The percentage of Gypsy and Traveller children attending school is unique in the region (80 per cent in our school). We focus on the reality of educating Gypsy and Traveller children in spite of the fact that 20 per cent of the children in this district are educated in a normal way and are prepared for secondary school.

One change which influences and distorts Gypsy culture, as it did in French society about twenty years ago, is the consumer society. Oral tradition is disappearing as family groups disperse over the region and is rapidly being replaced by a visual tradition. Families without TV and video in their caravans are rare. The attraction of visual images is easy to understand because it is possible to see and understand them without requiring prior learning. They are, therefore, valued by many of us in contrast to reading and writing.

Gypsies and Travellers have not been able to escape from the colonisation of visual images. For them television and video can be real learning tools as television and video are used in both communities and rely on language and communication for their impact. Thus, it becomes necessary to work on visual education because, without it, the child is left to consume random images in an unstructured way.

This reservoir of daily images is the only organising link in relation to teaching. It is a reservoir of knowledge and concepts valued by Gypsy and Traveller children and, as such, it is an indispensable resource for teachers who wish to lessen the resistance towards learning before starting to use method and content which have not been adapted.

Objectives of the Project
There were three objectives:
■ to eliminate the identified blocks against learning (coding and decoding) by shifting the emphasis in learning towards visual education
■ to develop discriminating viewers
■ to open up to the exterior world.

In fact, the image is not simply a reflection of reality, innocent and easy to understand. The image is a 'perceived reality'. This perception depends on cultural influences and, moreover, it functions almost like an icon. Throughout this double code it seems that the understanding of the significance of images operates through comparison and contrast, the basic elements of coding and decoding. By thus using a different approach, we want to try and teach the children the use of a code, of a syntax, of instruments for structuring (in time, in space) which can later be used in their approach to the written word.

Television offers the child many items of information which s/he has not yet asked for. Thus, it gives certain answers before the question has even been formulated. It is clear that if a child is capable of defining a question, it is sufficiently prepared to receive the answer. In cases where this natural process is reversed, a certain natural logic of the child is obscured. This means that one of the new tasks of the school will be to teach children to adjust to the mass of information they receive, to choose and to view critically. To achieve this it is necessary both to present learning material using the new educational technology and to incorporate television material in the total learning package.

Audio-visual 'messages' are produced by a small group of specialists. It goes without saying that the best way of understanding images is by producing them oneself. Moreover, these productions, apart from the work of elaborating and creating involved, will form a means to break the isolation of the school, offer an opening to the exterior world (parents, other schools, society) and enrich the collective memory of the school.

We see this project as complementary to the actions taken earlier in the school such as the creation of a Library Resource Centre and the use of information technology. Learning to use and understand images is of prime importance in a world which communicates more and more in a language of images. Visual education is imperative to enable the use and understanding of images and the school is the main instrument for this instruction. As Judith Lazar says in *Ecole, communication, télévision* (published by Presses Universitaires de la France): "In any case, it is not a question of renouncing the ancient, 'noble' culture but of taking that culture and making it part of a larger palette of different cultures in which all the colours of the universal culture blend one with another".

Detailed Objectives
The first objective is 'to see oneself'. One has to be able to develop oneself physically, psychologically and socially by learning to become acquainted with and using one's own body, for example, by the recording of physical exercise, such as swimming, skating and judo. One has to be able to distance oneself and to see oneself as part of a group by recording one's performance at work and at recreation, in team sports and in the canteen and one has to be able to fix oneself in time with reference to one's own history, that is, to see oneself on earlier recordings.

Secondly, one has to see beyond oneself. It is necessary to re-integrate more quickly into the life of the class after a period of absence: recording events like visits, trips, parties and shows will also provide a class diary which could play a part as the record of the school life of a child. The establishment of a school video library with tapes of television programmes (reports, documentaries, films) and documents produced by the teachers (cultural events, documents on geography, history, science and culture) helps to extend the child's knowledge and correspondence between schools by sending out and exchanging audio-visual productions helps to broaden his contacts with other people.

Learning Observation Skills
The improvement of observation skills will enrich the child's knowledge. By grasping the transient nature of events s/he has the option of reviewing an event as if s/he were reading a book and acquires the ability to rewind, dwelling a little longer on a detail in order to understand it better and to inspect it. S/he can 'read' the television by watching taped television programmes and learning to differentiate material by 'nature' (fiction, reality), 'type' (cinematic film, film for television, advertising, quiz games, reportage, news, clips) and 'technique' (filming of people, cartoons and animated objects, cutting). S/he discovers the rules, the syntax and their effects: the notion of time, the position and movements of the camera in relation to the subject, the movements of the subject through the field, the sound track, the interaction between sight and sound, special effects and editing. S/he gains knowledge about the subjectivity of the audio-visual message by changing the television programmes (modifying the sound track, producing other images with an original tape, producing fake interviews instead of real ones).

Production of images and sound
The child becomes acquainted with the techniques of making images and sound. By using a tape-recorder, video-camera and video cassette recorder s/he should discover the specific characteristics of electronic recording. S/he learns to use the above mentioned experiences to produce reports, documentaries,

stories or clips whilst respecting the rules of each genre. When s/he produces a sound track s/he must choose the music, record real or synthetic sounds and use voice-over and dubbing techniques. S/he will discover the constraints of the equipment and adapt to them. S/he will find the technical responses to overcome these problems and think out the project whilst considering the best technique to use. The production of the script will require her/his being capable of 'pre-thinking' about the production in every detail (chronology, choice of plans, continuity, contents of the sound track). S/he must get acquainted with editing techniques and learn to make use of documents from different sources: videotape recorders (television broadcasts), video-cameras (personal productions, slides), computers (computer animation, credit titles, inserts) and produce different versions of the same subject to create a different setting or relay a different message.

In other words, the child has at her/his disposal the means to create an account without the barrier of written language but, nevertheless, utilising a similar intellectual dialogue. Sh/e is able to tackle the problems of time and place, presenting people and their environment, putting an action or an event into its context and maintaining a chronological account.

Showing Productions
The child must choose good quality productions which are best suited to:
■ other pupils in the class
■ other classes in the school
■ other schools
■ parents
■ other teachers
■ socio-educational partners.

Evaluation of the Project
The teachers of the Jean Jaures schools have worked as a team for many years, giving up two hours a fortnight outside school hours to work on the quality of school life and to achieve a balanced and coherent pedagogical policy. They decided to work in terms of action-research on developing and refining this audio-visual project by introducing the different types of activity in a co-ordinated way.

Their immediate partners (District Resource and Exchange Centre, Centre for Liaison and Information, Travel/School, Paris V University, Gypsy Research Centre) served as resource centres to enrich the school project.

Evaluation work continues in the form of an analysis of perceived objectives, proposed approaches and activities and problems encountered. The analysis was indispensable for the success of the project in terms of the objectives attained, the improvements or modifications necessary to achieve progress in the future and to envisage the final adapted education (contents, methods, equipment).

Moreover, the teachers decided to keep a personal diary for each child, thus ensuring that each individual's achievements could be followed up within the overall collective project (changeover from infant to junior) and to offer the opportunity of concrete evidence of the productions by keeping the audio and video cassettes.

Demand and Allocation

The choice of material was determined by using the following criteria:

■ direct compatibility between the video camera and the video recorder (VHS-format) to enable the use of any cassette on any machine with the minimum of manipulations

■ the weight of the equipment to enable easy use by children (VHS-C)

■ the quality of the image on hold of a succession of discrete images to enable clear viewing and observation of view points and montages

■ audio and visual facilities on the video recorder to allow additions to be made to the sound track and to facilitate editing

■ the possibility of the incorporation of computer productions (RVB decoder and UHF signal).

The equipment used and its cost was as follows:

■ colour video film, 70cm, Pal-Secam, prise Peritel (7,000 FF)

■ VHS video recorder with audio and visual imput and output, numerical film counter and pause/hold facility (8,000 FF)

■ VHS-C video camera with zoom, mixer and memory counter (14,000 FF)

■ RVB/UHF converter.

An additional weekly meeting of one hour proved to be vital for the implementation of the project. There were ten teachers at the school for whom an allocation of ten additional hours per week would be budgeted.

Keywords

team work   life rhythms   field continuity

individualised teaching   reform   pilot project

operational   reciprocal transfer of knowledge

means of expression   content   information

methods   follow-up   ways of thinking

flexibility   contract   formulation of objectives

national   collection of material

opening up   documentation   refining organisation

change   exchanges   school policies

criteria   knowledge   take into account

school courses   Community   innovation

time   inter-cultural teaching material   diffusion

total relevance of the problems   in-depth understanding

proposals   experiences   analysis grid   space

References

1   LIEGEOIS, Jean-Pierre. *School Provision for Gypsy / Traveller Children; a synthesis report of a study undertaken by the States of the European Community.* Commission of the European Communities, 1986.

2   GRAMOND, Benoît. Beginners in the World of Writing: Current Questions and System of Analysis. In: *Gypsy Children in School, the Training of Personnel for National Education.* Report of the Summer University held at L'Ecole normale at Montauban, Centre for Gypsy Research/ Departmental Centre for Pedagogic Documentation 1988, p. 58-68.

Social and Professional Integration of Young Gypsies and Travellers (Group 3)

Danièle Granier (France), Nathan Lee (UK), Danielle Mercier (France), Martirio Muñoz (Spain), Félix Navarro (France), Jean-Marie Pichon (France), Marie-France Series (France), Santino Spinelli (Italy)

Background
Successful integration presupposes that the principal characteristics of the Gypsy community, should be taken into account and in particular that the families should be associated with the project on a contractual basis and that the creativity and expression of potential in each individual is respected. The forms of integration should be adapted to the way of life whether travelling or sedentary.

Action-research Proposal
A certain number of proposals can be made but it seemed best to us to centre our thoughts on an adaptation of the professional training approach aimed at young people leaving school.

Objectives and Content
The objectives should be practical and take account of the cultural habits of Gypsies and Travellers such as seasonal and daily discontinuity. The range of subjects should be widened to include traditional and new sectors – business activities, selling methods, maintenance of green space, seasonal work, lorry transport, business contacts, socio-cultural activities. The training should be given in such a way as to enable participants to perform practical activities in daily life and should provide them with an immediate source of income. Self-employment would be the preferred outcome of training. A grant system or reimbursement of fees would be looked at as an integral part of the course. The qualifications would be recognised by issuing a certificate from the joint members of the liaison group.

Structures
Training units linked administratively to a teaching structure (colleges, professional training colleges) should be created. The training unit would welcome pupils in the twelve to sixteen years age range without splitting them into classes according to age (cycle idea). The training unit would be a functional, not a geographical, idea and would form part of a larger scheme which could comprise departmental, regional and national units. The training would be broken down into manageable modules.

Personnel
The training units would ask for assistance from a number of Gypsy mediators in the context of a working group. These mediators would always be reimbursed, based on a standard rate. To achieve co-ordination between the units teacher exchange schemes would take place in the context of Community policy (grant system).

Participants in the Project
The participants in the project should include representatives of the Gypsies and Travellers through their families or their organisations as well as economic sector participants from a pool of employers who work together in a liaison group (for example in France: National Education Service, Directorate of the Department of Young People and Sport, Directorate of the Department of Health and Social Security, local organisations, Chamber of Commerce, associated sectors). On a decentralised level (at least on a departmental level for the National Education Service in France) a co-ordinator would be responsible for developing the projects, for liaison between the projects, for answering immediate questions and for liaising with other participants and the families. S/he would provide an annual report which would allow evaluation of the work of the project. The management of the budget would be as accessible as possible to the training units.

Proposals 1989-90
It was proposed that a link be established between existing projects by creating a national and Community network and that pilot projects be set up in regions where no project exists at present. Those pilot projects would have to have enough in common to allow for an evaluation of the whole network of projects. After a first evaluation has taken place, the network of projects would be extended.

Recommendation
It would seem important to appoint local and national observers to monitor the implementation of laws and regulations applying to minorities and to promote a positive image of minority cultures.

Keywords

professional integration   emergence

insertion   unemployment

justice   11-16 years

delinquency   school refusal   drug addiction

inter-generation conflicts

unreasonable or arbitrary requirements

school courses   professional training

adapted classes   remunerative activities

innovation   pre-professional training

Inter-culturalism (Group 4)

Maria Alcaloïde (France), Rosa Almeida de Medeiros (Portugal), Jean-Claude,, Bourgue (France), Claude Clanet (France), Michel Colanjon-Durand (France), Patricia Doublet (France), Georges Kautzmann (France), Mairin Kenny (Ireland), Nathan Lee (UK), Angel Marzo Guarinas (Spain), Secondo Massano (Italy), Sally Naylor (UK), Sheila Nunan (Ireland), Catherine Seguenot (France), Régine Tort-Nogues (France), Sacha Zanko (France)

Who is talking? What are they talking about?
What attitudes have been formulated?
Trainers of Teachers
What work should be done on respect for the cultural diversity of groups? Can inter-culturalism exist?

Gypsies
How can the contribution of the participant be valued? How can our culture be revalued? One should ask schools to provide material that allows everyone to recognise their culture and to identify themselves with that culture. There is a need to achieve an atmosphere of shared responsibility and mutual respect.

Social Workers
There is a need for mutual knowledge and interaction between cultures and research on inter-cultural attitudes and habits.

Teachers
What is inter-culturalism?
What is the inter-cultural attitude?
Which materials would help achieve inter-culturalism?
Can we talk about the inter-cultural in a 'homogeneous' Traveller milieu?
How can we reform structures to open them up to the exterior?
What account should be taken of the environment?
Which curriculum?

Methodology
Before discussing the theme the group identified a methodology which set out the steps and the organisation of the debate (plenary or group work) in the allocated time span. However, it should be noted that the group was not able to follow the entire workplan. After an attempt to categorise expectations it was proposed to work both on a definition of the concept of multi-culturalism (in a plenary session over a period of two hours) and also on the inter-cultural project. The latter was subdivided into three parts: structures, roles and liaison both within the organisation and externally with associated organisations and parents (time: one and a half hours); pedagogical tools; curriculum pro-grammes and learning cycles. The time allowed for each of these last two sections was thirty minutes. For each point an opening statement seemed necessary and the discussion could be led using these statements.

This plan was decided upon by a group where the majority of the participants were Gaujes; it emphasises the importance of the school over the other partners in the education process.

Research into Attempts to Define Inter-culturalism
Using the keywords provided by the organising team this group wondered whether there was any correlation between the group of keywords and the theme (the theme is possibly too restrictive). They also considered whether one should produce a definition of inter-culturalism or questions to outline the concept? The group felt that inter-culturalism was an ideal:
■ it is a moral attitude
■ it is necessary to be sensitive
■ it is an attitude of equality and respect.

Inter-culturalism is not an intrinsic aspect of everyone's behaviour and should be based on political, social and economic situations. It is necessary to identify areas of contact and of conflict between different cultures. Do these areas correspond with the fundamental values of the egalitarian society? Inter-culturalism and contradiction are inseparable. It is necessary to accept that conflicts need managing.

The group agreed to use a provisional definition: that inter-culturalism implies acceptance of the need to manage conflicting values. At this point, there was disagreement over whether the values should be ascribed to the group or to the individual. Do the values belong to the group or the individual (private/public domain)? Does the individual endorse all the values of the community to which s/he belongs? Are the values permanent? Are there universal values (Human/ Children's Rights)?

The Inter-cultural Project
It is impossible for the group to define the project as the necessary tools are lacking.

What are favourable conditions for the emergence and development of the project? Can the institution develop this project alone? Did the participants volunteer to co-operate? (Resistance towards a major change in attitudes). The group proposed a reiteration of the evaluation of the tools and the experiences and their dissemination, and also that the concepts in the training of teachers should be rethought. They recommended the definition of a European project to establish a basis for a general inter-cultural education.

Keywords

rights   society   integration   values

universal   cultural references   exchanges

inter-cultural dynamics   reciprocal   welcome

mutual exchange of knowledge   expectations

innovatory experiences   reciprocal acceptance

pluri-cultural dynamics   resource centre

process of collective learning   opening up

consensus   means to put inter-culturalism into practice

inter-cultural didactical tools   competence

inter-cultural pedagogical practices   time

interaction   transformation   understanding in depth

innovation   concerted action   projects   information

reflection   space   contract

documentation   teamwork

respect for the cultural and educational tradition of the ethnic group

Training (Group 5)

Claude Andrieu (France), Solange Denegre (France), Soledad Dubos (France), Jean-Joseph Gomez (France), Benoît Gramond (France), Françoise Malique (France), Evangelos Marselos (Greece), André Morzel (France), Annette Pougheon (France), Françoise Ventresque (France)

The starting point for the group discussion was the development of a mixed training centre (Gypsy/non-Gypsy), taking into account both the wish of Gypsies to manage the education of their own children and the wish of practitioners on the ground (at whatever level) to be officially recognised as competent participants in the field of training-research. It will, therefore, be necessary to leave the constraints of familiar processes behind and to innovate in order to integrate the thinking of Gypsies into our accustomed regulations and to introduce the notion of equality at all levels. Matters to be considered would be the percentage of each group (50:50?), recognition of competence and recognition of one social status (for salaries). The two communities would have to define the criteria for recruitment of personnel themselves.

It is evident that such a centre could never be a centralising body. It could exist wherever Gypsy children were educated and should be an officially recognised resource centre. The creation and organisation of these centres would constitute an action-research project which can be described as follows:

Diagram 1

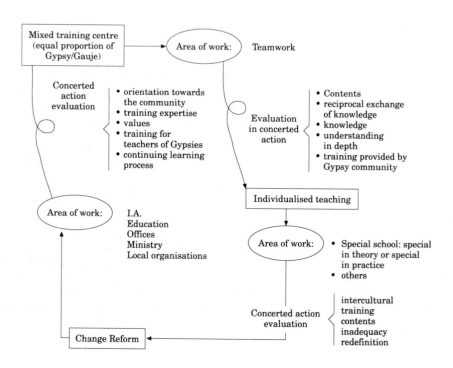

Keywords

values   redefinition   reform

inadequacy   knowledge   participation

documentation   individualised teaching

training for trainers   competence of trainers

education provided by the Gypsy community

community   understanding in depth   content

transformation   reciprocal exchange of knowledge

information   collective learning   continuity

training of Gypsies   team work

systematic training in inter-culturalism

An Example of Action-research Used to Support an Individual in their Professional Role (Group 6)

Maryse Alibeu (France), Marie Cannizzo (France), Ana Gimenez (Spain), Concha Gozalo Yagües (Spain), Harry Hutjens (The Netherlands), Jean-Paul Laffont (France), Arlette Laurent-Fahier (France), Josiane Perrin-Rostagni (France), Koen Van Ryckeghem (Belgium), Mary Waterson (UK)

The participants found it difficult to pinpoint their subject for discussion and action within the 'hazy' constraints set by the University organisers: to restate difficulties which have been repeatedly identified did not seem satisfactory. We found ourselves in the difficulty of identifying problems for Gypsies without a Gypsy present. On the other hand, to find solutions for a problem which is unsolvable within our sphere of action could be sterile.

Again, we found ourselves in a process of 'trompe l'oeil', of 'masking the reality' and we refused this piece of work. It would take too much time in a group, as in life, to define who is who (individual)? and who is what (function of individual)? To acknowledge this reality is to perceive the conflict. Everyone, according to his/her level and abilities, perceives problems which require changes. The urgent character of each individual and personal problem always appears most important to the individual concerned, as is his/her position in the hierarchical pyramid.

Diagram 1

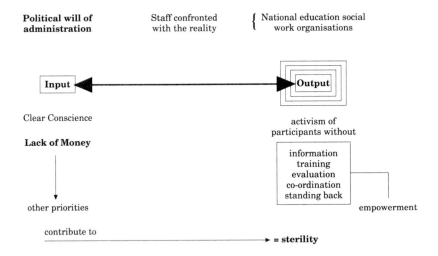

Project for Discussion and Research

To study one or more of the problems of life (in the output, at the base of the hierarchical pyramid) to determine a certain number of valuable tools whatever the initial problem has been. Each participant can fulfil a role by responding according to his/her abilities.

The Rules of the Game

In view of the heterogeneous character of the group (language, different competence), we found it necessary to set out some rules of the game:
■ an observer, who was not a participant, would lead the evaluation
■ the problem posed would be clear
■ the individual would be protected. It was necessary not to be dismissive of what anyone says
■ the aim of the work was to get a result and not to dwell on the details which might prevent the best result
■ the poser of the problem could deal with it
■ it was necessary to stick to the rules of the game without involving ideology of any kind.
   Within the constraints of the rules everything was allowed.

Dealing with Institutional Blockage

■ Successive analysis of interactions: conversations with interviewer
■ Successive evaluations
   Synthesis of the evaluations concerned:
■ the case involved is at the centre of the discussion
■ take sides with the person in difficulties to reassure that person, to make him/her feel confident
■ reflect on strategies leading to change
■ start at an emotional level to reach a rationalised level

■ team work and methodological work
■ problem of regulating the group process in terms of functions/blocks/support.

Diagram 2
Case X: a means
of dealing with a
situation of
institutional
blockage.

Tools used:
interaction of
two skills.

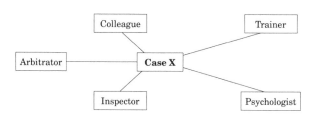

Evaluation of the Research
Participant A was familiar with the action-research method proposed by his colleague but he found it difficult to apply with novices. At the start, he was not convinced that this was the best method to use in the group. After the first conversations, he was amazed at the positive results. In fact, everyone had been involved and had benefited from describing the functions and blocks and had helped to produce evaluation results. He hoped that everyone was satisfied and regretted that one participant did not seem to be so. Participant A felt that it had not finished. He hoped to see everyone again and although he believed that this would not be possible but remained hopeful.

Participant B underlined the advantages and disadvantages of this method of work for the group. The problems were lack of time to define the tools and the fear of embarrassing or hurting a participant. It is a dynamic and positive method to develop, by certain simulations, a device for intervention but how to intervene and on behalf of whom? This positive personal involvement can become a negative feature if it opens up block situations or if emotional problems push an individual to the edge of a psychological crisis.

Participant C observed we were focusing on the evaluation of a method. The aim is not to 'train a group' but, using reality as a starting point, to look at the interaction of two competence and arrive at a definition of the tools necessary for the evolution of the situation. We did not pursue the procedure to its conclusion. Satisfactory work has to be planned in detail, taking account of all components which may prove to be obstacles, for example, language problems in this group. The evaluation enabled the study of different competence and their interaction in the area of work which interested us. Participant C thought the research was a 'vehicle' to progress further.

Participant D was satisfied with the model which seemed perfect to her for work with the Ministry. Working with Gypsies, she would have preferred a more practical research method. It is a mistake to study a problem concerning a group member because of danger of saturation.

Participant E was delighted. He discovered an innovative path of reflection, which enabled resolution (deblocking) of complicated situations.

Participant F thought that the aim of the Summer School would be to find means of influencing governments. Nonetheless, he endorsed the need to include this method of work in training for teachers.

Participant G was pleased to be a participant. He felt that the method could be tried out. He was disappointed about the lack of reflection on the relationship between input and output engendering change. He was convinced that investigations were not an adequate tool.

Participant H said that if the adult felt at ease with his/her situation so does the child. Difficulties encountered in properly leading the work in which we had been engaged could be used to acknowledge two important points. Both in the group work and in reality we encounter that time is necessary for all growth and the fact that communication necessitates listening and understanding but above all a feeling of individual well-being. The training of teachers must take account of psychological factors. This work, which she had found a positive experience, had enabled her to clarify her position and to identify the exact nature of the problem.

Conclusion
To use action-research we felt it necessary to clarify the position of all participants. The group did not have enough time to finish the work of defining the tools.

Development of the Procedure Adopted Initially
The introductory phase consists of:
■ Information about the method and procedures is given so that everyone can accept the project.
■ Proposal and acceptance of the 'rules of the game' examples of which have been outlined above.

Outlining the Problem
Case X: group discussion to establish the exact nature of the problem.

Interdisciplinary Approach
Various approaches were tried out by various participants. Everyone, using his/her position and competence, studied the problem (two participants in a team and one observer).

Evaluation in Three Stages
By those who studied the problem, those who outlined the problem and by the observer (analysis of the communication between the two participants).
We were not able to continue further.

The Tools
The first phase was a catalogue of facts, an examination, the development of theoretical models applicable in action-research. The second phase established the nature of action-research, that is, where possible actions would be used to effect change of practice.

Report of the Working Group on Co-ordination in France

All the participants from France

In the conclusions of the 1988 Summer School at Montauban the notion of consultation and co-ordination were identified as both necessary and imperative. In fact, after this meeting contacts were established giving certain participants the opportunity to envisage the creation of a local network, here and there enabling the exchange of competence and also enabling the Centre for Information and Liaison, Travel/School (CLIVE) to increase its audience. Nevertheless, everything still needs to be done to establish true co-ordination.

What Exists
There are support systems for co-ordination and some are more developed than others. These are:
■ for the families: Gypsy organisations
■ for the national education staff: CLIVE
■ for trainers: the CEFISEM resource (Centre for Training and Information in the Education of Migrant Children)
■ for the partners in education in the districts: a certain number of organisations
■ for research and documentation: the Centre of Gypsy Research.
    These support systems, therefore, exist both in and outside the educational system but, in spite of the necessary complementarity, there is hardly any liaison between them apart from that deriving from individual initiatives. In particular, it was noted that in the majority of cases there was an absence of co-ordination at a basic, local level. Finally, it was regretted that there was no-one with a national responsibility clearly designated as spokesperson on behalf of the National Ministry of Education to respond to all questions on the education of Gypsy and Traveller children.
    In these conditions should a voluntary solution be adopted by creating a national co-ordination structure which, though tentative and fragmentary in nature, would create the sought after dynamics? Or would it be preferable to build on a more modest scale a local or regional liaison resource where, on a more or less short term basis, the necessity for consolidating these efforts can be demonstrated?
    The group has not reached a decision on which of these two methods to adopt but it would seem that the regional level could provide a 'door opener' in terms of establishing a political, effective reality if it stays operational.
    Proposals have, nevertheless, been made. These proposals are on two levels. At local level, location of people and resources should be within National Education including teachers, development workers in the area of Priority Education, Departmental Inspectors of National Education, Training and Information Centre for the Education of Migrant Children, education welfare officer. In the voluntary sector (Gypsy organisations and other agencies) it is desirable to create, for example, a discussion group which can reflect on the local situation and would have representatives of Gypsy families and organisations and National Education staff. At national level, there should be an overview of the situation using a national questionnaire which would take account of the different attitudes of the people involved on the various aspects of the question, e.g. environment, education, health. This account could be

useful for university research at all levels. The results of this research would provide a solid and objective basis for dialogue with the authorities.

While awaiting the creation of true co-ordination the group participants have considered whether an organisation like CLIVE, independent of the school but on a more national level, could be one of the arbitrators in discussions with authorities, in particular with the National Ministry of Education. The trainers of the Training and Information Centres for the Education of Migrant Children who hope to see a clear political line of action in the near future, will raise their concerns about the education of Gypsy and Traveller children with the appropriate authorities as soon as an opportunity arises. In the meantime, regional restructuring is envisaged. However, in order to achieve a true national co-ordination from the efforts to establish co-ordination at a local level, it is vital that the educational institutions provide real means of exchange between persons whose expertise needs to be recognised. For example, there might be the possibility of initiating training beyond the constraints of the Department or the College and in the context of training, the possibility to call on persons in the field, (teachers or otherwise) whose experience and expertise in the schooling of Gypsy and Traveller children is recognised. As there are not many such persons in the whole country it would be necessary for them to travel from one district to another. Universal adoption of the principles of certain departments was recommended: staff designated for the education of Gypsy and Traveller children and liaison with schools, families and teachers. Moreover, two practical means have been proposed to ensure liaison between interested parties and the dissemination of information via the creation of a newsletter and the use of telematic networks, in particular by using EDUTEL.

Finally, this Summer School has demonstrated the need to develop exchange at a European Community level. We intend to do this in the short term through the medium of projects which already exist and await the setting up of a European pilot project.

Report of the Working Group on Co-ordination in the European Community

Adoption of the following principles was proposed by all participants of this group. The following countries were represented: Belgium, Spain, France, Greece, Ireland, Italy, Holland, Portugal, the United Kingdom.

First Principle
The principle of establishing a European forum was adopted unanimously. Members of this group should be chosen to be as representative as possible.

Second Principle
The Commission of European Communities will be the provisional co-ordinating body responsible for establishing the European forum (unanimous).

Third Principle
Everyone present takes the responsibility of consulting organisations and agencies in his/her country on the representation in the European forum as described in the first principle (unanimous).

Fourth Principle
We ask the Commission of European Communities to invite all representatives of national commissions to disseminate the information received at the Summer School to the appropriate persons in its country (unanimous). We hope that the Commission of European Communities will invite representatives of each nation by the 19 February.

We regret the absence of our colleagues from West Germany who had to leave early and Luxembourg and Denmark who sent no participants.

Action-research and Co-ordination: Some Proposals

Jean-Pierre Liégeois, Director of the Centre for Gypsy Research, University René Descartes, and Consultant to the Commission of the European Communities

The inclusion in these pages of the keynote address and the preliminary reports from the workshops has made for a somewhat lengthy text but gives the reader a clear picture of the context in which the meeting took place, the varying situations in the ten States represented and the agreed priorities of the participants. The present chapter will serve to emphasise some particularly striking findings, significant in that they indicate what should follow from our meeting.

As I mentioned in the keynote address, this seminar had several complementary objectives: training and informing the participants, developing dialogue and exchange between individuals professionally involved in various capacities in school provision for Gypsy and Traveller children and compiling guidelines to be used as a basis for action at both State and Community level, particularly in connection with the adoption of the Resolution of 22 May 1989 (see Appendix 2). The dynamics of our interaction in groups small and large, structured and informal, over eight intense days, has led to the emergence of several transversal themes to be treated as priorities, notably:

■ the necessity for significantly increased Gypsy participation in the planning and implementation of action concerning the schooling of their children

■ the necessity of developing (or of initiating) various forms of exchange both of personnel (placements, reciprocal visits) and of documents and other materials. There is a desperate need for information. At this meeting, as at previous ones, we have collectively gorged on it. Each participant has received hundreds of pages of published reports and hundreds more photocopied pages of documents prepared especially for this meeting. We have swapped even more documents amongst ourselves and look forward to our own findings being published. Yet this has not quenched our thirst for knowledge and many participants continue to ask the organisers for further information

■ the necessity for a vast investigation to give a clear and practical picture of what is being done throughout Europe with a view to establishing a repertoire which would provide an overview to all involved and at the same time enable them to contact each other directly

■ the desire to work in concert (beginning by increasing contact between colleagues and setting up think tanks), to promote co-ordination which would benefit so many regional, national and European projects and, with a clear eye to the future, the proposal of definite timetables, even precise deadlines, for the achievement of goals.

These are the themes which crop up again and again in plenary sessions, in conferences held in most Member States and in the debates which have followed them, as well as in the synthesis reports from the workshops here. Needless to add, our main themes of training, action-research and co-ordination, to which I will return, have also figured prominently.

First of all I would like to draw attention both to the total convergence of priorities and aspirations expressed by the participants in this conference regardless of their State of origin and to the total convergence of these priorities and aspirations with the analyses and guidelines evolved in the course of other studies and meetings (see the documents listed in Appendix 1). Summing up a meeting in 1988 (*Gypsy Children in School: Training of Teachers and other Personnel*, see Appendix 1) I remarked that the convergence of conclusions and propositions reinforces them and confirms their validity; one could add that this in turn legitimises our efforts to see them implemented. It is disturbing, even heartbreaking, to note that despite the passage of years we are still demanding the same basic necessities and still waiting for the implementation of a few principles essential to an improvement in the situation: the necessity that all policy be based on Gypsy/Traveller dynamics, the necessity for consultation, the necessity for precision and for realism and the necessity for study and reflection. (These principles are developed in *Gypsies and Travellers* and *School Provision for Gypsy and Traveller Children*, see Appendix 1).

Winding up the 1988 seminar, I finished on a positive note, emphasising the marked convergence between the conclusions we had just reached and the guidelines laid out by many officials from the field of education, notably during the Permanent Conference of European Ministers of Education (Helsinki, May 1987 where twenty-four States were represented) as well as those expressed by various professional associations, committees of experts and senior officials. In time, I said, this convergence should generate sufficient movement to accomplish what has to be done. Winding up this meeting, in 1989, I would like once again to develop an optimistic thought or two.

Here in Carcassonne the expression of these priorities and needs has been repetitious for some, a revelation for others, yet all participants have shown a firm commitment to go beyond a simple expression of ideas to an implementation of those steps which they believe to be crucial.

This meeting of ten different nationalities and a range of cultures has been a living illustration of multi-culturalism but not always an easy one because of our lack of practice. Working together on shared problems has left most participants mutually enriched and encouraged. Each of us will draw ideas and information from this meeting to be applied in our work; the personal contacts we have made here will enable us to exchange ideas directly over the coming months without waiting for the establishment of more formal channels. This dialogue and co-operation at State and Community level will be reinforced by the fact that all of the participants in this meeting on co-operation at European level are also committed to developing consultation within their respective States, with the aim of setting up working groups at national level which can in turn participate in co-operation at European level.

If those who have participated in this meeting, or even half of them, make an effort to keep the commitments they have made, the situation could improve, under favourable conditions, for a variety of reasons. The trend towards awareness and consultation may snowball. The number of individuals actively and directly involved may become significant enough to allow for organised co-operation which in its turn will strengthen the potential for action of the individuals and groups thus linked. (This tendency is already in evidence in States and regions where organisations linking teachers and others involved in school provision for Gypsy and Traveller children exist). Being partially outside formal institutional channels has many advantages, notably that it allows for grassroots flexibility since those involved are voluntary participants, motivated and active, rather than passive recipients requested to implement plans from above. The fact that proposals emerge in this way, that is, from the bottom up, is one of the conditions favouring the development and establishment of suitably adapted innovation. (For a detailed analysis, see the report entitled *School Provision for Gypsy and Traveller Children: Evaluating Innovation*, Appendix 1).

Participants in a meeting such as this thus bear a considerable responsibility: beforehand, to prepare for it conscientiously; during, to participate actively and constructively so as to make of it a forum for critical evaluation and the expression of carefully considered priorities; and afterwards, to become involved in the implementation, never easy and all too often postponed, of the emergent recommendations. Similarly, administrators and institutions bear vital responsibility at local, national and international level: beforehand, in facilitating meetings of this kind to take place; during, to ally themselves with the event in as many ways as possible, preferably including direct participation; and afterwards, to be attentive to the recommendations which emerge and to open up consultation which will help establish priorities and plan for implementation. In this way teachers and parents, with their concrete knowledge of the terrain, may find a platform for expressing their priorities and developing mutual help and appreciation with the administration which must ensure the functioning of schools adapted to the children attending them who would benefit from the findings of consultation between specialised and motivated personnel.

Participation in such a meeting is not easy. Apart from the disorientating effects of the cultural mix, the tiresome necessity for several working languages and the uncertainty, despite the well-defined framework, of working on themes left open by the organisers, the theme itself – action-research – entails a fundamental questioning of established practice without offering instant alternatives. On the contrary, it leads to further questioning and is thus destabilising. Such considerations for the most part go beyond the topic of school provision for Gypsy and Traveller children. Attention has been drawn to these matters in other contexts such as teacher training, distinguishing the classic teacher-trainer from the trainer/counsellor or trainer/researcher.

"The individual who occupies a position as teacher-trainer is often guided by traditional methods of teaching while the trainer/counsellor is concerned with new technology, different ways of teaching adapted to each case.

"The first essential difference between the two is that the teacher-trainer seems to know the answers as if they were recipes while the trainer/counsellor will look for underlying reasons in order to reach an understanding of the 'right' way to teach and to educate. The second essential difference is that the teacher-trainer often assumes a consensus of opinion on the situation and context while the trainer/counsellor usually seeks out the conflicts and contradictions between the situation and the practice. The third difference lies in the fact that while the teacher-trainer bases his work on specific tasks and subjects of teaching, the trainer/counsellor's acts are based on a broader concept of education. We note, however, that teachers themselves generally prefer the teacher-trainer, who offers instruction directly applicable to immediate classroom problems, to the trainer/counsellor who proposes options rather than offering solutions" (1).

Action-research is thus not easy to put into practice since the researchers are actors and the actors researchers. The usual methods, roles and frameworks no longer apply. The researcher, being an actor, is an implied object of his own research alongside the actor who is participating in the research yet who remains an actor. The familiar guidelines are gone but their absence leaves the field open for a new adaptability, innovation, flexibility and openness (see *School Provision for Gypsy and Traveller Children: Evaluating Innovation*, Appendix 1). I would like to share with you now some quotations from various texts emerging from reflection at European level, not on the subject of school provision for Gypsy and Traveller children but specifically on training and action-research, the pivotal questions we have gathered to consider. I would like to suggest that whatever the difficulties involved action-research is a working method offering multiple advantages. In effect it is an approach, a state of mind, more than a precise formula. Neither before nor during our encounter have we defined it; on the contrary, our discussions have revealed its complexity since, as Marcel Mauss would have put it, any pedagogical act is always also a "total social phenomenon". As an approach, we could phrase it thus: that action-research (whether by this or some other name) is character-ised by actors engaged in a critical analysis of their own skills and a develop-ment of self-assessment with a view to adapting approaches to the task in hand. Without being applied research, action-research is nonetheless inher-ently geared towards adaptability: to engage in action-research is to evaluate in order to evolve.

The Theory/Practice Relationship

This is a constant preoccupation of pedagogical texts, particularly those written for trainee teachers. Yet the theme is more often approached in terms of separation or opposition than with a view to how the two should relate to each other. Many questions are asked about what pedagogical use can be made of research.

"Extremely interesting research has been undertaken in all the major universities of Europe, the US and the Soviet Union. The findings have given rise to reports but have these insights been incorporated into teacher training? And if it does occur that some of this knowledge finds its way into the teacher/

training programme, how does the young teacher use it in the classroom?" (2).

"It often happens that researchers delay in releasing their findings and that research has no real impact on innovation. Should research in the field of education concern itself more with testing the effects of innovation on a reduced scale before going on to more generalised application, the 'hothouse' function of research?" (3).

Other broadly based synthesis documents at European level, recognising the gap between theory and practice, suggest:

"even if the universities cannot themselves respond to the full range of training needs, it is equally impossible to devise a complete and effective training package without their participation. In effect, it is only through the universities that the necessary links can be established between training and research. Yet these links remain insufficiently developed and in many countries the majority of universities are not as yet sufficiently concerned with in-service teacher training. It is thus necessary to tighten the links between education research and teacher training: to give teachers an opportunity to acquaint themselves with research findings, or better yet to participate in action-research themselves; to integrate the problems arising during the course of training, into new research approaches" (4).

They go on to propose that teachers, in the spirit of action-research, should themselves practice research:

"in order to combine theory and practice in the training of teachers and utilise research results more efficiently, teacher participation in research activity could offer a solution. It is only logical that teachers, the fulcrum of the school system and promoters of innovation, should be more directly associated with such activities. In order to do this, in-service training and pedagogical research should be combined in those establishments equipped to provide both. Every teacher should be familiar with those aspects of pedagogy which will enable him to collaborate with researchers" (5).

"We feel it preferable to encourage teachers to be authentic researcher/practitioners, innovative and capable of coming forward with their own initiatives but also having a basic minimum of training in the epistemology of research and having undergone the essential distancing procedure of putting it into writing. While we feel that every teacher should become a researcher/practitioner, it would be over optimistic to expect all of them to formalise their work. At the same time, formalisation should always be encouraged and supported (for example, through study circles or participation in certain university courses) in order to set up a pool of recognised researcher/practitioners with a sound grasp of the methodology of action-research. These can go on to fulfil a role as 'training companions', capable of working side by side with other teachers in seeking out new solutions yet also capable of maintaining a critical distance which will be rendered both acceptable and effective by their solidarity. The teacher-trainer on the team will thus occupy a role for which we have no adequate term: in tune with the participants, respectful of their problems however trivial they may appear, working with them to devise possible solutions, examining methodology as well as content, drawing on the consensus which links him/her to the team in the first place in seeking to evaluate results. It would thus appear to be useless and perhaps even perverse to aim towards establishing statutory guidelines for teacher-trainers; it seems wiser to envisage a researcher/practitioner who would temporarily also engage in training functions. Institutionally speaking, budgetary provision should be made for the researcher/practitioner, based on what s/he has published or the qualifications s/he has received from university courses involving research (notably in the Educational Sciences)" (6).

One could quote other reflections noting the possibility, indeed the necessity, of linking theory/research with practice:

"the directors of studies participating in this project favour a teacher training model which could take as its motto, 'practice shapes theory'" (7).

On the subject of the structures of in-service training, there has been an observed tendency

"springing from the emergence of new forms of training organisation. This tendency manifests itself, in a number of cases, in a direct link between in-service training, scholastic innovation and applied research. From this point of view the most interesting case is doubtless that of the IRRSAE in Bologna: simultaneously a centre for training teacher-trainers, capitalising on innovations from the field, a documentary resource centre and a research institute. On a different scale, though in a much more academic way, the experience of the Danmark Laererhojskole is a very interesting one to analyse since this is a university institution with the dual mission of research and in-service training" (8).

Teacher Participation
This is another recurring theme and one for which it would be easy to find many relevant and quotable extracts. I shall cite only one of them, part of a summary from a workshop within a specialised European conference:

"an all-too-rare method of teacher training is to allow them to participate in pedagogical research, to involve them in the research process. After all, every teacher needs to have an attitude of research. But we can go much further than this, allowing teachers real participation in scientifically constructed research. Unfortunately this link between research and teacher training is not a systematic one as yet and this fact should in itself be the object of a study. Such a strategy would require basic training to include familiarisation with research methods (statistics, observation methods) as is already the case in Luxembourg and Portugal" (9).

The action-research approach carries within itself the implication of the teacher within the research: a learning situation, to be sure, but one which goes beyond mere training in that it has a direct impact on the teacher's classroom practice. The action-research approach is also significant in that it encourages the participation of the all too often silent partners in the school equation – the Gypsy/Traveller parents and other Gypsy/Traveller organisations. Action-research postulates maximum participation from all concerned and actively encourages ongoing consultation alongside reflection, instead of, as is often the case, seeing it as an extra to be undertaken afterwards, if at all.

Adapting to the Individual Teacher's Situation

This topic inevitably crops up when discussing teacher training and research. Much has been written on it; I will limit my quotations to a single source, a summary of the views of ATEE (Association for Teacher Training in Europe) formulated in preparation for the fifteenth session of the Permanent Conference of European Ministers of Education (May 1987) on inter-cultural education:

"research work must be undertaken in the following directions: first of all, in identifying the pedagogical problems recognised by teachers themselves. Research at this level could take the form of observation of work in the classroom as well as interviews with the teachers. Inevitably, this raises the question as to whether the problems perceived by the teachers are a manifestation of deeper problems which should be attributed to pluralism. It is essential that research carried out at this level be founded to a large degree on a detailed observation of work in the classroom. This observation of pedagogical practice must also, along with the study of thematic pedagogical documentation, serve as the basis for the third level of research: identifying pedagogical problems which are not recognised by the teachers but which nonetheless spring from pluralism. The working group is convinced that the results obtained by such a three-tiered research approach would have a decisive importance for the implementation in the pluralist societies of Europe, of a practical and theoretical framework for multicultural education, on the basis of which future education policies could be developed" (10).

It is easy to see how action-research is capable of fulfilling these needs, since it enables the formulation of continuous, precise analysis/evaluation of the classroom situation, an analysis in which the teachers themselves participate and from which they simultaneously benefit since it gives them first hand experience of training adapted to their individual situation. (I am limiting my observations in this context to the relationship between training and action-research).

Holistic Stocktaking

Even careful study of classroom reality must not blind us to the socio-cultural and political environment and the living conditions of the families themselves. The absolute necessity of taking into account the full range of factors comprising a given situation has already been amply demonstrated in the reference documents with which you are familiar (see Appendix 1). Action-research, being both action and research, demands this approach so that analysis and evaluation cover the overall situation. Action-research encourages us to:

Go Beyond the Confines of the Strictly Pedagogical
"the question of evaluation poses the problem of which criteria should be applied. Generally speaking, the public judges teaching efficiency in relation to the attainment of strictly educational goals such as scholastic results, while

other equally or even more important criteria would include the general development of the pupils and their preparation for taking an active, responsible and constructive role in society" (11)

Be Flexible
Work with a flexibility which enables us to adapt to the individual pupil and which in turn enables him to respond in individual rather than predetermined ways:

"as for the philosophy of education itself, if the methodologies described above were to be formally applied and if didactic procedures were to be too tightly adjusted to the personality of the pupils, we would run the risk of generating mechanisms encouraging parroting, dependence, confinement. On the other hand, the very fact of engaging in action and of monitoring its development by observing its effects, by its very imperfection enables the pupil to disengage from the process of teaching and, by confronting procedures with results, to construct his own anatomy... The 'applicationist' model which supposes the existence of solutions developed by specialists outside the classroom, that is, outside the school situation, which teachers have only to put into practice... should be rejected in favour of a 'regulative' model characterised by the fact that it seeks to place the teacher in a situation of action-research, which is to say, to call upon both his didactic inventiveness and his ability to regulate this in accordance with his observations of its effects... Seen from this perspective the teacher has, to be sure, a need for tools but these must be of an open and dynamic character; they must be tools of exploration and/or regulation, employed in a loop which enables activity to be adjusted as necessary" (6)

Respect Diversity
Respect diversity and base our approach on it:

"given that unity and diversity are inextricably mixed in Europe, it is incumbent on pedagogical research to determine where, how and to what degree these two principles must be taken into account in the reality of national education systems and in the day-to-day problems encountered by both teachers and learners in the society of their country. If we ignore the permanent tension between these two principles, we risk losing sight of situational diversity and of rushing into superficial constructions presenting a mere illusion of unity" (12).

Adopt a Structured Approach
We must approach our task in a structured rather than a haphazard way, in a framework of continuity and regular evaluation and with an eye to the broader issues of the educator's role.

Complementarity with Other Actions
Action-research is not a panacea. It is an approach of great richness and usefulness which offers a number of advantages but which must remain complementary to other approaches:

"there is often over reliance on training courses to the detriment of other forms of action, such as mutual observation, visiting other establishments and action-research, which are in fact responses adapted to real needs, on condition, of course, that they are integrated into a well-planned programme" (4).

"It has been observed that, where innovation has continued beyond the action of in-service training undertaken by the researchers, a social dynamic was created around the innovating teachers. This interactive dynamic, which to some degree links into the training framework maintained by an outside agent, appears to be a sine qua non if innovations are to have stability... This reflection leads us to conceive in-service training no longer solely in terms of individual learning but also in terms of social interaction. Let us emphasise this point as there is great danger of being misunderstood: it is a question of combining an approach centred on the cognitive transformation of the individual, with an approach oriented towards the interactive but not of substituting one for the other" (13).

By the same token, classical research and action-research can only gain from combining their activities and comparing results, particularly in the field of schooling; moreover, since the teacher is of necessity motivated to constantly review his/her own actions and their effects, conditions are clearly favourable for fruitful collaboration. I will add that action-research is, by virtue of its holistic approach as outlined above, also in a position to collaborate in actions of other kinds, for example, in relation to accommodation or health.

Mention could be made of yet other positive aspects of action-research but I think that the above remarks, while not exhaustive, are nonetheless sufficient and also offer an insight, through their discussion of the relationship between action-research and training, into the convergence of reflections and conclusions expressed in recent, often under-publicised, documents issuing from meetings at European level. Similarly, participants here at Carcassonne have confirmed that the theme of action-research and the proposals put forward for practising it are adapted to the context of school provision for Gypsy and Traveller children. I would add that this adaptability applies both to a general movement of renovation in education policy and to a sense of respect for specific characteristics, especially of a cultural nature. Let me illustrate both these aspects.

"Adapting education to the economic and social context and to individual needs is hampered by the system's incapacity to generate or manage innovation and change. The generation, financing and implementation of innovation in the school system should be a political priority of the first order. The conditions for change must be created, indeed, brought together out of concrete recognition of the need for them in order to encourage schools and teachers in the field to become involved in innovation and to learn how to generate it themselves. One important way of achieving this would be to guarantee more autonomy and flexibility to individual establishments, to enable them to respond to their own changing needs. It is essential that the heads of these establishments, and the teachers, be trained and made aware in order to motivate and prepare them to take up such initiatives and to take on responsibility for such innovative work. It is also important to reinforce the role to be played by inspectors, pedagogical counsellors and other services in stimulating and supporting these processes within the schools. Actions of the pilot project or educational innovation-zone type should be used more systematically as instruments for development and for the application of innovation." (Working document of the Commission of the European Communities, October 1988).

"Situations and aspirations vary greatly; in order to respond to them we need a range of micro-developments, micro-projects (and this is where short term approaches and those based on immediate circumstances have a role to play) but within the framework of ongoing consultation, co-ordination and assistance which is both all-encompassing and structural. Successful projects will not provide recipes but will reveal tendencies and convergence need not necessarily occur where we normally expect it to. There can be no doubt that it is to be found more in processes such as consultation or basing approaches on internal dynamics than in end products (this or that concrete result). Going back to the sociology of development, we see yet again that, while one can attempt to construct theory on a basis of practice, it is often somewhat irrelevant to base practice on theory. The necessity for flexibility mentioned above is based on observation of the fact that it is preferable that projects not be fitted into a rigid, preconceived theoretical and practical framework; a flexible, evolving framework which allows for innovation and new developments is far more capable of allowing the desired development to occur. This observation will appear tritely self-evident to some but heretical or anarchic to others. It is true that an approach of this kind, to recognise and make use of uncertainty in order to encourage innovation and the expression of internal dynamics, is politically and intellectually speaking disquieting. It has often been said that within the realm of the social sciences there is no science of ends, only of means. We would add that the science of means is to be used with much caution, as it is most often a mere impression of knowing or an alibi for power" (14).

Yet proposals for action-research are relevant only if made in tandem with proposals for co-ordination. This is another point insisted upon by document after document from various European organisations (see Appendix 1) as well as by the participants at this meeting. It would be well to re-examine these documents to understand the reasons for this insistence on co-ordination and to look again at various ways of putting it into practice. The priorities of individuals involved in co-ordination focus on direct contacts (document exchange, participation in joint action-research, exchange visits) and on setting up centres at regional, national and community level to facilitate the organisation and running of networks of mutual assistance, expertise, the distribution of information, evaluation, centres for various types of resources geared towards the interlinking of actions both within the field and with actions being undertaken in other domains, so as to avoid repetition or isolation; geared, too, towards opening up existing networks to all concerned bodies. These priorities are in tune with the proposals of the Resolution adopted on 22 May by the Council and the Ministers of Education. Teachers and other personnel wish to break out of their isolation, to form groups which will evolve into teams of collaborators who can develop mutual exchanges to help each other adapt their professional practices to present realities and particularly to the demands and the rewards of the pluri-cultural. Alongside a new Europe, united socially and economically, a new, united Europe for education practitioners is desired, desirable and possible. It is up to each of us to work towards it.

References

1   OLSEN, Tom Ploug. La nécessité du formateur ou une 'joint venture'. In: *La formation continue des professeurs en Europe: expériences et perspectives; Université d'été, Madrid, 12-19 July, 1987.* Commission of the European Communities.

2   ATEE (Association for Teacher Training in Europe). *Les perspectives en matière de formation des enseignants.* Council of Europe Doc. M ED-15-HF-49.

3   TILLEMA, H. Les nouveaux défis à relever dans l'enseignement. In: *4e Conférence Paneuropéennes de Directeurs d'Instituts de Recherche en Education (Report of the Fourth Pan-European Conference of Directors of Research in Education Institutes); Eger (Hungary), 13-16 Octobre 1986.* Council of Europe Doc. DECS/Rech (86)22. Council of Europe. 1986.

4   BLACKBURN, V. and MOISAN, C. *La formation continue des enseignants.* Conclusions and proposals, pp.57 – 61. Maastricht: Presses Interuniversitaires Européennes, n/d.

5   ANDERSEN, Henning. Défense de l'approche pragmatique In: *4e Conférence Paneuropéennes de Directeurs d'Instituts de Recherche en Education (Report of the Fourth Pan-European Conference of Directors of Research in Education Institutes); Eger (Hungary), 13-16 Octobre 1986.* Council of Europe Doc. DECS/Rech (86)51. Council of Europe. 1986.

6   MEIRIEU, P. La formation continue des enseignants centrée sur les problèmes pratiques de la classe. In: *La formation continue des professeurs en Europe: expériences et perspectives; Université d'été, Madrid, 12-19 July, 1987.* Commission of the European Communities.

7   BERNBAUM, Gerald. Formation des enseignants en Angleterre et au Pays de Galles: tendances et innovations In: *4e Conférence Paneuropéennes de Directeurs d'Instituts de Recherche en Education (Report of the Fourth Pan-European Conference of Directors of Research in Education Institutes); Eger (Hungary), 13-16 Octobre 1986.* Council of Europe Doc DECS/Rech (86)45. Council of Europe. 1986.

8   PIETTRE, François. Evolutions constatées et problèmes posés par les différentes stratégies de formation continue des enseignants. In: *Analyse des stratégies de formation continue des enseignants dans les pays de la Communauté Européennes*; Working Paper of the European Commission, pp. 40-41. Commission of the European Communities. 1989.

9   COUNCIL OF EUROPE. *Report of the Fourth Pan-European Conference of Directors of Research in Education Institutes*; Eger (Hungary), 13-16 October 1986. Council of Europe Doc. DECS/Rech 86-75, p.73. Council of Europe, 1986.

10   ATEE. Op. cit., pp.17-18

11   COUNCIL OF EUROPE. Council of Europe Doc M ED-15-3.

12   Op. cit. see ref.9, p.13.

13   CRAHAY, Marcel. Comment transformer la pratique des enseignants en formation. In: *La formation continue des professeurs en Europe: expériences et perspectives; Université d'été, Madrid, 12-19 July, 1987.* Commission of the European Communities.

14   LIEGEOIS, Jean-Pierre. Formation, leadership, mutation: quelques réflexions sur un contexte. In: *Tsiganes: identité, évolution;* conference at Georges Pompidou Centre, Paris, December 1986.

Appendix 1
Documentation: Texts published by or for the Commission of the European Communities and the Council of Europe on the subject of school provision for Gypsy/Traveller Children

1   LIEGEOIS, Jean-Pierre. *La scolarisation des enfants tsiganes et voyageurs (School Provision for Gypsy/Traveller Children)*, a synthesis report of a study undertaken by the States of the European Community. Commission of the European Communities, Série Documents, 1986.

Published in English, French, German, Italian and Spanish. The English edition is out of print but photo copies can be obtained from:
Office for Official Publications of the European Communities, 2 Rue Mercier, L2985, Luxembourg.

2   LIEGEOIS, Jean-Pierre. *La scolarisation des enfants tsiganes et voyageurs: Documentation d'orientation pour la réflexion et pour l'action (School Provision for Gypsy/Traveller Children: Orientation Document for Reflection and Action)*. Paris: Centre for Gypsy Research, 1989.

Produced for the Commission of the European Communities, widely distributed and published in various publications in Europe (currently available in English, French, German, Italian, Portuguese and Spanish). The English edition (price £1 including post and packaging) can be ordered from: Manchester Traveller Education Service, Parkside Centre, Sheepfoot Lane, Prestwich, Manchester M25 8BW. Telephone 061-740 1465.

3   LIEGEOIS, Jean-Pierre. *Tsiganes et Voyageurs, données socio-culturelles, données socio-politiques.* (Gypsies and Travellers, social cultural data, social political data). Council of Europe, 1985.

Published in English, French, Italian, Portugese and Spanish. The English edition (ISBN 9287107912) can be ordered by post from HMSO, UK agents for the Council of Europe. Cheques (£12.70 including postage) should be made payable to Her Majesty's Stationery Office and sent to:
HMSO Publications Centre, PO Box 276, London, SW8 5DT. Telephone orders: 071-873 9090. Telephone enquiries: 071-873 0011.

4   COUNCIL OF EUROPE. *La formation des enseignants des enfants tsiganes (Teacher training for the teachers of gypsy children);* report of the twentieth seminar of the Council of Europe held at Donaueschingen on 20-25 June, 1983. Council of Europe Document DECS/EGT 83(63).

An English edition is obtainable free of charge from:
Division de l'Enseignement scolaire, Conseil de l'Europe BP 431 R6, F 67006 Strasbourg Cedex, France.

5   COUNCIL OF EUROPE. *La scolarisation des enfants tsiganes: l'évaluation d'actions novatrices (The education of gypsy children: evaluation of innovative programmes);* report of the thirty-fifth seminar of the Council of Europe held at Donaueschingen on 18-23 May, 1987. Council of Europe Document DECS/EGT 87(36).

An English edition is obtainable free of charge from:
Division de l'Enseignement scolaire, Conseil de l'Europe BP 431 R6, F 67006 Strasbourg Cedex, France.

6   COUNCIL OF EUROPE. *Les enfants tsiganes à l'école: la formation des enseignants et autres personnels (Gypsy children at school: the training of teachers and other personnel);* report of a Summer School, organised by the Centre for Gypsy Studies at Montauban, France, held on 4-8 July, 1988. Council of Europe Document DECS/EGT 88(42).

An English edition is obtainable free of charge from:
Division de l'Enseignement scolaire, Conseil de l'Europe BP 431 R6, F 67006 Strasbourg Cedex, France.

Complementary volume:
Les enfants tsiganes à l'école: la formation des personnels de l'Education nationale (Gypsy children: the training of personnel in the French education system).

Available from: Centre Departementale de Documentation pédagogique du Tarn-et-Garonne, 65 avenue de Beausoleil, 82013 Montauban Cedex, France.

7   COUNCIL OF EUROPE. *Vers une éducation interculturelle: la formation des enfants ayant des élèves tsiganes (Towards an intercultural education: the training of children with Gypsy pupils);* report of a Council of Europe Seminar held at Valencia, Spain on 9-13 June, 1989. Council of Europe Document DECS/EGT 89(31).

An English edition is obtainable free of charge from:
Division de l'Enseignement scolaire, Conseil de l'Europe BP 431 R6, F 67006 Strasbourg Cedex, France.

8   COUNCIL OF EUROPE. *La scolarisation des enfants tsiganes et voyageurs: enseignement à distance et suivi pédagogique (The education of Gypsy and Traveller children: distance learning and pedagogic follow-up);* report of the seminar organised at Aix-en-Provence, France, 10-13 December 1990. Council for Cultural Co-operation, Council of Europe, DECS/EGT 90(47).

An English edition is obtainable free of charge from:
Division de l'Enseignement scolaire, Conseil de l'Europe BP 431 R6, F 67006 Strasbourg Cedex, France.

9   CENTRE FOR GYPSY RESEARCH. *Interface*; free termly bulletin
     published by the Centre for Gypsy Research with the help of the
     Commission of the European Community in implementation of the
     Resolution of the 22 May 1989 of the Council of the Ministers of
     Education on the education of Gypsy and Traveller children.

English, French, German and Spanish editions are available from:
Centre for Gypsy Research, 106 quai de Clichy, F-92110-Clichy, Paris, France.

Appendix 2

Resolution of the Council and the Ministers of Education Meeting within the Council of 22 May 1989 on School Provision for Gypsy and Traveller children (89/C 153/02)

From the Official Journal of the European Communities, number C 153 of the 21 June 1989, p3.

The Council and the Ministers for Education meeting within the Council, having regard to the resolution of the Council and of the Ministers for Education, meeting within the Council, on 9 February 1976 (1) comprising an action programme in the field of education.

Considering that on 24 May 1984 the European Parliament adopted a resolution on the situation of Gypsies in the Community (2) in which it recommended in particular that the governments of the Member States co-ordinate their approach and called on the Commission to draw up programmes to be subsidized from Community funds aimed at improving the situation of Gypsies without destroying their separate identity.

Considering that Gypsies and Travellers currently form a population group of over one million persons in the Community and that their culture and language have formed part of the Community's cultural and linguistic heritage for over 500 years.

Considering that the present situation is disturbing in general, and in particular with regard to schooling, that only 30-40 per cent of Gypsy and Traveller children attend school with any regularity, that half of them have never been to school, that a very small percentage attend secondary school and beyond, that the level of educational skills, especially reading and writing, bears little relationship to the presumed length of schooling, and that the illiteracy rate among adults is frequently over 50 per cent and in some places 80 per cent or more.

Considering that over 500,000 children are involved and that this number must constantly be revised upwards on account of the high proportion of young people in Gypsy and Traveller communities, half of whom are under sixteen years of age.

Considering that schooling, in particular by providing the means of adapting to a changing environment and achieving personal and professional autonomy, is a key factor in the cultural, social and economic future of Gypsy and Traveller communities, that parents are aware of this fact and their desire for schooling for their children is increasing.

Noting the results and recommendations of studies carried out on behalf of the Commission on the schooling of Gypsy and Traveller children in the twelve Member States of the Community and the guidelines emerging from the summary report, consultations of Gypsy and Traveller representatives and discussions between experts and representatives of the Ministries of Education.

Hereby adopt this resolution: The Council and the Ministries for Education, meeting within the Council, will strive to promote a set of measures concerning school provision for Gypsy and Traveller children aimed without prejudice to any steps already taken by Member States to cope with specific situations which they face in this area, at developing a global structural

approach helping to overcome the major obstacles to the access of Gypsy and Traveller children to schooling.
These measures will aim at:
- promoting innovatory initiatives
- proposing and supporting positive and appropriate measures
- ensuring that achievements are interrelated
- widely disseminating the lessons learned
- promoting exchanges of experience.

At Member State Level
Within their constitutional and financial limits and the limits of their own specific national policies and structures, the Member States will make every effort to promote:

Structures:
- support for educational establishments, providing them with the necessary facilities for catering for Gypsy and Traveller children
- support for teachers, pupils and parents.

Teaching methods and teaching materials:
- experiments with distance teaching which is better adapted to the reality of nomadic life
- the development of forms of educational follow up
- measures to facilitate transition between schooling and continuing educational training
- consideration for the history, culture and language of Gypsies and Travellers
- use of new electronic and video methods
- teaching materials for educational establishments involved in the schooling of Gypsy and Traveller children.

Recruitment and Initial and Continuing Training of Teachers:
- adequate continuing and additional training for teachers working with Gypsy and Traveller children
- the training and employment of teachers of Gypsy or Traveller origin wherever possible.

Information and Research:
- increased provision of documentation and information to schools, teachers and parents
- encouragement of research on the culture, history and language of Gypsies and Travellers.

Consultation and Co-ordination: Promotion of Social-mindedness among the Population:
- appointment of trained staff to carry out co-ordination tasks
- the encouragement of liaison groups bringing together parents, teachers, representatives of local authorities and school administrations
- designation, where necessary, of a State authority or authorities involved in the schooling of Gypsy and Traveller children in States with a large number of Gypsies and Travellers to assist in co-ordination of the necessary measures including, where appropriate, those relating to the training of teachers,

documentation and the production of teaching material.

At Community level

Community involvement in this field is useful for encouraging national initiatives concerning the exchange of experience and for promoting innovatory pilot schemes.

Organisation of exchanges of views and experience by means of meetings at Community level of the various partners concerned and more particularly of representatives of Gypsies and Travellers, young Gypsies and teachers.

The Commission will continuously document, promote, co-ordinate and assess all the measures at Community level with the assistance of an outside body if necessary.

The Commission will ensure that these measures fit in with the other Community measures already planned in the field of education. It will ensure in particular that these activities are compatible with other Community activities such as those of the European Social Fund and with those of other international organisations, especially the Council of Europe.

A report on the implementation of the measures provided for in this resolution will be submitted to the Council, the European Parliament and the Education Committee by the Commission before 31 December 1993.

References

1 *Official Journal* No C38, 19 February 1976, p.1.
2 *Official Journal* No C172, 2 July 1984, p.153.

Appendix 3
List of Participants in the Summer School of the Ecole normale de l'Aude, Carcassonne, from 5-12 July 1989 on *School Provision for Gypsy / Traveller Children: Action-Research and Co-ordination*

Seminar Staff

Maria ALCALOIDE
Primary teacher, member of the
administrative committee of CLIVE
(Centre for Information and Liaison, Travel/School)
Ecole des Chênes
Bd de Verdun
95220 HERBLAY
France

Benoît GRAMOND
Primary teacher, member of the
administrative committee of CLIVE
(Centre for Information and Liaison, Travel/School)
Ecole J Jaurès primaire mixte
Rue des Cailloux Gris
95220 HERBLAY
France

Arlette LAURENT-FAHIER
Centre de Recherches Tsiganes,
Université René Descartes
Teacher trainer from CEFISEM
(Centre for Information and Training in the
Schooling of the Children of Migrants)
56 Bd des Batignolles
75017 PARIS
France

Jean-Pierre LIEGEOIS
Teacher-researcher
Centre de Recherches Tsiganes
Université René Descartes
106 quai de Clichy
92110 CLICHY
France

Staff from the Ecole normale de l'Aude

Jean COMMETS, Director
Marie-Claire BIAU, Administrator
Michel MILIAN, Senior tutor
Ecole normale de l'Aude,
122 Av Général Leclerc,
11000 CARCASSONNE,
France

List of Participants

Maryse ALIBEU
Nursery teacher
Ecole maternelle
Les Platanes
11000 NARBONNE
France

Rosa Maria ALMEIDA DE MEDEIROS
Primary teacher
Escola No 189 CURRALEIRA
Rua ENGo SANTOS SIMOES
1900 LISBOA
Portugal

Maria de Lurdes ALMEIDA GIL DA SILVA
Co-ordinator of the national project to support
the schooling of Gypsy children
Av.24 de Julho
1388-5o
1399 LISBOA
Portugal

Pedro AMAYA MUNOZ
Outreach teacher
Plan Integral Can Tunis
Paseo Luis Antunez
BARCELONA 08004
Spain

Claude ANDRIEU
Social worker
Lycée Paul Sabatier
11012 CARCASSONNE
France

Paule BABOULIN
Social worker
Centre Médico Scolaire
3 Quai du port
11400 CASTELNAUDARY
France

Michael BALDWIN
Advisory teacher with a co-ordinated service for
the education of Travelling children
West Midlands Education Service For Travelling Children
Broad Lanes
BILSTON WV14 OSB
England

Elisabeth BISOT
Teacher trainer
CEFISEM de l'Académie de Versailles
Ecole Normale d'Instituteurs
45 Av des Etats Unis
78000 VERSAILLES
France

Jean Claude BOURGUE
Teacher trainer
CEFISEM
30 Rue E CAS
13004 MARSEILLE
France

Marie CANNIZZO
Teacher
7 Chemin des Plates
69120 VAULX EN VELIN
France

Maria Assumpcio CASAS
Teacher
Rda Sant Marti S/N
BARCELONA 08020
Spain

Claude CLANET
Teacher-researcher
Université de Toulouse Le Mirail
5 Allées Antontio Machado
31058 TOULOUSE CEDEX
France

Maria Teresa CODINA
Co-ordinator of the educational diversity programme
Area d'Educacio Ajuntament de Barcelona
BARCELONA 08001
Spain

Michel COULANJON-DURAND
Director of the voluntary organisation AAAMMPG
13 Rue Félix Aldy
11000 NARBONNE
France

Solange DENEGRE
Teacher trainer
CEFISEM E N F
181 Av de Muret
31076 TOULOUSE
France

Patricia DOUBLET
Teacher
Les Dinandiers
Rue Django Reinhardt
15000 AURILLAC
France

Soledad DUBOS
Teacher
16 rue Marnata
83000 TOULON
France

Eliane FRANCO
Teacher
Ecole Publique de VERLHAGUET
82000 MONTAUBAN
France

Ana GIMENEZ
Anthropologist
Partida Bovalar
S/N BUZON 7
12004 CASTELLON
Spain

Jean-Joseph GOMEZ
Teacher training co-ordinator
Var Tziganes
2 rue Vincent Allègre
83000 TOULON
France

Concepción GOZALO YAGUES
Educational psychologist
Avda Toreros No 22
28028 MADRID
Spain

Danièle GRANIER
Var Tsiganes
Centre Social La Ripelle C D 46
83200 TOULON
France

Lucienne GUIBERT
Retired primary teacher, voluntary association member
Laissaud
73800 MONTMELIAN
France

Marie-Jo HIRIGOYEN
PhD student
6 rue Francis de Pressensé
69100 VILLEURBANNE
France

Harry HUTJENS
National co-ordinator, education advisor
K P C Postbus
482 5201 AL'S Hertogenbosch
NETHERLANDS

Jacqueline IMBERT
County education inspector
Circ de Montauban II Insp. Académique
Av Ch de Gaulle
82000 MONTAUBAN
France

Mirella KARPATI
Lecturer in education, teacher trainer,
editor of the review of Gypsy Studies *Lacio Drom*
Centro Studi Zingari
Via dei Barbieri 22
00186 ROMA
Italy

Georges KAUTZMANN
Teacher in charge of the Travellers'School
Ecole des Voyageurs
rue de l'Aéropostale
67100 STRASBOURG
France

Mairin KENNY
Headteacher, member of
Dublin Travellers' Education Development Group
St Kieran's N S for Travellers
c/o Mt St Mary
Alley River Road
BRAY
Co WICKLOW
Ireland

Jean-Paul LAFFONT
County education inspector (nursery)
I A 56 Av H Goût
11000 CARCASSONNE
France

Nathan LEE
Representative of the National Gypsy Education Council
13 Caravan Site
Clays Lane
Stratford
LONDON E15
England

Jean-Marie LEGRAND
Social worker
LET Couffignal
67000 MEINAU
France

Katharina LENNER
Adult literacy tutor/trainer
Feilitzschstr 9
D 8000 MUNCHEN 40
Germany

Francoise MALIQUE
Teacher trainer
CEFISEM de l'ESSONNE
CDDP de l'ESSONNE BP
163 91000 EVRY
France

Evangelos MARSELOS
Expert attached to the
Secretariat of the Ministry of Education
(secondary teaching)
Secretariat Gal de l'education des Adultes
ACHARNON 417
11143 ATHENS
Greece

Angel MARZO GUARINOS
Teacher
Association de ensenantes con Gitanos
c/Lele del Pozo 20
MADRID 28018
Spain

Secondo MASSANO
Headteacher (primary)
Scuola M L King
V Germonio 4
10142 TORINO
Italy

Danielle MERCIER
Tertiary education advisor, teacher trainer
CEFISEM
Chateau Bourran
33700 MERIGNAC
France

André MORZEL
County education inspector
42 Bd Castel
22600 LOUDEAC
France

Martirio MUNÕZ ENRIQUE
Headteacher
C Luisa de Marillac
Almanjayar Bajos del BL 18
GRANADA
Spain

Félix NAVARRO
Nantes University medical advisor
Rectorat BP 972
44076 NANTES CEDEX
France

Sally NAYLOR
Representative of the
National Association of Teachers of Travellers
Travellers Education Centre
c/o Templars Infants School
Cressing Road
WITHAM
Essex
England

Sheila NUNAN
Teacher
Department of Education
Marlborough Street
DUBLIN
Ireland

Josiane PERRIN-ROSTAGNI
Teacher
Ecole Jules Vallès
91 ST GERMAIN LES ARPAJON
France

Gerrit PETERINK
National Co-ordinator,
Catholic Pedagogical Centre
Postbus 482
5201 AL'S Hertogenbosch
NETHERLANDS

Jean Marie PICHON
County education inspector
Inspection Acad. Circ Rennes VIII
1 Quai Dujardin
35000 RENNES
France

Sylvain POIRIER
Teacher, co-ordinator in an education priority area
AIS II
26 R Kleber
ou Ecole Cité St Louis
111 Av du Rove
13000 MARSEILLE
France

Annette POUGHEON
Educational psychologist
GAPP Ecole Nuyens
54 rue Nuyens
33000 BORDEAUX
France

Lydie RECIO
Teacher
Ecole des Platanes
Route d'Armissan
11000 NARBONNE
France

Catherine SEGUENOT
Teacher
Ecole Les Voyageurs
Rue Django Reinhardt
21000 DIJON
France

Marie-France SERIES
Primary teacher
Ecole Littré
Place Bertier
31300 TOULOUSE
France

Santino SPINELLI
Director of the Centre of Italian Music
Studio Musicale Alexian
12 rue S M Maggiore
66034 LANCIANO
Italy

Regine TORT-NOUGUES
Senior county education social worker
Inspection Académique de l'Aude
11000 CARCASSONNE
France

Koen VAN RYCKEGHEM
Assistant Project Manager EFECOT
Rue del'Industrie 42/10
B-1040 Brussels
Belgium

Francoise VENTRESQUE
Teacher trainer, CEFISEM
Ecole Normale
122 av du Général Leclerc
11000 CARCASSONNE
France

Mary WATERSON
Administrator of ACERT
(Advisory Council for the Education of Romany and other Travellers)
Keepers
High Wych
SAWBRIDGEWORTH
Herts CM21 OLA
England

Sacha ZANKO
President of the Association Tchatchipen
Quartier Mataffe Bâtiment E
83400 HYERES
France